Husbands That Cook

Husbands That Cook

More Than 120 Irresistible Vegetarian Recipes and Tales from Our Tiny Kitchen

Ryan Alvarez and Adam Merrin

St. Martin's Griffin 🐎 New York

www.stmartins.com

All photos by Ryan Alvarez and Adam Merrin, except for the following:
Cover, center photo: Emma K. Morris
Page iii, center photo: Emma K. Morris
Page x: Emma K. Morris
Page 139: Kenneth Requa
Page 168: Tory Stolper
Page 179: Jeaneen Lund
Page 216: Emma K. Morris
Page 225: Jeaneen Lund
Page 237: Eric Cwiertny
Page 253: Emma K. Morris
Page 266: Emma K. Morris
Page 287: Kenneth Requa

The Library of Congress Cataloging-in-Publication Data is available upon request.

ISBN 978-1-250-15154-4 (paper over board)
ISBN 978-1-250-15155-1 (ebook)

Our books may be purchased in bulk for promotional, educational, or business use. Please contact your local bookseller or the Macmillan Corporate and Premium Sales Department at 1-800-221-7945, extension 5442, or by email at MacmillanSpecialMarkets@macmillan.com.

First Edition: March 2019

10 9 8 7 6 5 4 3 2 1

This book is dedicated to you—

may it bring a smile to your face and

joy to your kitchen

Contents

Entrées   95

Sides   141

Desserts   167

Drinks 217

Entertaining 249

Condiments 277

Ryan and Adam

Introduction

Ryan

Food is love.

All my life, food has been a way for my family to express affection—well, *most* of my family. My older brother David would tell me that I wasn't actually related to them, that I was found in a Dumpster behind the local Albertsons under a pile of wilted lettuce, because clearly, with my baby-blond hair and blue eyes, I did not fit in with the rest of our dark-haired, brown-eyed family. Much of my childhood was spent in the kitchen with my mother and grandmother, learning how to cook by their sides, and while their methods could not have been more different—my mother has shelves overflowing with cookbooks while my grandmother never followed a recipe in her life—they both shared the same love of cooking.

Even as an infant, I was interested in everything my mom did in the kitchen. When I was fussy, she would calm me down by putting me in a baby backpack while she washed the dishes. I would peer over her shoulder, intently watching all the action—and to this day, I still enjoy doing dishes, which is fairly helpful since Adam and I don't have a dishwasher. She encouraged my interest from the beginning, teaching me how to measure ingredients, how to follow a recipe, and techniques for everything from boiling an egg to baking a triple-layer cake. Her collection of cookbooks was diverse, featuring dishes from around the world, and when I moved out on my own, most of my recipes came from her.

My grandmother, on the other hand, cooked only by memory and intuition. Born in Argentina, she lived her adult life in Cuba before immigrating to the United States, so whenever I would visit my *abuelita,* her kitchen was filled with delicacies, from Cuban Black Beans and Rice (page 127) to Spanish Tortilla (page 156) and golden Cuban Empanadas (page 122), and there was always a creamy flan (page 202) chilling in the fridge. Every time I walked in the door, she greeted me with warm hugs and laughter, and the first question in her cheery Spanglish was always, "You got a hungry?" And my answer was always yes.

When I first met Adam, I was still a baby: a bright-eyed nineteen-year-old freshman at USC, just out of high school. I was living in cramped university housing—with antisocial roommates who never seemed to leave—so our only opportunities to cook together were at his tiny bachelor pad in Hollywood. He had only one pan in his kitchen, and we had to chop ingredients using a butter knife, but some of our most memorable meals came from that one-room apartment, sitting on the floor around an old coffee table. Three years later, once I graduated from college, we decided we'd had enough of the city—especially driving around for nearly an hour every day looking for parking—and moved into our first apartment together, with a full-size kitchen and two parking spots!

I did most of the cooking at first, but we both shared a love of food, and anytime we followed a recipe, we would take detailed notes on ways to improve it. Eventually, the collection of loose papers grew so out of hand that we organized them into a three-ring binder, each page filled with meticulous corrections, scribbled reminders, and numerous handwritten changes. That green folder, which still sits on our kitchen shelf, became our go-to cookbook containing all our favorite recipes. Eventually, Adam became so inspired and interested in the process that we began to split the cooking duties: every week we planned recipes and candlelit dinners to prepare for each other, and once he joined me in the kitchen, we never looked back.

In January 2015, I casually mentioned to Adam, "I think I'd like to start a cooking blog," and he immediately replied, "I want to do it with you!" We were photography novices, so it took us a few months to shoot food photos that were publicly presentable (our early pictures are kept in a hidden folder on our computer titled "Do Not Open" and for very good reason), but on April 29, 2015, we jumped into the world of blogging and officially launched *Husbands That Cook*.

Since we started the site, we've written hundreds of posts, but this book represents something special. Most are recipes we've never shared with anyone before—along with dishes that brought us together, like the Indian Curry with Chickpeas and Cauliflower (page 109) inspired by our first date, and those that tested our resolve as a couple, like the Communication Breakdown Carrot Cake with Whipped Goat Cheese Frosting (page 169) from one of our most epic fights. There are a handful of classics from the blog (like the showstopping Ratafruitie, page 265), but the remaining 125 recipes have never been seen before. Adam and I spent a delicious year roasting, toasting, testing, and tasting them, and every single one received an enthusiastic "Mmm!" from us—and our neighbors, who were the lucky recipients of our extra treats. We're excited for you to try them all, so come join us in the kitchen, pour some cocktails, and let's get the cooking party started!

Food is love, and this is our love letter: to each other, to our families and friends, and to you.

Enjoy!

Adam

Hello! I'm happy you're here! I am happy to be here!

You're probably wondering, who are these drop-dead gorgeous guys on the cover, and what is this cookbook all about? Light a few candles, pull up a comfortable chair, and allow me to tell you the story of how it all began . . .

Never in a million years did I think that I would one day write a cookbook. In fact, when I was in my early twenties, my friends used to tease me, saying I should open a restaurant dedicated entirely to microwaveable cuisine—I was *that* good. I didn't even like cooking until recently. I never had interest in following a recipe, felt overwhelmed by a messy kitchen with piles of dishes, and was intimidated by my lack of experience. Sound familiar? If you're anything like me, it is my goal to rid you of your cooking fears and show how fun and rewarding it can be!

Music was my life until just a few years ago. When I was still in diapers, I would pound away on the family room piano my dad won on an episode of *Hollywood Squares.* I begged my parents for music lessons, and at every recital, I was the eager student with his hand in the air requesting to perform first. I spent hours every day practicing and making up songs, and at age twelve, I became obsessed with musicals, landing lead roles at the community theater in plays like *Grease, Bye Bye Birdie,* and *A Chorus Line.* My parents supported me through every artistic adventure, despite the fact that I had a difficult time paying attention in class and was quite the handful growing up!

On the last day of high school, I formed a rock band with my best friend, and we made a career of it for almost twenty-five years. You've probably even heard some of our music! Our band, The 88, had songs featured in dozens of TV shows, movies, and commercials, and if you ever watched the NBC sitcom *Community,* you heard our theme song start the show every week. In 2010, our dreams came true when we got the call to be the opening act for Ray Davies—lead singer and songwriter of the Kinks—and joined him onstage during his set to play classic Kinks songs on multiple tours throughout the United States and overseas. We accomplished more than I could have ever imagined, but life had other plans in store for me.

Just as The 88 was taking a break in 2015, *Husbands That Cook* started to take off. So how did I go from musician and microwave man to cookbook author? Over the past several years, something inside me changed, and I fell completely in love with the process. Developing a recipe is just like writing a song, experimenting with the right combination of ingredients until the perfect flavors are achieved, and now I wake up every day excited to start cooking. And eating!

We want to welcome you to our cozy hilltop home and introduce you to our pumpkin-loving kitty, Sylvia—who will be making appearances here, since she is an important part of our story too. This book and these recipes are inspired by the spirit of our relationship—seventeen years of cooking, gardening, and traveling the world together. From Calzones with Broccoli, Pesto, Artichoke Hearts, and Sun-Dried Tomatoes (page 103), inspired by one of our first microwaved meals together back in my tiny studio apartment, to a Cinnamon Crumb Coffee Cake (page 186) my grandma Gertrude entered in a 1964 *Los Angeles Times* contest (winning the grand prize, a whopping five dollars!), this cookbook has a bit of everything. Oh, and it happens to be vegetarian too! So pick up some fresh, colorful ingredients, put on your favorite tunes, and happy cooking!

Basics

Preparing a special meal is a wonderful and creative way to spend your time. Surrounding yourself in the kitchen with fresh ingredients and aromatic fragrances—a hot skillet of sizzling garlic or a bubbling pot of butterscotch caramel—is a relaxing way to escape from the noise of daily routines, even if for just a brief moment. In this chapter, we will cover all the basics you will need to make any recipe in this book. It was important to us when creating these dishes that we use common, everyday ingredients, making them easily accessible so anyone can cook along. Throughout these next few pages, we cover everything from how to stock your pantry and fridge to kitchen tools that will help you decorate a gorgeous cake. You certainly don't need to own every kind of tool and cookware we are about to mention, so do not feel overwhelmed. Only a few items are truly necessary, and some are just suggestions to help make the process a little quicker and easier. There is no need to rush out to a kitchen supply store and purchase everything all at once, since cooking is a lifelong hobby; once you begin preparing more recipes and celebrating more birthdays, your collection will gradually grow over the years. Take it one day at a time, one recipe at a time, and we hope you learn a thing or two along the way and get as much joy and pleasure from cooking, eating, and sharing these recipes as we did while creating them.   —*Adam and Ryan*

Ingredients

Have you ever wondered what the difference is between soy sauce and tamari? Have you ever felt confused at the grocery store, trying to decide between cage-free, free-range, and pasture-raised eggs? In this section, we will answer all your questions, share food storage tips, and let you in on some clever substitution tricks—from how to make your own powdered sugar in a food processor to homemade buttermilk with just two ingredients. We will highlight a few pantry staples, and for more unusual ingredients, we will explain exactly what they are and where to find them. Join us in our kitchen as we open our cabinets and discuss the types of flours, oils, vinegars, and salts you will be using throughout this book. Have you ever questioned why some olive oils are labeled as *extra-virgin*? Did you know that cilantro stems have just as much flavor as the leaves? Sit back and relax, make a cup of our Soothing Ginger-Honey Tea (page 239), and let's chat about ingredients!

Pantry

HERBS

Since fresh herbs are often expensive at the store and wilt quickly, the best and cheapest way to enjoy them is by keeping small pots of living herbs on a bright windowsill. Even if you do not have outdoor space, a mini indoor herb garden will save you time and money and provide fresh herbs on a daily basis. We keep a small basil plant in our kitchen window, which we cook with almost every day, and once all the leaves are gone, we simply replace it with a new plant, which will last for months.

SPICES

Dried herbs and spices lose flavor over time, so when possible, buy in the bulk foods section of your grocery store and purchase only the amount you need, rather than picking up a large bottle that may go to waste.

- Smoked Paprika: Also known as *pimentón de la vera,* this lightly spiced paprika has a smoky, bold flavor. It is featured throughout the book, and a sprinkle of this bright red spice is a tasty garnish for savory dishes. We always use smoked paprika in our recipes since it is far more flavorful than standard paprika and works perfectly in any recipe that calls for it.

- Cayenne Pepper versus Red Pepper Flakes: Typically, we use red pepper flakes as a garnish and use cayenne for cooking since it is finely ground and disappears into the texture of a dish. Both have quite a kick, so feel free to adjust the amounts to your personal heat preference.

LIQUID CONDIMENTS

- Soy Sauce versus Tamari: In general, soy sauce and tamari are interchangeable. While they are both fermented soy products, traditional soy sauce is made with wheat while tamari is not, making it a convenient gluten-free substitute. Tamari is slightly less salty with a less intense flavor and makes a wonderful base for dipping sauces.

- Liquid Smoke: This aromatic ingredient adds smoky, bacon-y flavor without using any meat, like in our shiitake bacon (page 40) and Barbecue Baked Beans (page 151). It is made from the condensed smoke of hickory or mesquite chips and typically found in grocery stores in the baking aisle.

- Worcestershire Sauce: This British sauce has a tangy, salty, savory flavor and is used in our California Gumbo (page 118), Cheddar-Beer Fondue (page 275), and classic Bloody Mary cocktails. It traditionally contains anchovies, but there are vegetarian brands available at natural food stores and online.

FLOURS

We store flours in separate labeled containers, which keeps them fresh, easy to find, and organized. When adding flour to a mixing bowl, pour it through a fine-mesh strainer to remove any lumps.

- All-Purpose Flour: You will use this flour for most of the baking recipes in this book since it works in almost any situation. In stores, look for flour labeled as "unbleached," since it is not treated with harsh chemicals and is more nutritious and less processed.

- Bread Flour: This is best for baking bread since its higher protein content results in chewy, dense loaves like our Moroccan *khobz* (page 85). If you do not have bread flour, you can substitute all-purpose flour.

- Cake Flour: This is best for baking light, airy cakes like our I'm Dreaming of a White Christmas Cake (page 212). It is lower in protein and more finely ground, resulting in extra-soft layers. If you do not have cake flour, you can substitute all-purpose.

- Cornmeal and Masa Harina: These are two different types of corn flour. Cornmeal is coarsely ground, slightly gritty, and commonly used for corn bread and polenta, while masa harina is softer and treated with lime, used for tamales and tortillas in Mexican cuisine. They are very different products and cannot be substituted for each other.

OILS

For maximum freshness, store oils in a cool, dark place. As convenient as it may be to keep bottles of oil next to the stove, the heat will negatively affect the flavor.

- Extra-Virgin Olive Oil: The term *extra-virgin* means that the oil is unrefined, so it is higher quality and retains more of its natural olive flavor.

In stores, look for a dark glass bottle, since the flavor is affected by light.

- Vegetable Oil: This refers to any neutral-flavored oil used for frying, baking, or anytime the flavor of olive oil is not desired. Canola, safflower, and peanut oil all work in any recipe that calls for vegetable oil.

- Coconut Oil: This is sold in two varieties, *virgin* and *refined*. It is solid at room temperature, making it an ideal replacement for butter in vegan baked goods. Virgin coconut oil has a strong coconut flavor and is delicious in curries and coconut desserts. Refined coconut oil is flavorless, making it a versatile ingredient for both savory and sweet dishes.

VINEGARS

Vinegar is produced from the fermentation of alcohol. It adds tangy flavor and bright acidity when cooking, and it will last for five to ten years if stored in a cool, dark place. In baking, combining vinegar and baking soda can provide leavening for baked goods like our Vegan Chocolate Puddle Cake (page 171). There are five different kinds of vinegars in this book, each one with a different flavor profile and each used for a different purpose.

- White Vinegar: This clear vinegar has a neutral, clean, tangy flavor. It is the only vinegar we use in our baking recipes, but it can also be found in Cuban dishes like Yuca con Mojo (page 158). When poaching eggs, adding a splash of vinegar to the simmering water helps bind the whites together for perfectly poached eggs every time.

- White Wine Vinegar: Similar to white vinegar, but a little sweeter and with a hint of white wine flavor, this is commonly used in dips, salad dressings, and in our Curry Deviled Eggs (page 268).

- Balsamic Vinegar: Balsamic is a concentrated, aged vinegar made from grapes, which is dark in color and slightly thick and syrupy. It is sweeter and tangier than white wine vinegar, useful for salad dressings, and when combined with a splash of olive oil, it makes a delicious dip for slices of crusty bread.

- Apple Cider Vinegar: Made from apples, this amber-colored vinegar has a slight apple flavor with a hint of sweetness. Unfiltered varieties can be cloudy in appearance with material floating near the bottom, but this is normal; just give the bottle a shake before use.

- Rice Vinegar: Made from fermented rice, this vinegar is less acidic and has a mild flavor, perfect for sushi rice and other Asian dishes.

SALT

Salt can make or break a recipe, so in this book, we provide exact measurements every time. You won't find the words *salt to taste* here—we like being specific so you never have to guess.

- Table Salt: There are many types of salt available, but in our recipes, we cook with table salt—finely ground, refined white salt with no additives, like Morton Salt. Other types can vary widely in flavor and sodium levels, but table salt gives the most consistent results. It is available in plain and iodized varieties, and since the flavor is identical, feel free to use either one. The only difference is that iodized salt has added iodine, an essential nutrient for healthy thyroid and hormone function.

- Flaky Sea Salt: We use flaky sea salt as a final garnish for recipes rather than during cooking. It is less salty than table salt and has more flavor since it contains trace amounts of natural ocean minerals. Maldon salt works well because its large sparkling flakes make a pretty garnish while adding an irresistible crunchy texture.

- Coarse Kosher Salt: This coarse salt can vary in saltiness between brands, so for consistency, we use table salt when cooking. Kosher salt appears in just one recipe in this book, as a topping for Everything Pretzels (page 260).

SUGAR

Just like flour, we store sugars in sealed, labeled containers for easy use and to maintain freshness.

- Granulated Sugar: This is an all-purpose refined white sugar used in almost every dessert recipe in our book. Stored in a sealed container in a cool, dark place, it will last indefinitely in the pantry.

- Brown Sugar: Brown sugar is a partially refined sugar with a sweet molasses flavor, sold in light and dark varieties. Both types can be used interchangeably, but we like dark brown sugar because of its robust molasses flavor. When measuring, use the back of a spoon to pack it tightly into the measuring cup, as this will eliminate air pockets, ensuring accurate measurements every time. Brown sugar can dry out and harden over time, so be sure to store it in a sealed container. To prevent it from hardening, place a slice of apple in the container with the sugar. The sugar absorbs the moisture in the fruit, keeping it from drying out.

- Powdered Sugar: Also called confectioners' or icing sugar, this is perfect for frostings, fillings, and any recipe where a silky-smooth texture is desirable. The flavor is identical to granulated sugar; the only difference is that it is more finely ground. If a recipe calls for powdered sugar and you don't have any, make it yourself by blending granulated sugar in a food processor until it turns into powder. When using powdered sugar in a recipe, sift it through a fine-mesh strainer so the final product is smooth and creamy and doesn't contain any lumps.

GRAINS

- Arborio Rice: This is a short-grain rice from Italy with a high starch content, making it ideal for creamy risottos (page 99). We also use arborio when making our Vegetarian Paella (page 130), since it is much more widely available than traditional Spanish varieties of rice.

- Long-Grain Rice: This all-purpose rice is ideal for use in stews like our Cuban Black Beans and Rice (page 127) and California Gumbo (page 118) since the soft, fluffy texture helps the rice absorb the flavors around it.

- Short-Grain/Sushi Rice: This short-grain rice has a chewy texture and is somewhat sticky, used to make rice balls for sushi and *onigiri* (page 145) and in other Asian dishes like Bibimbap (page 133).

- Basmati: Basmati rice is a long-grain variety with an aromatic fragrance and flavor, traditionally used in Indian and South Asian cooking.

- Quinoa: This small South American grain is high in protein and fiber, making it more nutritious than rice. It needs to be thoroughly rinsed before use, since each grain is coated with a bitter substance known as *saponin*. It is cooked the same way as rice—in a pan on the stove until soft and fluffy.

OTHER PANTRY INGREDIENTS

- Cocoa: There are two types of cocoa: natural and dutch processed. Natural cocoa has a reddish-brown color and an intense bittersweet chocolate flavor. Dutch-processed cocoa is much darker in color, resulting in baked goods that appear almost black, with a slightly less bitter flavor—similar to an Oreo cookie. In this book, they can be used interchangeably, as it is simply a matter of preference.

- Chocolate: We use three kinds of chocolate in this book: milk, semisweet, and bittersweet. Milk chocolate is the sweetest with 20–30 percent cacao, and it contains dairy for a smooth, creamy flavor. Semisweet chocolate is a combination of sweet and bitter, containing 50–55 percent cacao. And bittersweet or dark chocolate contains 70–85 percent cacao for a more intense chocolate experience. Look for brands with as few ingredients on the label as possible: dark chocolate should contain cocoa, cocoa butter, sugar, vanilla, and nothing else. Avoid brands that contain lecithin or other stabilizers, as they have a waxy texture. Also, many brands of dark chocolate are vegan, but be sure to check the label to confirm.

- Instant Coffee: Instant coffee is useful for baking, as it is an easy way to bring the flavor of coffee to a recipe without adding excess liquid. There are two types available: coffee crystals, which add a light coffee flavor like in our Gooey Butterscotch Blondies (page 215), and instant espresso powder, which is darker, finely ground, and more intensely flavored, used in our Affogato Milkshake with Toasted Marshmallow (page 244).

- Yeast: We use two types of yeast in this book—active dry and instant. Active dry yeast needs to be proofed before mixing into dough, which is the process of soaking the yeast in a warm liquid to activate it. Instant yeast—also labeled as bread machine yeast—does not need to be proofed and causes breads to rise more quickly.

- Garlic: Individual garlic cloves can vary widely in size. In this cookbook, one large clove equals 5 grams, ensuring consistent results every time. You may need two or three to equal one large clove if they are too small. When sautéing garlic, cook it for no more than 30 seconds, as it can burn very quickly.

- Lentils: There are two types of lentils used in this book—red and brown. Red lentils are common in Indian cuisine and become creamy when cooked, like in Mulligatawny Soup (page 59). Brown lentils are chewy and hold their shape, making them an ideal replacement for meat in recipes like Cuban Empanadas (page 122) and Lentil-Stuffed Cabbage (page 124).

- Canned Beans: Canned beans are more convenient than dried beans. Dried beans are time-consuming, since they must be soaked overnight, taking hours to fully cook, but canned beans can be used immediately, saving time in the kitchen. Since sodium levels vary, check the labels and experiment with different brands to find one you like. In general, it is best to drain canned beans into a colander and rinse with cold water before use.

- Bread Crumbs: We use three types of bread crumbs in this book: finely ground plain bread crumbs, Italian-style bread crumbs—which have an herb seasoning blend added—and panko bread crumbs, which have larger pieces, giving a crispy texture to foods like onion rings (page 106). All three types are useful for absorbing moisture and helping to hold ingredients together, like in our Kale Bites with Lemon Ranch Dressing (page 257) and Tots Two Ways (page 251).

- Ground Flaxseeds: Ground flaxseeds are high in fiber and healthy omega-3 fatty acids. The only recipe in this book that calls for them is the Morning-After Smoothie with Blueberry and Banana (page 31), but they can also be used to create a vegan egg replacement in baking. To make a "flax egg," stir together 1 tablespoon of ground flaxseeds and 2½ tablespoons of water in a small bowl, and let rest for ten minutes. To prolong shelf life, store flaxseeds in the refrigerator for up to one year.

- Nutritional Yeast Flakes: This flaky yellow powder is high in protein, fiber, and vitamins, and has a savory, cheddar-like flavor. It is an excellent replacement for cheese in vegan sauces and is a delicious topping for popcorn and pastas. Look for it in the bulk section of natural food stores.

- Nut Butters: We use two nut butters in this book: peanut butter and almond butter. In most recipes, it is best to use a creamy all-natural kind that requires stirring, since they are healthier than processed brands. However, in certain recipes, like our Molten Peanut Butter Chocolate Cakes (page 210), we recommend a no-stir peanut butter, since the all-natural variety can become oily during baking. In recipes where a peanut flavor is not desirable—like our Gooey Butterscotch Blondies (page 215)—we use almond butter, since it has a milder flavor.

Fridge and Freezer

- Seasonal Produce: For the most flavorful results, try to purchase produce when it is in season. The difference between a fresh summer heirloom tomato and a crunchy grocery store tomato in winter is night and day. Some produce is flavorful year-round, but for fruit like peaches and cherries, it is best to enjoy them during the summertime, since off-season produce is often disappointing.

- Lemon and Other Acids: Acidic ingredients like lemon, lime, and vinegar lose their flavor when cooked, so they are best when added at the end, immediately before serving. If simmered for too long, their flavor will diminish.

- Milk: Since Adam is slightly lactose intolerant, whenever a recipe calls for milk, we use unsweetened almond milk, as the texture and flavor is similar to dairy. In this book, whenever a recipe calls for *milk of your choice,* feel free to use dairy milk, almond milk, soy milk, rice milk, or hemp milk. Whichever variety you choose, make sure it is unsweetened so it does not affect the flavor of the recipe.

- Buttermilk: Despite the name, buttermilk does not contain any butter. It is a low-fat cultured dairy product similar to a thin, pourable yogurt that adds a rich, tangy flavor to baked goods. If you do not have buttermilk, it is easy to make a substitute. Combine one cup of milk of your choice with one tablespoon of lemon juice or white vinegar, then let it sit for five minutes before use.

- Canned Coconut Milk: Canned coconut milk is thick and creamy, and it adds richness to curries and coconut desserts. It is normal for the milk to solidify inside the can, so simply stir it until smooth. When using coconut milk in a curry, it is important to keep it from boiling too heavily, as it will curdle and separate, so be sure to simmer it gently as it cooks.

- Yogurt: In stores, there are two common types of yogurt—plain and greek. In this cookbook, we only use greek yogurt, as it is creamier, higher in protein, and richer in flavor. Some brands add thickeners like pectin or gelatin, which makes the texture and flavor inferior, so look for brands that only contain milk, cream, and active cultures.

- Eggs: When buying eggs, there are several options available, each kind determined by the chickens' living conditions. Standard eggs are usually laid by chickens packed in tight cages inside factories. Cage-free chickens are not kept in cages but still live in cramped indoor communal spaces. Free-range chickens have access to the outdoors, but it may be limited to a tiny, fenced-in concrete patio. Pasture-raised chickens live freely outside, pecking in the grass for food in the sunshine. Not only is this the most humane option, but the difference in the eggs is incomparable; the yolks are deep orange, buttery, and far more flavorful.

- Butter versus Vegan Butter: In any recipe that calls for butter, feel free to substitute vegan butter, as the flavor and texture are nearly identical.

When baking, we always use unsalted butter for consistency, since every brand of salted butter contains different amounts of salt.

- Mayonnaise versus Vegan Mayo: Vegan mayo and regular mayo are essentially identical and can be swapped in any recipe.

- Tofu: Tofu is available in silken, soft, firm, and extra-firm varieties. In this book, we exclusively use firm and extra-firm. Since tofu absorbs all the flavors around it, it is extremely versatile and can be used in a wide variety of dishes. When cooking with tofu, first drain the water, place the block on a cutting board, set a paper towel on top, and press down gently to remove excess water before dicing.

- Whole Cheese versus Grated: When cooking with grated cheese, we recommend buying blocks of cheese and grating them yourself; pre-shredded cheese is coated with cellulose and other additives that can negatively affect the flavor and texture of the dish.

- Miso: This is a fermented soybean paste used in Japanese cuisine, found in three common types: white, yellow, and red. In this book, we use red miso exclusively, as it is the most savory and intensely flavored of the three. Miso is filled with healthy probiotics and will keep indefinitely in the fridge.

- *Gochujang:* This fermented red Korean chili paste is spicy and savory with a hint of sweetness. It is common in Korean cooking and a key ingredient in Bibimbap (page 133). Look for it in Asian grocery stores, and keep it in the fridge after opening.

- Pomegranate Molasses: This thick, intensely tart syrup is made from concentrated pomegranate juice and can be found in natural food markets and grocery stores that cater to a Middle Eastern clientele. It brightens our tangy pomegranate vinaigrette (page 72) and is also the secret ingredient in the Mediterranean dip known as muhammara.

- Parsley: When shopping for parsley, always look for italian parsley, also known as flat-leaf. It has a more robust flavor than curly parsley, which is more commonly used as a garnish. When chopping parsley, be sure to include the stems, since they have just as much flavor as the leaves.

- Cilantro: Just like parsley, when chopping cilantro for a recipe, use the stems along with the leaves, since they are also very flavorful.

- Scallions: Also known as green onions, these long and thin sprouts have a milder flavor than yellow onions. When chopping, use the entire scallion, including all the white and green parts, as they are equally flavorful.

- Jalapeño versus Serrano Peppers: Serrano peppers are slightly spicier than jalapeños, but both are similar enough to substitute in any recipe. Most of the heat is contained in the seeds and white ribs, so for milder results, remove and discard them before use. When handling hot peppers, be sure to wear gloves, or wash your hands immediately afterward, since the juice from the peppers can irritate your skin and eyes.

- Capers: There are two types of capers available: salt-packed and brined. When using salt-packed capers, be sure to rinse them before use; otherwise, the excess salt will affect the flavor of the dish.

- Frozen Bananas: A delicious addition to smoothies, frozen bananas can also be blended up into a silky-smooth gelato-like "nice cream" (page 204). Simply peel and chop the bananas at room temperature, place the slices in a single layer in a ziplock bag, and freeze until firm. The frozen slices will stay fresh for up to two months.

- Frozen Spinach: In recipes that use a large amount of spinach, like our Spanakopita Quiche (page 26), it is cheaper and easier to use frozen spinach, since it takes four to five bags of fresh leaves to equal one small block of frozen. The flavor and nutritional value are identical, and it is far more convenient.

- Vegetable Broth: When testing all the recipes for our cookbook, we used our homemade Vegetable Bouillon (page 46). Since store-bought broth varies in quality and is often disappointing and expensive, we make our own bullion base and store it in the freezer for use throughout the year. It is fresher, much tastier, and more economical, as it allows you to make broth in small amounts rather than buying large containers that often go to waste. If you purchase broth from the store, make sure it is flavorful, as it is an important foundation to any recipe. Since every packaged broth varies in sodium levels, you may need to adjust the salt in recipes to compensate.

Equipment

Cookware

- Saucepans: It is helpful to have four different sizes of pans: small (1–2 quarts) for simmering sauces, medium (3–4 quarts) for cooking rice and grains, large (4–6 quarts) for soups, and extra-large (6–8 quarts) for larger stews and boiling pasta. Each pan should have a tight-fitting lid and heatproof handles so they can be used on the stove and in the oven.

- Skillets: Every kitchen should have at least one medium nonstick skillet (8–10 inches) and one large, deep, oven-safe skillet with a lid (10–12 inches). When cooking on a nonstick skillet, be sure to use wooden or plastic utensils, as metal can scratch the finish. When purchasing nonstick cookware, look for brands that use nontoxic

ingredients, as traditional Teflon pans can be hazardous to the environment and your health.

- Cast-Iron Skillets: These classic skillets are useful since they are oven-safe and will last for generations. The care and cleaning of cast iron is different from other cookware; you almost never use soap, and it must be seasoned to work effectively. To season a cast-iron pan, once it is clean and dry, rub the surface with a light coating of neutral vegetable oil. When cleaning cast iron after cooking, scrub the pan with a bristled brush using hot water, and avoid using soap, as it will strip the oil—although a small amount of soap is sometimes necessary for tougher cleaning jobs. Rinse the pan thoroughly in hot water, pat it dry immediately after washing, and reapply a thin coat of oil over the entire surface. Doing this over time will make it nearly as nonstick as a Teflon pan. To help maintain the finish, do not use the pan to cook highly acidic foods, as they can corrode the iron.

- Steamer Basket: These collapsible baskets are useful for steaming vegetables like the broccoli in our calzones (page 103), and since they will fit inside pans of almost any size, they allow you to cook everything from tiny brussels sprouts to giant globe artichokes and any vegetable in between.

- Grill Pan: These ridged pans are a convenient way to achieve seared grill marks on the stove without using an outdoor barbecue. It is not essential to own one, but they are an indoor alternative that allows you to grill throughout the year.

- Double Boiler: This is a type of bowl-shaped pan that rests on top of another pan on the stove. The lower pan is filled with a few inches of water, and when placed on the stove, the steam from the water gently heats the upper pan, which is ideal when working with delicate ingredients like melting chocolate or when cooking a silky flan (page 202). When buying a double boiler, look for one that dips several inches into the lower pan, rather than simply sitting on top. If you do not own a double boiler, you can easily use a heatproof mixing bowl instead: simply select a bowl that rests snugly in the pan you are using. When filling the lower pan, leave space between the water level and the double boiler, as the bottom of the pan should not touch the water directly.

Baking

- Cake Pans: We use two sizes of round cake pans in this book—8 and 9 inches. We recommend having two pans in each size, with sides about 2 inches tall. It can also be helpful to have a pair of 6-inch pans for serving smaller groups, since any full-size cake recipe can be cut in half to make a 6-inch cake that serves 6 to 8 people. When baking cakes, we always grease the pans with butter or vegan butter, then line the bottoms with a circle of parchment. To create a circle of parchment, place the cake pan on a flat sheet then trace around the bottom with a pencil. Cut the parchment into a circle, and press it into the bottom of the pan. This helps release the cakes smoothly after baking.

- Baking Sheets: Also known as cookie sheets, these flat pans are available in different sizes, but the most common type is called a *half sheet* pan, measuring 13×18 inches. Look for a pan with sides at least ½ inch tall to prevent leaks or spills in the oven. Also, pans with dark finishes absorb heat faster, which will cause food to brown more quickly, so keep an eye on the oven as it cooks and adjust baking times as needed. To prevent sticking and help with cleanup, we often line our baking sheets with a reusable silicone mat or parchment paper, both of which are oven-safe for temperatures up to 480°F/250°C.

- Baking Pans: In this book, we use two sizes of baking pans: an 8-inch square pan and a 9×13-inch rectangular pan. Any time a recipe calls for a 9×13-inch pan, it can be cut in half to fit perfectly in an 8-inch square.

- Mixing Bowls: It is helpful to own a set of mixing bowls in a variety of sizes. Heatproof bowls made from tempered glass are preferable, since they can also be used as double boilers, heated in the oven and microwave, and kept in the fridge. Deep bowls with tall sides are better than shallow, wide bowls, as they are more effective at preventing spattering when mixing.

- Dry Measuring Cups: A complete set of dry measuring cups should include: ¼ cup, ⅓ cup, ½ cup, ⅔ cup, ¾ cup, and 1 cup. The most durable kinds are made from metal with the size clearly etched into each handle. Plastic cups with printed numbers often fade, leaving you guessing which size is which.

- Liquid Measuring Cups: It is helpful to have three sizes of liquid measuring cups: 1 cup, 2 cup, and 4 cup. Those made from tempered glass are best, since they are heatproof and microwave-safe.

- Measuring Spoons: Just like dry measuring cups, we prefer to use metal measuring spoons, since they are more durable than plastic. It can be helpful to own two sets, because in baking, recipes often use multiple spoons for measuring ingredients. Each set should include ⅛ teaspoon, ¼ teaspoon, ½ teaspoon, ¾ teaspoon, 1 teaspoon, and 1 tablespoon. Look for spoons that are long and thin rather than wide and round since they fit more easily into small spice jars.

- Cooling Racks: We use metal wire cooling racks to cool all our baked goods. It is helpful to have at least two racks, which should provide enough space for an entire batch of cookies.

CAKE-DECORATING EQUIPMENT

With just a few simple tools, you can create a sleek cake that will impress your guests without any classes or training. While none of these tools are necessary to prepare the cakes in this book, they will allow you to decorate them with smoother edges and cleaner lines.

- Pastry Bag: These long, thin bags can be filled with frosting or whipped cream and fitted with tips of different shapes to create cake decorations. Look for them in the baking section of grocery or kitchen supply stores. They can be reusable or disposable, but if you don't have any, you can substitute a ziplock bag: fill it with your desired frosting, snip off one corner using a pair of scissors to your desired width, and voilà—an instant pastry bag!

- Piping Tips: While there are thousands of differently shaped tips available, you only need two for a basic cake decorating set: one round tip and one star tip. Round tips are useful for writing on cakes or for making polka dots, while star tips are used for making swirls of frosting and decorative shell borders around the sides of cakes.

- Cake Leveler: A cake leveler is an adjustable wire tool that allows you to slice cakes into thin, perfectly even layers. If you do not own one, simply use a long, serrated knife and cut slowly and carefully, making the layers as even as possible. If they are not perfect, don't worry—any sloping layers can be leveled out with frosting and won't be noticeable once the cake is assembled.

- Turntable: A small turntable or lazy Susan makes frosting cakes easier, since you can keep your hands still while the cake rotates, resulting in smoother finishes and more accurate piping.

- Offset Spatula: These metal tools are useful for smoothing the tops and sides of cakes as well as spreading fillings and batters. They are easier to use than straight spatulas, since the bent angle of the blade allows you to spread a smooth surface comfortably and evenly.

Kitchen Tools

- Knives: While many knife sets contain over a dozen types of blades, you only need four: one small paring knife, one medium knife for chopping vegetables, one large chef's knife, and one long, serrated knife for cutting breads and cakes. To keep your knives sharp, do not wash them in the dishwasher; simply clean them by hand and towel-dry. Also, do not leave them in the sink with other dirty dishes or keep them in drawers with other utensils, as this will cause the blades to get chipped and dull more quickly.

- Mandoline: This extra-sharp cutting tool has an adjustable blade for making thin, even slices of any thickness. A knife will do the same job, but a mandoline makes it quicker, easier, and more precise. They are especially useful for slicing firm produce like potatoes, apples, onions, and squash, as well as fresh fruit like in our rainbow-colored Ratafruitie (page 265). Many mandolines include a hand guard, so be sure to use it to avoid cutting your fingers.

- Pastry Knife: This horseshoe-shaped tool, also known as a pastry blender, has rows of thinly spaced blades used for cutting butter into dry ingredients for pie and pastry crusts. If you do not own one, you can use two knives in a scissoring motion to do the same job, but since a pastry knife is inexpensive and works much better, we recommend buying one if you plan on baking.

- Rubber Spatula: These versatile kitchen tools are also called rubber scrapers. They are used to stir and scrape the sides of bowls when baking and can also be used when cooking on the stovetop if they are made of heatproof silicone.

- Spatula: Wide, thin, flat spatulas are versatile tools and essential for everything from flipping pancakes and burgers to lifting cookies onto a cooling rack. They are useful for sautéing vegetables in a skillet, as well as tossing roasted potatoes in the oven.

- Wooden Spoons: When cooking on the stovetop, we almost always use wooden spoons. Since wood does not conduct heat, you can comfortably stir a simmering pot without the handle getting hot, and they can be used on any material, including nonstick pans, since they do not scratch the finish like metal utensils.

- Whisk: This essential kitchen tool is used for everything from mixing dry ingredients for a cake to simmering caramel on the stove. If you don't own an electric mixer, you can use a whisk and a bit of elbow grease to create smooth frostings, delicate meringues, and fluffy whipped cream.

- Spider Strainer: This is a wide, cup-shaped wire strainer with a long wooden handle. It is useful for lifting food out of hot liquids, such as doughnuts from hot oil or vegetables from a pot of simmering water.

- Tongs: A set of long-handled heatproof tongs is useful for various kitchen tasks, like flipping roasted vegetables in the oven, tossing mixed salads, and making a stir-fry on the stovetop.

- Candy Thermometer: Also known as a deep-fry thermometer, this tool is useful for melting sugar, deep-frying, making candy, and testing the liquid temperature when proofing yeast for bread. It can be conveniently clipped onto the sides of pans for easy measurement and will ensure consistent results when cooking.

- Oven Thermometer: Every oven heats a little differently. Some ovens run hotter or colder than the displayed temperature, so the best way to ensure successful baking is to simply test your oven temperature. Small, inexpensive, clip-on thermometers are widely available in grocery and kitchen supply stores and tell you the exact temperature of your oven so you can adjust accordingly, if needed.

- Salad Spinner: These large spinning bowls are great for drying leafy greens and fresh herbs, and they remove much more water than simply draining them in a colander. Although they are often bulky, we are happy to make space in our kitchen, since they work so well.

- Colander: A wide colander with large holes is useful for draining pasta, rinsing beans, and washing vegetables. Look for one at least 10–12 inches wide.

- Wire-Mesh Strainer: Fine-mesh strainers have a variety of uses. Larger sizes (8–10 inches) are useful for sifting dry ingredients, straining custards and fruit purées, and rinsing grains like rice and quinoa. Small strainers (4–5 inches) are useful for dusting baked goods with cocoa or powdered sugar.

- Rolling Pin: This essential baking tool is used to make piecrusts and cookies like our Strawberry Apricot Rugelach (page 193). Look for a rolling pin at least 12 inches wide for maximum coverage. If you do not own one, a wine bottle is a convenient substitute.

- Pizza Cutter: This rolling tool can be used for more than just cutting pizza. It can also cut pastry dough cleanly and evenly, and is helpful when making homemade pasta like our Cheesy Artichoke-Stuffed Ravioli (page 116).

- Citrus Squeezer: Handheld citrus squeezers are the quickest and easiest way to juice citrus in small batches. They are available in different sizes—often color-coded for limes, lemons, and oranges—but if you buy just one, pick out the largest size, since it will fit all types of citrus.

- Microplane versus Standard Grater: Microplanes are useful for zesting citrus, fresh ginger, and hard cheeses like Parmesan and pecorino. They are extremely sharp, so use with caution. Standard graters with larger holes are used for grating softer cheeses, as well as fruits and vegetables, like the grated apples for our Mulligatawny Soup (page 59).

- Garlic Roller: There are countless techniques for peeling garlic, but one of the easiest ways is to use a garlic roller—a flexible rubber tube that peels cloves in seconds. This comes in handy when you have to peel large amounts of garlic, like in our twenty-clove Yuca con Mojo (page 158).

- Potato Masher: These flat tools are useful for making smooth mashed potatoes and puréed beans. If you do not own one, a fork works nearly as well—although it may take a bit longer to achieve the same creamy results.

- Brushes: A kitchen brush is useful for spreading glazes on baked goods and coating food with sauce. Look for brushes made from heatproof silicone, as natural-bristle brushes can sometimes leave fibers on your food.

- Nut Milk Bag versus Cheesecloth: Nut milk bags are reusable, ultrafine-mesh bags used for making homemade milks, such as for our Horchata with Almond Milk (page 247). They are also useful for removing pulp from juices like in our Post-Hike Pick-Me-Up (page 243). If you do not own one, you can use several overlapping layers of cheesecloth as a substitute, although it is not as fine and may allow some pulp to slip through.

- Pasta Machine: This countertop hand-cranked roller makes perfectly even, thin sheets of pasta. We use it for our Cheesy Artichoke-Stuffed Ravioli (page 116), but if you do not own one, we provide instructions on how to make ravioli by simply using wonton wrappers.

- Gnocchi Board: This small wooden board with ridges is used to make textured lines on gnocchi and cavatelli. If you do not own one, you can also make ridges using a fork.

- Mortar and Pestle: We use a mortar and pestle to mash garlic into a paste for Yuca con Mojo (page 158), and they are also useful for grinding spices and seeds. Look for a mortar with a capacity of at least one cup.

Electronics

- Kitchen Scale: In this book, we provide exact weight measurements for almost every ingredient, because cooking by weight is more precise than cooking by volume. This is especially important in baking. For instance, when measuring flour, one "cup" can contain drastically different amounts simply because of how firmly it was packed, but if you know that one cup of flour weighs 120 grams, the results will be consistent every time. We also include weights for produce because simply calling for "one onion" can be fairly vague—since onions range in size from a golf ball to a softball, we always provide exact measurements for consistency. When weighing ingredients, we set the scale to metric, as it is easier to measure whole numbers like *250 grams* rather than awkward measurements like *8.82 ounces*. Also, kitchen scales are useful in helping to cut down on dishes. For instance, when baking a cake, instead of individually measuring each ingredient with separate cups and spoons, you can simply place an empty mixing bowl on the scale, press Tare to set it to zero, and add the first ingredient until the correct weight is reached. Then set it to zero again, repeat with the next ingredient, and so on. Fewer dishes *and* more accuracy? Win-win!

- Food Processor: These powerful machines are useful when making purées, grinding dry ingredients, and making creamy hummus (page 262). When fitted with a grater attachment, it makes shredding vegetables like carrots and potatoes quick and easy.

- Blender: A blender is useful when making smoothies, sauces, and puréed soups. High-powered blenders can even crush ice with no difficulty, creating extra-creamy drinks—the more powerful the blender, the smoother the results. When blending hot soups, only fill the blender halfway, making sure the lid is tightly secure, as steam can cause hot liquid to spray out. If your blender is tough to clean around the blades, try adding a few drops of dish soap, fill it halfway with warm water, run the machine until clean, then thoroughly rinse and dry.

- Immersion Blender: This handheld tool can blend soups and sauces as they simmer on the stove. They are safer and easier to use than a standard blender when dealing with hot liquids, as there is less chance of spilling. When preparing a soup that requires blending, use a deep pan and be sure to completely immerse the blades in the liquid to minimize spattering.

- Stand Mixer: This is a baker's best friend, since it does all the hard work for you. When whisking egg whites or whipped cream, you can turn on the mixer and walk away while it works its magic. If you do not own one, a handheld electric mixer works just as well.

- Electric Juicer: This is helpful for making refreshing fruit and vegetable juices, since it filters out all the pulp. If you do not own a juicer, you can purée fruits and vegetables in a blender, then filter out the excess pulp using a nut milk bag or cheesecloth.

- Rice Cooker: A rice cooker is an easy, hands-off way to cook rice and other grains. It is convenient, since it cooks a perfect bowl of rice with the push of a button, but if you do not own one, you can easily cook grains on the stovetop instead.

Kitchen Tips

- How to Organize a Cabinet: Keeping your cabinets neat and organized makes it easy to find what you need, when you need it. We store our baking ingredients and grains in clear containers, making it apparent when anything is running low and needs to be replaced. They are sealed to keep everything fresh and free from pests, and since many baking ingredients look alike, when the containers are labeled, it is easy to tell them apart. With this tidy method, you will never confuse salt and sugar again—like Adam once did when he added several spoonfuls of salt to his morning coffee.

- Pinch versus Teaspoons: For the purposes of this book, we consider "a generous pinch" to be about $\frac{1}{16}$ teaspoon, while "a pinch" is approximately half of that. In general, we use the word *pinch* when referring to ingredients used as a garnish, since we prefer to use specific measured amounts in our recipes.

- Broiling: This oven technique uses high heat directly above the food, searing just the top. It is useful for toasting bread, searing vegetables, and melting cheese. To use the broil setting on your oven, place the oven rack in the highest position, just underneath the heating element, and set the oven to 500°F/260°C. While broiling, keep the oven door open—this allows you to keep an eye on the food so it doesn't burn and prevents the oven interior from becoming too hot and baking the food.

- Cooking with Wine: When cooking with wine, there is no need to spend money on a high-end bottle—any inexpensive wine will work perfectly with these recipes.

Bar Basics

We love mixing drinks for friends; it is cheaper than going out and fun to experiment with fresh fruit and homemade simple syrups (page 280). Stocking a home bar is easy, and with a few basic tools and supplies listed below, you can create dozens of classic cocktails.

Tools

- Shaker with built-in strainer
- Two-sided jigger with ½- and 1-ounce cups
- Muddler
- Citrus squeezer

Glassware

- Martini or coupe glasses
- Old-fashioned glasses (short and wide)
- Collins glasses (tall and thin)
- Pitcher for batch cocktails

Liquor

- Vodka
- Gin
- Bourbon
- Rum
- Tequila

Mixers

- Ice
- Citrus (limes, oranges, lemons)
- Simple syrup (plain or flavored, see page 280)
- Angostura bitters
- Ginger beer
- Soda and tonic water

Garnishes

- Maraschino cherries (look for brands with no artificial color, such as Luxardo)
- Tajín spice for rimming glasses
- Cocktail picks
- Cocktail umbrellas

Breakfast

Rise and shine! Open the curtains and start that pot of coffee. The sun is out, and we have thirteen delicious reasons for you to get out of bed today. Whether you are craving something sweet or savory, hearty or light, your breakfast basics are covered, from tropical smoothies to towering stacks of pancakes. Looking for a simple week-day breakfast? Our Avocado Toast with Sautéed Onions and Shiitake Bacon (page 40) or Chunky Apple Spice Granola (page 42) will certainly put a spring in your step. Planning your next brunch? Recipes like Orange-Pecan Overnight French Toast (page 32) and Spanakopita Quiche (page 26) are prepared the night before, making Sunday morning entertaining a breeze. Put on your robe and slippers, come join us in the kitchen, and let's get cooking!

Eggs Florentine with Garlicky Swiss Chard

Serves 4 to 6 • Gluten-Free Option

Extra! Extra! Read all about it! The secret to the perfectly poached egg has been revealed. While you can't believe everything you read, here the proof is in the poaching. The tips we're sharing result in consistently tender whites and soft golden yolks every single time. Here, a delicate poached egg rests on a healthy bed of garlicky swiss chard and a crispy homemade English muffin. Topped with a lemony hollandaise sauce, flaky sea salt, and a pinch of red pepper flakes, this breakfast is making all the headlines.

FOR THE ENGLISH MUFFINS (MAKES 8)

2¼ cups (270 g) all-purpose flour
1 teaspoon salt
¾ cup (177 ml) milk
1 tablespoon granulated sugar
1⅛ teaspoons active dry yeast
1 large egg
1½ tablespoons unsalted butter, melted
Vegetable oil, for greasing the dough bowl
2 teaspoons cornmeal or farina (Cream of
    Wheat), plus more if needed

FOR THE HOLLANDAISE SAUCE

3 large egg yolks
1 tablespoon heavy cream
8 ounces (226 g) unsalted butter, melted and
    cooled to room temperature
1 tablespoon lemon juice
½ teaspoon salt
dash of ground cayenne pepper

FOR THE GARLICKY SWISS CHARD

2 tablespoons extra-virgin olive oil
4 large garlic cloves (20 g), minced
2 bunches swiss chard, stems removed, leaves
    roughly chopped (370 g of leaves total)
½ teaspoon salt

FOR THE POACHED EGGS AND ASSEMBLY

splash of white vinegar
8 large eggs
flaky sea salt, for garnish
freshly ground black pepper, for garnish
red pepper flakes, for garnish

TO MAKE THE ENGLISH MUFFINS

In a large mixing bowl, combine the flour and salt, whisk briefly, and set aside. In a glass measuring cup, combine the milk and sugar, stir to dissolve, and heat to 110–115°F/43–46°C (see note about how to save time). Add the yeast, and stir until the lumps are broken up. Let rest for about 5 minutes, until foamy.

When foamy, pour the milk mixture into the mixing bowl with the flour, then add the egg

and melted butter. Stir until the dough is evenly blended—if it is too wet, add 1 tablespoon of flour at a time; if it is too dry, add 1 teaspoon of milk at a time. If you are using a stand mixer, use the dough hook and knead on medium speed for 5 minutes, until the dough is smooth and elastic. If kneading by hand, place the dough onto a floured work surface and knead until stretchy, about 10 minutes. Form the dough into a ball, then lightly oil the inside of the mixing bowl with a few drops of vegetable oil, and place the ball in the bowl. Cover the bowl with a kitchen towel and let rise for 1 hour.

Preheat oven to 350°F/177°C. Place a large heavy skillet, about 10 to 12 inches in diameter, on the stove, but do not turn on the heat. Sprinkle a few teaspoons of cornmeal or farina in the skillet. Uncover the dough, then transfer it to a clean work surface. Divide into 8 equal portions, and roll each one into a 3-inch ball. Flatten slightly to a disc shape, then place in the skillet, on top of the farina. Space the discs 1 inch apart, and do not crowd the pan too tightly. (You may have to do this in two batches, depending on the size of the skillet.)

Heat skillet on low and cook until the underside of each muffin is dark brown, 7 to 15 minutes. If they puff too much, use the back of a spatula to flatten them again. Flip and cook until the second side is deeply browned as well, another 7 to 15 minutes. Transfer the muffins to a baking sheet and bake for 10 minutes.

Muffins will keep for a week in a sealed container at room temperature. Be sure they are fully cooled before storage.

TO MAKE THE HOLLANDAISE SAUCE

Place the egg yolks and cream in a heatproof mixing bowl, and whisk to combine. Find a saucepan that the bowl will fit on top of. Pour an inch or two of water in the pan, ensuring that the water does not touch the bottom of the bowl. Whisking constantly, turn the heat to medium-low and bring the water to a bare simmer. Make sure that the water is not boiling. If the water begins to boil, lower the heat. The mixture will thicken slightly once the water is simmering. Continuing to whisk constantly, add the melted butter extremely slowly, a few drops at a time, whisking until blended after each addition. Once all the butter has been added, slowly add the lemon juice in the same manner. Continue to whisk until the sauce is the consistency of cake batter (it will thicken as it cools), then whisk in the salt and cayenne pepper, and remove from heat. Let cool briefly before serving. If the sauce thickens too much for your liking, thin it out by adding a few drops of warm water and whisking to combine.

TO MAKE THE GARLICKY SWISS CHARD
Place the oil and garlic in a skillet, and turn the heat to medium. When the garlic begins sizzling, add the chard, and toss to combine. Cook, stirring occasionally, until the chard is wilted and tender, about 3 to 4 minutes. Add salt, stir to combine, and remove from heat.

TO POACH THE EGGS
Place a medium saucepan filled with several inches of water over high heat. Add a splash of white vinegar, bring to a boil, then lower heat to a simmer. Place a fine-mesh strainer over a small bowl. Crack an egg into the strainer, and let it sit for 1 minute to let the watery part of the egg white drain out. At this point, the egg can be poured directly into the simmering water, or if you want to cook multiple eggs simultaneously, pour the drained egg into a small cup. Repeat with the remaining eggs, then add up to 4 at once to the simmering water, distributing evenly around the pan so they do not crowd each other. Once the eggs enter the water, set a timer for 2½ minutes. When the time is up, use a slotted spoon to remove them from the water.

TO ASSEMBLE THE DISH
Use a fork to split an English muffin in half. If desired, toast the muffin halves (either in a toaster or a dry skillet over medium heat) until golden brown, then place them cut-side-up on a plate. Top with a layer of sautéed chard, then a poached egg. Pour a generous amount of hollandaise sauce over the egg, then sprinkle with a pinch of flaky sea salt, a few grinds of black pepper, and a pinch of red pepper flakes. Serve immediately, and enjoy!

Notes

- Time-Saving Tips: The English muffins can be made ahead of time and will stay fresh for a week. They are delicious and flavorful, but if you are pressed for time, then store-bought will work too. The hollandaise is silkiest and smoothest the day it is made, but it can be prepared ahead of time too; when reheating, heat slowly and gently on the stovetop or in the microwave, whisking often and adding drops of warm water if too thick. The sautéed chard can also be made ahead of time; just reheat when ready to assemble.

- The milk and sugar can be heated in the microwave or in a pan on the stovetop. A candy thermometer works best to test the temperature, but if you do not own one, you can carefully test it with your finger. The milk should feel quite warm, but not hot.

- To make this Gluten-Free: serve with gluten-free English muffins.

Breakfast Enchiladas with Crispy Spiced Potatoes

Makes 10 to 12 enchiladas, serves 5 to 6 • Vegan Option

Los Angeles is known for its authentic Mexican cuisine. We feel lucky because within walking distance of our house, there are dozens of options to choose from. From the friendly older couple running their taco cart outside our local bar every weekend, to the trendy vegan trucks lining the boulevard and offering meatless versions of our favorite Latin dishes, the city is brimming with choices. Inspired by our scrumptious surroundings, we created a breakfast that brings a little taste of our neighborhood into your home. This homemade enchilada sauce is so tasty, it almost made it into the drinks chapter! Say good-bye to canned and bland sauce, and treat yourself to (cue the music) "a whole new world" of enchiladas. If only every day can start with crispy garlicky potatoes, sautéed spinach, scrambled eggs, and melty cheese wrapped in warm corn tortillas . . . oh, wait, now it can!

FOR THE ENCHILADA SAUCE
3 tablespoons vegetable oil
3 tablespoons all-purpose flour
6 tablespoons chili powder
¾ teaspoon garlic powder
¾ teaspoon salt
½ teaspoon ground cumin
½ teaspoon dried oregano
3 cups (710 ml) vegetable broth (page 46)

FOR THE SPINACH FILLING
2 tablespoons extra-virgin olive oil
1 large yellow onion (300 g), thinly sliced
5 ounces (142 g) spinach, roughly chopped
¼ teaspoon salt
¼ teaspoon freshly ground black pepper

FOR THE POTATOES
3 tablespoons extra-virgin olive oil
12 ounces (340 g) Yukon Gold potatoes, unpeeled and cut into ½-inch cubes
½ teaspoon salt
¼ teaspoon freshly ground black pepper
¼ teaspoon ground cumin
½ teaspoon chili powder
¼ teaspoon garlic powder
3 tablespoons water

FOR THE SCRAMBLED EGGS
5 large eggs
¼ teaspoon salt
1 tablespoon unsalted butter

FOR ASSEMBLY AND SERVING
10 to 12 corn tortillas
1¼ cups (142 g) shredded monterey jack cheese, divided
1¼ cups (142 g) shredded cheddar cheese, divided
coarsely chopped cilantro, for garnish
sliced avocado, for garnish

TO MAKE THE ENCHILADA SAUCE
In a medium saucepan, heat the oil over medium heat. When hot, add the flour and whisk for 1 minute. Add all the spices, whisk to combine, then add the broth. Raise heat and bring to a boil. Lower to a simmer and cook uncovered, stirring occasionally, until slightly thickened, 10 to 15 minutes. Remove from heat and let cool. Use right away, or cool completely and store in the refrigerator in a sealed container for up to a week.

Notes

- The sauce, spinach filling, potatoes, and even the eggs can all be made up to a week in advance, so it is easy to make this at your own pace. That way, when it's time for brunch, all you have to do is roll up the enchiladas, and you're ready to go.

- To make this Vegan: omit the scrambled eggs, and use a vegan cheese blend.

TO MAKE THE SPINACH FILLING

In a large skillet, heat the olive oil over medium heat. When hot, add the onion and sauté, stirring occasionally, until softened and beginning to turn golden brown, 7 to 10 minutes. Add the spinach and toss to combine. Cook until the spinach wilts, 2 to 3 minutes. Remove from heat, add the salt and pepper, and stir to combine. Use right away, or cool completely and store in the refrigerator in a sealed container for up to a week.

TO MAKE THE POTATOES

Set the oven to 375°F/191°C. In a large oven-safe skillet with a lid, heat the oil over medium heat. When hot, add the potatoes, salt, pepper, cumin, chili powder, and garlic powder, and toss to combine. Cook uncovered for 5 minutes, stirring occasionally. Turn heat to high, add the water, cover the pan, and sauté until the water evaporates, 3 to 4 minutes, stirring occasionally. Remove from heat, then transfer the uncovered pan to the oven, and bake until creamy inside and crispy outside, 18 to 25 minutes. Use right away, or cool completely and store in the refrigerator for up to a week. Note that the flavor will stay fresh, but they will lose their crispness quickly. (Note: if you do not have an oven-safe skillet, simply transfer the potatoes to a baking sheet lined with parchment or a silicone mat and bake as directed.)

TO MAKE THE SCRAMBLED EGGS

In a medium bowl, whisk together the eggs and salt until evenly blended. Heat a large nonstick skillet over medium heat, and when hot, add the butter. When the butter melts, give the egg mixture a few more whisks and pour it into the pan. Use a spatula to gently nudge the eggs around, scraping the bottom to prevent scorching. Once the eggs are cooked to your liking, remove the pan from heat and transfer the eggs to a plate to prevent them from cooking further in the hot skillet. Use right away, or cool completely and store in the refrigerator for up to 3 days.

TO ASSEMBLE THE ENCHILADAS

Preheat the oven to 350°F/177°C. If warming the tortillas on the stovetop, place a large heavy skillet over low heat. In a small bowl, mix together ¾ cup (85 g) of the jack cheese and ¾ cup (85 g) of the cheddar. Pour enough enchilada sauce in a 9×13-inch glass baking dish (or other similarly sized baking dish) to cover the bottom in a thin layer. Set up an enchilada assembly line by laying out all the components within reach: tortillas, spinach mixture, scrambled eggs, potatoes, the cheese blend, a clean cutting board, and the baking dish.

Now, start by placing a tortilla in the skillet, and heat it for 30 to 45 seconds until warm and soft, or place it in the microwave and warm for about 15 seconds. Lay the warm tortilla on a cutting board. Place a few tablespoons of the spinach mixture down the center of the tortilla, leaving a few inches of space on each side, then a few spoonfuls of scrambled eggs on top, followed by the potatoes and a generous sprinkle of the cheese blend. Roll the tortilla over the filling, forming a tube. Place the enchilada seam-side-down in the baking dish, against one of the sides. Repeat the process with the remaining tortillas and filling, laying each enchilada next to the previous one in the dish. You will end up making 10 to 12 enchiladas, depending on how you fill them. Pour the remaining sauce over the enchiladas, making sure to thoroughly coat all the tortillas. Sprinkle over the remaining cheese, and bake uncovered for 25 minutes. Serve hot, garnished with cilantro and avocado, and enjoy!

Spanakopita Quiche

Makes one 9-inch quiche, serves 6 to 8

Special Tools: Food Processor

One of our favorite Greek dishes is spanakopita, a savory pastry filled with sautéed spinach, feta cheese, and fresh dill wrapped in crispy phyllo. In this recipe, we take those same flavors and transform them into a golden quiche nestled in a flaky, buttery crust. Perfect for weekend brunches with friends, you can even prepare it the night before for an easy and stress-free morning.

FOR THE CRUST

1¼ cups (150 g) all-purpose flour
½ teaspoon salt
1 stick (113 g) unsalted butter, cut into cubes
¼ cup (59 ml) ice water

FOR THE FILLING

1 tablespoon extra-virgin olive oil
4 scallions, finely chopped
2 large garlic cloves (10 g), minced
1 pound (454 g) frozen spinach, thawed,
    drained, and squeezed dry
¼ cup (12 g) packed italian parsley, finely
    chopped
¼ cup (12 g) packed fresh dill, finely chopped
½ cup (118 ml) plain greek yogurt
1 cup (237 ml) heavy cream
3 large eggs
1 teaspoon salt
¼ teaspoon freshly ground black pepper
pinch of ground cayenne pepper
½ cup (57 g) gruyère cheese, grated
¼ cup (28 g) Parmesan cheese, grated
½ cup (57 g) feta cheese, crumbled

TO MAKE THE CRUST

In a food processor, combine the flour and salt, and pulse a few times to combine. Add the cubes of butter and process until it has a sandy texture. With the machine running, slowly add the ice water just until the mixture begins to clump together, then stop. Gather the dough into a ball, wrap tightly in plastic, and let rest in the refrigerator for at least 1 hour, or up to several days.

Preheat oven to 400°F/204°C. Unwrap the dough and place on a lightly floured work surface. Roll out to a circle 11 to 12 inches in diameter. Transfer the dough to a 9-inch tart pan with a removable bottom, pressing the dough into the bottom and sides of the pan (one easy way to do this is to gently fold the circle in half, then in half again, transfer to the tart pan, then unfold in the pan). Trim any overhang, using any extra scraps to make patches for holes or to thicken areas that might be too thin, as needed. Poke holes over the bottom of the crust with a fork. Cover with foil, pressing the foil directly onto the surface of the crust. Fill the foil with a layer of pie weights or dry beans, and bake for 15 minutes. Remove the weights and foil, and let the crust cool slightly. Lower the oven temperature to 300°F/149°C.

TO MAKE THE FILLING

Set the olive oil in a large skillet over medium heat. Add the scallions and garlic, and cook for 1 minute until sizzling. Add the spinach by hand, breaking up any clumps with your fingers. Toss to combine, then add the parsley and dill, and remove from heat. Toss to combine, and transfer to a large mixing bowl to cool briefly. Add the yogurt and cream, and stir to combine. Add the eggs, salt, black pepper, cayenne pepper, gruyère, and Parmesan, and stir until evenly blended.

Place the prebaked crust on a rimmed baking sheet. Pour the spinach mixture into the crust, then top with the crumbled feta. Bake for 1 hour, then let cool for 15 minutes. Serve warm, room temperature, or even chilled, if desired, and enjoy!

Notes

- Once the crust dough is resting in the fridge, it can stay there for up to 3 days before baking, if needed.

- The quiche will stay fresh for up to 3 days in the fridge, so it can be made ahead of time and reheated (or not) when it's time to eat. To reheat, cover with foil and bake for 15 minutes at 325°F/163°C.

Peach Dutch Baby with Raspberry Purée

Serves 2

Special Tools: Food Processor or Blender

Making a dutch baby is like performing a magic trick. A skillet full of thin, watery batter enters the oven, and moments later emerges as a puffy golden cloud with crispy edges and a smooth, almost custard-like interior. Even a plain dutch baby without any toppings is a thing of beauty, but here we raise the stakes with fresh sautéed peaches baked right inside. Drizzled with a tart ruby-red raspberry purée and a dusting of powdered sugar, watch how quickly it disappears before your very eyes.

FOR THE RASPBERRY PURÉE
1½ cups (170 g) fresh or frozen raspberries
2 tablespoons powdered sugar
1 teaspoon lemon juice

FOR THE DUTCH BABY
½ cup (60 g) all-purpose flour
1½ tablespoons granulated sugar
¼ teaspoon salt
½ cup (118 ml) milk of your choice
2 large eggs
1 teaspoon vanilla extract
1 to 2 tablespoons unsalted butter
1 peach, thinly sliced, pit removed

FOR GARNISH, AS DESIRED
peach slices
fresh raspberries
powdered sugar
maple syrup

TO MAKE THE RASPBERRY PURÉE
Combine the raspberries, powdered sugar, and lemon juice in a food processor or blender, and blend until smooth. Pour through a fine-mesh strainer to remove the seeds, and transfer to a small measuring cup or pitcher for serving. The purée can be made up to 3 days in advance and kept in a sealed container in the fridge until ready to serve.

TO MAKE THE DUTCH BABY
Preheat oven to 425°F/218°C. In a medium bowl, combine the flour, sugar, salt, milk, eggs, and vanilla, then whisk until smooth and set aside.

Place a 10-inch oven-safe skillet (cast iron is ideal) over medium heat. Add the butter and tilt the pan to slide the butter around, coating the bottom and sides of the skillet. Once the butter is melted, lay the peach slices in a single layer over the bottom of the pan—if you have peach slices left over, reserve them for garnishing later. Cook the peach slices without stirring for 2 to 3 minutes, then pour the batter over the peaches. Cook for 1 minute without stirring—the batter will still be liquid at this point—then carefully transfer the hot skillet to the oven. Bake for 12 to 15 minutes, until puffed and golden. Serve immediately, topped with the raspberry purée, additional peach slices, raspberries, and powdered sugar or maple syrup as desired. Enjoy!

Winter Shakshuka

Serves 6 • Gluten-Free

Shakshuka is a one-pan brunch superhero. Traditionally made by poaching eggs in a spicy tomato sauce, our wintry version—which can be enjoyed all year round—adds tender cauliflower florets, wilted red chard, and sautéed leeks for a hearty and satisfying breakfast. Topped with toasted pine nuts and a tangy lime yogurt, this brunch also happens to be gluten-free, so if you have friends who can't eat wheat, this Middle Eastern delicacy is here to save your Sunday morning.

FOR THE SHAKSHUKA

- 3 tablespoons extra-virgin olive oil
- 1 head cauliflower (about 1 lb / 454 g), center stem removed, florets cut into bite-size pieces
- 1 leek, leaves removed, halved lengthwise and thinly sliced (see note)
- 1 large bunch (about 12 oz / 340 g) red swiss chard, leaves roughly chopped, stems sliced separately
- 1 teaspoon salt, divided
- 1 serrano pepper, halved lengthwise and thinly sliced
- 1 28-ounce (794 g) can diced tomatoes
- ½ teaspoon freshly ground black pepper
- 1 teaspoon ground cumin
- 6 large eggs
- ¼ cup (35 g) pine nuts

FOR THE LIME GREEK YOGURT

- ¾ cup (198 g) plain greek yogurt
- 1 tablespoon lime juice
- ¼ teaspoon salt

Place the olive oil in a 12-inch heavy skillet over medium heat. When hot, add the cauliflower, leeks, swiss chard stems (set aside the leaves for later since they cook more quickly than the stems), and ½ teaspoon of salt, and sauté for 4 minutes. Add the serrano pepper and cook, stirring occasionally, until the cauliflower is al dente, about 5 minutes. Add the tomatoes, the remaining ½ teaspoon of salt, black pepper, and cumin, and bring to a simmer. When simmering, scatter the chard leaves over the top of

the mixture, then cover, turn heat to medium-low, and cook for 2 minutes. Remove lid, toss to combine, then cover again for 2 minutes. Stir again to combine, and check to see if the chard is tender and wilted. If it is not, cover for another 2 minutes. When the chard is tender, make 6 indentations in the simmering mixture evenly spaced around the pan, and crack an egg into each one. Cover, turn heat to low, and simmer until the whites are set and yolks are a little runny, 4 to 5 minutes.

While the eggs are cooking, make the lime greek yogurt by combining the yogurt, lime juice, and salt in a bowl. Whisk until smooth and creamy, then set aside. In a small, dry skillet over medium heat, cook the pine nuts, stirring often, until they are deeply toasted and fragrant, about 5 minutes.

Once the eggs are ready, top the shakshuka with toasted pine nuts and serve with lime yogurt on the side. Enjoy!

Notes

- Leeks are different from most vegetables, since you wash them after cutting, not before. Because sand and grit can get deep within its thin layers, it is best to slice up the leek, then place the slices in a colander to rinse them off.

Morning-After Smoothie with Blueberry and Banana

Serves 1 to 2 • Vegan, Gluten-Free

Special Tools: Blender

We've all been there before. You had a little too much fun last night, stayed out past your bedtime, and probably shouldn't have accepted that last mojito that was handed to you. Or maybe you handed it to yourself . . . your recollection is fuzzy. Regardless, have no fear—your morning-after smoothie is here! This powerful remedy blended with frozen bananas, blueberries, apples, and vanilla will have you feeling fine in no time.

6 ounces (170 g) frozen banana slices (see note)
¾ cup (97 g) frozen blueberries
2 tablespoons (34 g) creamy natural peanut butter
½ teaspoon vanilla extract
½ tablespoon ground flaxseeds
1 cup (237 ml) milk of your choice
one handful (about 5 g) spinach
¼ Granny Smith apple (50 g)

Combine all ingredients in a blender and process until smooth. Makes one very large serving (about 12 ounces) or two medium servings. Pour into glasses and enjoy!

Notes

- To freeze the bananas, cut them into 1-inch slices, then place in a single layer in a ziplock bag. Keep in the freezer until ready to use, up to two months.

Orange-Pecan Overnight French Toast

Serves 6 to 8 • Gluten-Free Option

Hosting brunch is fun, but let's be honest, spending all morning cooking is not. The solution? Overnight french toast. In this easy recipe, all the work is done the night before: you assemble the dish in the evening and let it chill overnight while you get your beauty rest. The next morning, you just pop it in the oven and bake, leaving plenty of time to relax—or frantically clean the house before your guests arrive, like we usually do. With crispy edges, a soft custardy interior scented with orange and vanilla, and a crunchy spiced pecan topping, this dish will have you wondering why you don't host brunch more often.

FOR THE FRENCH TOAST
1 loaf brioche or challah (about 1 lb / 454 g)
6 large eggs
2 tablespoons orange zest (from two large oranges)
⅔ cup (158 ml) orange juice, fresh squeezed if possible
⅓ cup (79 ml) milk of your choice
¼ cup (59 ml) maple syrup
1½ teaspoons vanilla extract
¼ teaspoon salt
¼ teaspoon ground nutmeg
3 tablespoons Grand Marnier liqueur (see note)

FOR THE SPICED PECAN TOPPING
¾ cup (85 g) coarsely chopped pecans
1 tablespoon unsalted butter, melted
½ teaspoon ground cinnamon
pinch of salt

TO SERVE
maple syrup
fresh fruit
powdered sugar, if desired

TO MAKE THE FRENCH TOAST
Butter a 9×13-inch baking pan (or similarly sized baking pan), and set aside. Slice the bread into 1-inch-thick slices, and lay the pieces in the prepared baking dish, overlapping to fit them in as evenly as possible. In a medium bowl or quart measuring cup, mix together the eggs, orange zest, juice, milk, syrup, vanilla, salt, nutmeg, and liqueur until combined. Pour over the bread slices, coating them evenly. Cover with plastic or foil and refrigerate overnight.

The next morning, preheat the oven to 375°F/191°C. Place the dish in the center rack of the oven uncovered and bake until fully cooked, about 30 minutes. You can test if it's done by inserting a knife into the center of the casserole and moving it slightly to make a small hole; if you see liquid inside, it is not finished cooking.

WHILE THE FRENCH TOAST IS BAKING, MAKE THE PECAN TOPPING
Place the pecans in a dry skillet, and heat over medium heat, stirring occasionally, until they become toasted and fragrant, 6 to 8 minutes. When finished toasting, transfer to a heatproof bowl to stop the cooking process. Let cool briefly, then pour over the butter, cinnamon, and salt, and toss to coat.

TO SERVE
Once the french toast is done, top with the pecans and serve along with syrup, fruit, and powdered sugar, if desired, and enjoy!

Notes

- Grand Marnier is an orange-flavored brandy liqueur. If you don't have it, you could substitute another orange liqueur, such as triple sec, or leave it out entirely if you'd like to omit alcohol.

- To make this Gluten-Free: substitute gluten-free bread for the brioche.

Sharp Cheddar Waffles with Scallions and Sautéed Wild Mushrooms

Makes about 12 4-inch waffles

Special Tools: Waffle Iron

Can we let you in on a little secret? This may sound preposterous, but it's true: you don't need to submerge your waffles in sweet syrup and pyramids of butter in order for them to taste good. Make no mistake, there is absolutely nothing wrong with starting your day with toasted cake flooded with liquid sugar, but dessert doesn't always sound appetizing at eight o'clock in the morning. Enter the savory waffle. Oozing with melted sharp cheddar cheese and studded with scallions, these crispy, golden beauties are topped with sautéed wild mushrooms and minced garlic. What's the saying? Once you've tried a savory stack, there's no going back!

FOR THE WAFFLES
2 cups (240 g) all-purpose flour
2 teaspoons baking powder
1¾ teaspoons salt
2 large eggs
2 cups (473 ml) milk of your choice
8 ounces (226 g) unsalted butter, melted
6 ounces (170 g) sharp cheddar cheese, shredded
½ cup (35 g) thinly sliced scallions

FOR THE SAUTÉED MUSHROOMS
2 tablespoons extra-virgin olive oil
1 medium onion (about 330 g), coarsely chopped
¾ teaspoon salt
1 pound (454 g) assorted wild mushrooms, cleaned, trimmed, and sliced if larger than bite-size
2 large garlic cloves (10 g), minced
½ teaspoon freshly ground black pepper

FOR GARNISH
sliced scallions
grated cheddar cheese

TO MAKE THE WAFFLES

Preheat oven to 200°F/93°C, and place a wire rack in the middle of the oven. In a large mixing bowl, whisk together the flour, baking powder, and salt, and set aside. In a medium bowl, whisk together the eggs and milk. While whisking, slowly add the melted butter, and whisk until smooth. Pour the liquid mixture into the bowl with the dry ingredients, and stir until evenly blended. Add the cheddar and scallions, and stir to combine. Heat your waffle iron according to manufacturer's instructions, and ladle the batter onto the hot iron. When each round of waffles is ready (look for the steam to subside) transfer them to the oven so they stay warm and crispy.

WHILE THE WAFFLES ARE COOKING, MAKE THE MUSHROOMS

Place a large, deep skillet over medium heat. When hot, add the olive oil, then add the onion and salt and sauté until the onion has softened and begins to turn golden, about 7 to 8 minutes. Add the mushrooms and cook until they soften and release their juices, about 8 minutes. Add the garlic and cook for another 1 to 2 minutes. Add the black pepper and remove from heat.

TO SERVE

Serve the waffles hot topped with a generous amount of mushrooms, accompanied by sliced scallions and grated cheddar at the table. Enjoy!

Notes

- Use whatever types of mushrooms you like—the more variety of sizes and flavors the better!

Spiced Apple Blintzes

Makes about 15 blintzes

Ryan and I come from different backgrounds, and over the years, we have introduced each other to all kinds of new dishes. Before we met, he was unfamiliar with traditional Jewish food and had never experienced the magic of a blintz, while I hadn't discovered the wonders of Spanish and Cuban cuisine. When I was growing up, my mom did all the cooking. Today, she is a health-conscious pescatarian on a low-sodium, low-sugar diet, but in the 1970s and '80s, our eating habits were quite different: packaged frozen dinners and canned vegetables were weeknight staples, with Barry Manilow and Neil Diamond in heavy rotation, and on evenings when she was too busy to cook, my brother, Josh, and I were treated to drive-throughs with chocolate milkshakes, cheeseburgers, and french fries. Nowadays, she would never dream of ordering fast food and is an excellent cook who takes pride in preparing recipes and puts thought and love into every presentation. One of my favorite dinners during those carefree days were packaged frozen blueberry blintzes: thin crêpes lightly brushed with butter, with a sweet blueberry filling. I would cover mine in powdered sugar, of course, and although it felt more like a dessert than an entrée, I most certainly kept that secret to myself, not wanting to spoil the party. In this easy breakfast inspired by those fond freezer-food memories, Granny Smith apples are sautéed until soft and ultra-tender. Spiced with brown sugar, cinnamon, nutmeg, cardamom, and vanilla, and snuggled in a delicate crêpe blanket, these blintzes are topped with a dollop of honey-whipped goat cheese, making all your childhood dreams come true.   —*Adam*

FOR THE SPICED APPLE FILLING

2 pounds (907 g) Granny Smith apples
  (about 4 medium)
4 tablespoons (56 g) unsalted butter, cut
  into pieces
½ cup (106 g) brown sugar, packed
1 teaspoon ground cinnamon
¼ teaspoon ground nutmeg
¼ teaspoon ground cardamom
¼ teaspoon salt
1 cup (237 ml) apple cider (see note)
4 teaspoons cornstarch
1 teaspoon vanilla extract

FOR THE CRÊPES

1¾ cups plus 2 tablespoons (444 ml) milk,
  at room temperature
6 large eggs, at room temperature
1½ cups (180 g) all-purpose flour
heaping ¼ teaspoon salt
4½ tablespoons (64 g) unsalted butter, melted
  and cooled slightly

FOR THE WHIPPED HONEY GOAT CHEESE

8 ounces (227 g) goat cheese, at room
  temperature
2 tablespoons honey
½ cup plus 2 tablespoons (148 ml) cream

TO MAKE THE SPICED APPLE FILLING

Core, peel, and slice the apples as thinly as possible, less than ⅛-inch thick. Place the apple slices in a medium saucepan with the butter, brown sugar, cinnamon, nutmeg, cardamom, and salt. Toss to combine, and place over medium heat. Cook covered, stirring occasionally, until the apples have softened to your liking, about 20 minutes. In a measuring cup or small bowl, combine the cider and cornstarch, whisking well to dissolve the starch completely. Add the cider mixture to the saucepan with the apples, stir to combine, and cook for 2 minutes more. Remove from heat, stir in the vanilla, and let cool. The apples can be used immediately or cooled completely and then stored in the refrigerator for up to a week. If storing, be sure to warm them thoroughly in a saucepan or the microwave before use.

TO MAKE THE CRÊPES

Combine the milk, eggs, flour, and salt in a medium bowl, and whisk until smooth. While whisking, slowly add the melted butter and whisk until combined. Cover the bowl and refrigerate for 1 hour, or up to overnight, but no longer.

When ready, heat a nonstick (or very well-seasoned cast iron) skillet over medium-low heat. Test if the temperature is correct by flicking a few drops of cold water from your fingers onto the skillet. If the droplets don't move, it is too cool. If the droplets immediately evaporate, it is too hot. If they dance and sizzle, you're ready to start making crêpes. Pour about ¼ cup (59 ml) of batter in the skillet, using the back of the measuring cup or ladle to spread the batter into a 6- to 8-inch circle. Cook until the bottom begins to turn deep golden brown in several spots; you can tell it is getting close when bubbles on top of the crêpe start to pop and stay open. Check for doneness by carefully lifting a corner of the crêpe.

If it's done, flip onto the second side and cook until lightly browned, another 30 seconds. Stack finished crêpes on a plate and cover to keep warm.

TO MAKE THE HONEY GOAT CHEESE

Combine the goat cheese, honey, and cream in a small bowl and whip with a whisk or fork until blended and fluffy. Use immediately or store in the refrigerator for up to a week. Return to room temperature before serving.

TO MAKE AND ASSEMBLE THE BLINTZES

Lay a crêpe flat on a plate or cutting board. Scoop about ¼ cup (59 ml) of apple filling onto the lower third of the crêpe. Begin rolling the bottom edge of the crêpe over the filling, then fold the sides in and continue rolling up, creating a sealed blintz. Repeat until you run out of crêpes or filling. Heat the skillet over medium-low heat, and lay as many of the blintzes as will fit comfortably seam-side-down in the pan, with at least an inch between them. Cook until lightly browned on the bottom, 2 to 3 minutes, then flip and repeat on the other side. Serve warm, topped with whipped goat cheese, any extra apple filling, and a sprinkle of powdered sugar, if desired, and enjoy!

Notes

- For the apple cider, look for nonalcoholic, unfiltered, unprocessed apple juice.
- The apple filling and whipped goat cheese can both be made days ahead, and the flavor of the batter tastes even better when allowed to rest overnight.

Banana Chocolate Chip Pancakes
with Peanut Butter Drizzle

Makes about 12 6-inch pancakes • Gluten-Free Option, Vegan Option

My older brother Michael, who has been blind since birth, describes himself as a banana connoisseur. He has been obsessed with anything banana-flavored his entire life, so his birthday is often filled with banana-themed presents: from beverages and snacks to cookies and candies, and one year, he even received a bottle of banana-infused BBQ sauce. So in honor of him, this recipe is overflowing with bananas. With semisweet chocolate chips and swirls of creamy peanut butter, all combined in one towering stack of warm, fluffy pancakes, this is a breakfast that will make any connoisseur go bananas.

—Ryan

FOR THE PANCAKES
1½ cups (180 g) all-purpose flour
¼ cup (50 g) granulated sugar
1½ teaspoons baking powder
1 teaspoon salt
½ teaspoon ground allspice
1½ cups (355 ml) milk of your choice
2 large eggs
½ teaspoon vanilla
½ cup (130 g) mashed bananas
3 tablespoons (42 g) unsalted butter, melted
1½ cups (227 g) thinly sliced bananas (about
    2 whole bananas)
6 tablespoons (70 g) mini chocolate chips

FOR THE PEANUT BUTTER DRIZZLE
½ cup (135 g) creamy peanut butter
½ cup (118 ml) maple syrup
½ teaspoon ground cinnamon

FOR GARNISH
sliced bananas
mini chocolate chips
maple syrup

TO MAKE THE PANCAKES

In a small bowl, whisk together the flour, sugar, baking powder, salt, and allspice, and set aside. In a medium bowl, whisk together the milk, eggs, and vanilla until smooth. Add the mashed bananas and melted butter and whisk to combine. Add the flour mixture and whisk until blended. Add the sliced bananas and mini chips and stir to combine.

Preheat the oven to 200°F/93°C, place a plate or platter in the oven, and preheat a cast iron or nonstick skillet over medium-low heat. Test if the temperature is correct by flicking a few drops of cold water from your fingers onto the skillet. If the droplets don't move, it is too cool. If the droplets immediately evaporate, it is too hot. If they dance and sizzle, you're ready to start making pancakes. If using a cast-iron skillet, drizzle a few drops of vegetable oil into the hot skillet, using a paper towel to spread it into a thin sheen over the surface of the pan. If using a nonstick pan, oil is not necessary. Scoop ⅓ cup of batter and pour it into the skillet,

using the back of the measuring cup to nudge the batter into a circle. Cook until bubbles form on top of the pancake, the edges begin to dry out, and the bubbles near the edge pop and stay open. Flip, then cook until the other side is lightly golden brown. Transfer to the plate in the oven to stay warm while you make the remaining pancakes. You may need to adjust the heat as you cook. If the pancakes are browning too quickly, turn the heat down, and if they are taking too long, turn the heat up.

TO MAKE THE PEANUT BUTTER DRIZZLE

Add the three ingredients in a small bowl and stir to combine. If desired, the drizzle can also be served warm; heat it in the microwave or in a small pan on the stove.

TO SERVE

Serve the pancakes warm, topped with peanut butter drizzle, additional sliced bananas, mini chips, and maple syrup, if desired.

Notes

- This recipe is best with bananas that are fully ripe: completely yellow without a hint of green, with a few small freckles of brown.

- Feeling ambitious? Try heating multiple skillets to cook several pancakes at once. Just be aware that different pans will cook at different rates and will need their heat levels adjusted individually.

- To make this Gluten-Free: use a gluten-free flour blend in place of all-purpose flour.

- To make this Vegan: use nondairy milk and butter, and replace the eggs with flax eggs (page 8). Also be sure to use vegan chocolate chips.

Avocado Toast with Sautéed Onions and Shiitake Bacon

Serves about 4 • Gluten-Free Option, Vegan

My dad constantly makes fun of us for being vegetarian. In fact, when I announced to my parents that I was no longer eating meat, their reaction was far worse than when I came out of the closet. When I told them I was gay, they laughed and said, "Yes, we know. We love you, and were wondering when you would tell us!" But when I informed them about my desire to become vegetarian, they nearly flipped out. They were very disappointed, expressing concerns about my health and how this decision would negatively impact my life. Thankfully, they've gotten used to it over the last eighteen years, but the teasing from my dad still continues. Every time we visit, he thinks it's absolutely hilarious to ask us whether fish counts as a vegetable, and he loves telling horrific food stories from his travels to see how we'll react. One of his favorite phrases is "Bacon is a gateway drug for vegetarians," and he cracks himself up every time he says it. While we admit that the aroma of bacon can be appealing, we would never eat it and don't miss it, especially since discovering a meatless alternative. Ladies and gentlemen, please welcome shiitake bacon: with its charismatic crispiness and smoky flavor, it is divine on this avocado toast. Topped with caramelized onions and a pinch of red pepper flakes, this addictive breakfast might even stop my dad from teasing . . . for at least a minute or two.

Looking for other ways to use shiitake bacon? Make a BLT, use it as a salad topping, or sprinkle it over a bowl of spicy California Gumbo (page 118). While no one would be fooled that this is bacon, the crunchy texture and savory flavor are so tempting, you may just find yourself hovering over the pan and snacking on it by the handful—we're speaking from experience here.   —*Ryan*

Notes

- The shiitake bacon and sautéed onions can be cooked up to three days ahead of time, cooled completely, then stored in airtight containers in the refrigerator. After three days, they will still be delicious, but the bacon may begin to lose its crispness and the onions may start to become soft.

- The avocado spread, on the other hand, should be used immediately after making, so it does not turn brown.

- To make this Gluten-Free: use slices of gluten-free bread, and use tamari instead of soy sauce.

FOR THE SHIITAKE BACON
1 tablespoon liquid smoke
1½ tablespoons tamari or soy sauce
2 tablespoons nutritional yeast flakes
¼ cup (59 ml) extra-virgin olive oil
1 tablespoon toasted sesame oil
½ teaspoon smoked paprika
6 ounces (170 g) shiitake mushroom caps (about
    12 to 15 large caps), cut into ⅛-inch slices

FOR THE SAUTEED ONIONS
2 tablespoons extra-virgin olive oil
1 medium onion (about 300 g), thinly sliced
½ teaspoon salt
½ teaspoon freshly ground black pepper
pinch of red pepper flakes

FOR THE AVOCADO SPREAD
2 large avocados (400 g)
2 to 3 teaspoons lime juice
½ teaspoon salt

FOR ASSEMBLY
½ baguette or other crusty loaf of bread
flaky sea salt
freshly ground black pepper
red pepper flakes

TO MAKE THE SHIITAKE BACON
Preheat the oven to 350°F/177°C, and line a rimmed baking sheet with parchment or a silicone baking mat. In a large mixing bowl, combine the liquid smoke, tamari, nutritional yeast flakes, olive oil, sesame oil, and paprika, and whisk to blend. Add the sliced shiitakes and toss gently with a rubber spatula to coat the mushrooms without breaking them apart too much. Cover the bowl with plastic wrap and let them marinate for 20 to 60 minutes at room temperature. Spread the mushrooms and their sauce on the prepared baking sheet, and arrange into

a single layer. Bake until crispy, 40 to 55 minutes, tossing occasionally. When testing for doneness, keep in mind that the mushrooms will become crispier as they cool.

TO MAKE THE SAUTÉED ONIONS
Heat the oil in a skillet over medium heat. When hot, add the onion, salt, pepper, and red pepper flakes, and cook until softened and just beginning to caramelize, 7 to 10 minutes.

TO MAKE THE AVOCADO SPREAD
Cut the avocados in half, remove the pits, and scoop the fruit into a small bowl, discarding the skin. Mash the avocados with a fork to your desired texture. Add the lime juice and salt, and stir to combine. Taste for salt and lime, and adjust as desired.

TO ASSEMBLE
Cut the baguette into two 4-inch slices, then cut each slice in half horizontally. If the skillet is still hot from cooking the onions, keep the heat on, push the onions to the side of the skillet, and place the bread facedown on the pan until it is nicely browned and toasted. If you made the onions ahead of time, you can either toast the bread slices in a dry skillet over medium heat or simply in a toaster if they fit.

Once the bread is toasted, top it with a layer of avocado, then a generous serving of the onions, followed by the shiitake bacon, a sprinkle of flaky sea salt, a few grinds of black pepper, and a pinch of red pepper flakes, if desired. Serve immediately, and enjoy!

Chunky Apple Spice Granola

Makes about 4 cups • Gluten-Free Option, Vegan Option

It took us several tries to get this recipe right. We knew exactly what we wanted: big, crunchy clusters of granola with the proper balance of nuts, fruit, and spices. We realized our determination had paid off when our neighbors filed a noise complaint due to the loud crunching noises emanating from our kitchen. Barely dodging a hefty fine, we shared our illicit granola with the kind police officer who knocked on our door, and once she realized it was simply a noisy snack filled with rolled oats, sliced almonds, dried apples, and chopped pecans, she had a change of heart, ripped up the ticket, and let us off the hook. Okay, while that story might be a slight exaggeration, this breakfast is bound to attract some attention. Sweetened with honey and vanilla and seasoned with cinnamon, ginger, nutmeg, and allspice, this granola may be deafening, but it makes a wonderful snack and a healthy way to start the day . . . just make sure everyone is awake in your house before taking a bite.

1½ cups (150 g) rolled oats
¼ cup (30 g) sliced almonds
¼ cup (30 g) coarsely chopped pecans
1 teaspoon ground cinnamon
½ teaspoon ground ginger
¼ teaspoon ground nutmeg
¼ teaspoon ground allspice
¼ teaspoon salt
½ cup (36 g) dried apples, cut into ¼-inch pieces
1½ tablespoons melted coconut oil
2 tablespoons (26 g) brown sugar
¼ cup (61 g) unsweetened applesauce
½ teaspoon vanilla extract
2 tablespoons honey

Preheat oven to 300°F/149°C, and line a baking sheet with parchment or a silicone baking mat.

In a large mixing bowl, combine the oats, almonds, pecans, cinnamon, ginger, nutmeg, allspice, salt, and apples, and toss well to combine.

In a small bowl, combine the oil, sugar, applesauce, vanilla, and honey, and whisk until blended. Pour over the oat mixture, and stir well. Spread the granola mixture on the prepared baking sheet in one solid single layer. Bake until crispy and golden on the edges, 40 to 45 minutes. Do not stir the granola as it bakes. Once it is done, let the pan cool on a rack until the granola is cool enough to handle, then break into clusters by hand. Let the granola cool completely before storing in an airtight container at room temperature.

Notes

- Use the granola as a topping for the Island Breakfast Bowl (page 44) or the Morning-After Smoothie (page 31), or just enjoy it by the handful!

- To make this Gluten-Free: be sure to use oats that are labeled as gluten-free, as some brands contain trace amounts of gluten.

- To make this Vegan: substitute maple or agave syrup for the honey.

Island Breakfast Bowl

Makes 2 12- to 16-ounce servings • Gluten-Free, Vegan

Special Tools: Blender

On our last visit to Kauai, my clumsiness almost ruined the vacation. We planned to walk a portion of the Kalalau Trail, one of the world's most beautiful and treacherous hikes, and had been looking forward to this adventure for months. But on the first day, while strolling along a rocky beach watching the sunset, I slipped and fell directly on my right knee. As the sharp pain shot up my leg, my only thought was whether I could still do the hike, the centerpiece of our trip. Over the next few days, Ryan took care of me with lots of love and plenty of ice packs, so the swelling subsided, and I completed the full eight-mile journey with just a slight limp. We made it all the way to the spectacular three hundred–foot waterfall and back, exploring narrow trails winding through the rain forest with breathtaking ocean views of the Na Pali Coast, and we can't wait to visit again. In the meantime, Ryan has been coaching me on my constant clumsiness, and we created this rainbow smoothie bowl to remind us of that tropical slice of heaven. So pack your bags, prepare your palate for paradise, and we'll see you on the islands!

—Adam

1 pineapple
4 ounces (113 g) frozen mango chunks
8 ounces (226 g) frozen banana slices (see note)
1 tablespoon milk of your choice, if desired

TOPPING SUGGESTIONS
coconut flakes
blackberries/raspberries
kiwi
chia seeds
passionfruit
pomegranate arils

Lay the pineapple on its side on a cutting board. Using a long, serrated knife, cut it in half vertically from base to leaves. Lay the halves on a cutting board, and use a small paring knife to cut out the woody core of each half. Discard the cores, then cut and scoop out the fruit, leaving skin of the pineapples intact and forming boats for the smoothies. Place the pineapples on their serving plates—it's easier to move them before they are filled.

Place the pineapple fruit and juice from the "boats" in a blender, then add the mango and banana, and purée. If desired, add a tablespoon of milk of your choice to thin the smoothie to your liking. Divide the mixture evenly between the two pineapple halves, decorate each one with a variety of colorful toppings, and enjoy!

Notes

- To freeze the bananas, cut them into 1-inch slices, then place them in a single layer in a ziplock bag. Keep in the freezer until ready to use.

- In addition to the toppings listed above, try other fruits you have at home, or crunchy mix-ins like granola (page 42), puffed grains, or seeds.

Soups

Making a hot bowl of soup on a chilly day will warm your body and relax the soul. Travel with us across the globe from South America to Southeast Asia for an eclectic sampling of soups, and discover traditions and flavors from around the world. We'll journey to the mountains of Japan for Spicy Udon Noodle Soup with Tofu (page 52), sail to the Galapagos Islands for a creamy potato and cheese soup known as Locro de Papa (page 53), then make a brief stop in Mexico for a vegetarian version of classic Tortilla Soup (page 50). There's a quick recipe for a savory vegetable bouillon that you can make once, store in the freezer, and use all year long—and crispy croutons (page 54) that can be sprinkled over any soup in this chapter. These recipes are internationally delicious, so grab your passport and get ready for takeoff.

Vegetable Bouillon

Gluten-Free, Vegan

Special Tools: Blender

This recipe calls for a celebration! It can be difficult to find flavorful vegetarian broth, but once you realize how easy and fun it is to make your own, you will never use store-bought broth again. This savory broth is the base for every soup in this chapter and is useful for dozens of recipes throughout the book, from Spicy Five-Bean Chili (page 96) to our vegetarian version of classic Spanish paella (page 130). Set aside a little time to chop some fresh herbs and vegetables, and this quick batch of bouillon will last you more than a year.

150 grams leeks, thinly sliced, rinsed, and drained
100 grams fennel root, coarsely chopped
100 grams green bell pepper, seeded and coarsely chopped
200 grams carrots, coarsely chopped
100 grams celery, coarsely chopped
100 grams celeriac root, coarsely chopped
30 grams sun-dried tomatoes (dry, not packed in oil)
100 grams shallots, coarsely chopped
20 grams garlic, minced
300 grams salt
40 grams parsley
60 grams cilantro
½ teaspoon ground turmeric
1 tablespoon nutritional yeast flakes
1 teaspoon freshly ground black pepper
1 teaspoon vegetable oil
¼ teaspoon toasted sesame oil

Combine all ingredients in a blender, and process until smooth and blended. Transfer to a sealed container and keep in the freezer. The salt content will keep the bouillon from freezing solid, so whenever you need some for a recipe, just scoop out the amount that is required. If it is too firm to scoop, let the container sit at room temperature for a few minutes to thaw.

To use, combine 1 cup of boiling water to 1 teaspoon of bouillon.

Carrot Ginger Soup

Serves 3 to 4 • Gluten-Free, Vegan Option

Special Tools: Immersion Blender or Standard Blender

Seeking a simple soup to soothe your soul? Swiftly stop your search! This easy version of carrot ginger soup will have you feeling cozy in no time. With sweet roasted carrots, sautéed fresh ginger, minced garlic, and a pinch of spicy cayenne, this golden remedy will clearly combat the cold and cure your continuous carrot cravings while keeping you wondrously warm in the winter.

FOR THE ROASTED CARROTS
1 pound (454 g) carrots (about 4 large), cut into 2-inch pieces
1 tablespoon extra-virgin olive oil
½ teaspoon salt
¼ teaspoon freshly ground black pepper

FOR THE SOUP
1 tablespoon unsalted butter
½ onion (about 140 g), coarsely chopped
1 large celery rib (about 80 g), coarsely chopped
2 large garlic cloves (10 g), minced or pressed
1 tablespoon (16 g) freshly grated ginger
2 cups (473 ml) vegetable broth (page 46)
2 cups (473 ml) water
½ teaspoon salt
⅛ teaspoon freshly ground black pepper
pinch of ground cayenne pepper

OPTIONAL GARNISH
minced chives or scallions

TO MAKE THE CARROTS
Preheat oven to 375°F/191°C, and line a baking sheet with parchment or a silicone baking mat. Spread the carrots on the sheet, and sprinkle over the oil, salt, and pepper. Toss lightly to coat, then spread in a single layer. Bake until the carrots are soft and beginning to caramelize around the edges, 45 to 60 minutes, stirring once halfway through.

TO MAKE THE SOUP
Place the butter in a large saucepan and set over medium heat. When hot, add the onion and celery, and cook until slightly softened, about 5 minutes. Add the garlic and ginger, and cook for another 3 to 4 minutes. Add the roasted carrots, broth, water, salt, black pepper, and cayenne pepper, and stir to combine. Cover, raise heat and bring to a boil, then lower to a bare simmer and keep covered for 45 minutes, stirring occasionally. Purée the soup with an immersion blender or with a regular blender in 2 to 3 batches. Return to a simmer, turn off heat, then ladle into serving bowls and top with minced chives or scallions.

Notes

- To make this Vegan: use a vegan butter substitute.

Lemon Barley Soup

Serves 4 to 5 • Vegan

A few weeks after we moved into our house in Eagle Rock, I gave Adam a birthday present that keeps on giving: a baby lemon tree. We had never planted anything before and had very little experience gardening, but we were eager to learn, reading books, watching online videos, and even signing up for a few classes at the local plant nursery. That baby lemon tree is now over ten feet tall and bears juicy, flavorful lemons all year round. We've planted a dozen other fruit trees over the years, including navel orange, star ruby grapefruit, plums, and nectarines, but our little lemon will always hold a special place in our hearts. In this citrusy soup, the lemon takes center stage, with zest and freshly squeezed juice added just before serving. Made with tender pearled barley, wilted swiss chard, and creamy russet potatoes, this satisfying soup is seasoned and spiced with sliced scallions, cilantro, celery, and sunshine.

—*Ryan*

3 tablespoons extra-virgin olive oil
1 medium onion (about 300 g), coarsely
　　chopped
½ cup (68 g) coarsely chopped carrots
　　(1 to 2 medium carrots)
½ cup (68 g) coarsely chopped celery
　　(1 to 2 ribs)
4 large garlic cloves (20 g), minced or pressed
1 teaspoon ground turmeric
½ teaspoon ground cumin
½ teaspoon ground ginger
1¼ teaspoons salt
½ teaspoon freshly ground black pepper
6 cups (1.4 L) vegetable broth (page 46)
⅔ cup (127 g) pearled barley
¾ cup (130 g) peeled and cubed russet potato
　　(about ½ of a medium potato)
1 bunch chard, stems removed, leaves roughly
　　chopped (180 g after trimming, about
　　1½ cups)
¾ cup (50 g) thinly sliced scallions
¼ cup (12 g) italian parsley, coarsely chopped
¼ cup (12 g) cilantro, coarsely chopped
zest from one lemon
2 to 3 tablespoons fresh lemon juice

Heat a large pot over medium heat. Add the oil and when hot, add the onion, carrots, and celery. Sauté for 7 to 10 minutes, until softened. Add the garlic, turmeric, cumin, ginger, salt, and pepper, and cook for 1 minute. Add the broth, cover, raise heat, and bring to a boil. Add the barley and potato, and return to a boil. Cover, lower heat to a simmer, and cook until the barley and potatoes are both tender, about 45 minutes. Add the chard and scallions, and cook until the chard is wilted and tender, about 3 minutes. Add the parsley, cilantro, and lemon zest, and cook 3 to 5 minutes. Remove from heat, add lemon juice, and let cool for 5 to 10 minutes before serving.

Tortilla Soup

Serves 6 to 8 • Gluten-Free, Vegan Option

Special Tools: Blender

I never experienced true Mexican cuisine until moving to Los Angeles. Growing up in Portland, I was limited to Taco Bell and the occasional visit to Tex-Mex diners serving combo platters overflowing with lakes of melted cheese, rafts of refried beans, and unnaturally colored orange rice. But authentic Mexican cooking couldn't be more different, where seasonal vegetables, aromatic herbs and spices, and handmade ingredients are used to create delicious, healthy dishes like this vegetarian version of classic Tortilla Soup. With two types of dried chili peppers and fire-roasted tomatoes as a base, every bowl is a fiesta of flavor. Filled with black beans and diced avocado, and garnished with crispy golden strips of fresh corn tortillas, this hearty recipe is a meal in itself. *¡Buen provecho!*

—Ryan

FOR THE SOUP
- 3 large dried ancho chilies (sometimes sold as pasilla chilies)
- 1 dried guajillo chili
- 1 14.5-ounce (411 g) can fire-roasted tomatoes
- 2 tablespoons vegetable oil
- 1 medium onion (about 350 g), thinly sliced
- 3 large garlic cloves (15 g), minced
- 6 cups (1.4 L) vegetable broth (page 46)
- 2 cups (473 ml) water
- ¼ cup (12 g) cilantro, coarsely chopped
- 1¾ teaspoons salt
- 2 teaspoons ground cumin
- 1 teaspoon chili powder
- ¼ teaspoon smoked paprika
- 1 15-ounce (425 g) can black beans, drained and rinsed
- 1 avocado, cubed

FOR THE CRISPY TORTILLA STRIPS
- 8 corn tortillas, cut into strips ½-inch wide
- vegetable oil

FOR GARNISH
- half an avocado per serving, cubed
- cheddar or jack cheese, grated
- sour cream
- coarsely chopped cilantro
- 1 to 2 lime wedges per serving
- 1 to 2 sliced radishes per serving

First, roast the dried chilies. If you have a gas stove, turn a burner on to medium, and turn on the exhaust fan. Use tongs to hold one of the peppers just above the flame, turning it back and forth until it is charred and blistered on the outside. Repeat with the remaining peppers. If you do not have a gas stove, you can use the broiler instead: set the broiler to 500°F/260°C, lay the dried peppers on a baking sheet, and place it on the top oven rack closest to the broiler. With the oven door open, and watching carefully, cook the peppers until charred and blistered, then turn them over and repeat.

Once the peppers have been toasted, lay them on a cutting board until cool enough to handle safely. Remove the stem and all the seeds, then rip the peppers into large pieces and place them in a blender. Add the can of tomatoes, but do not turn the blender on yet.

In a large pot, heat the oil over medium heat. When hot, add the onions and cook until softened, 7 to 9 minutes. Add the garlic and sauté for 1 minute.

Add the onion mixture to the blender, and purée. Pour the purée back into the pot and cook until thickened slightly, about 6 minutes. Add the broth, water, cilantro, salt, cumin, chili powder, paprika, and black beans. Raise heat, cover, and bring to a boil. Then lower heat and simmer 15 minutes.

While the soup is simmering, place a deep heavy skillet over medium-high heat, and have a plate ready nearby, covered with a few layers of paper towels. Pour enough vegetable oil in the skillet to cover the bottom about ¼-inch deep. When hot, add a handful of tortilla strips, then cook, stirring occasionally until crispy, about 3 to 5 minutes. Use a slotted spoon or tongs to transfer them to the plate lined with paper towels to drain while you repeat with the remaining tortilla strips.

Once the soup has simmered for about 15 minutes, add the avocado, and simmer 5 minutes. Serve with crispy tortilla strips, more avocado, grated cheese, sour cream, cilantro, lime wedges, and radishes, if desired. Enjoy!

Notes

- The dried chili peppers can be found in the Latin section of many markets.
- As with all chili peppers, removing the seeds lowers the heat level. This is a mild soup, but if you're looking for a spicy kick, leave some or all of the seeds in the peppers, especially the guajillo.
- To make this Vegan: use vegan cheese and sour cream.

Spicy Udon Noodle Soup with Tofu

Serves 3 to 4   •   Gluten-Free Option, Vegan

In the summer of 2012, we visited Japan for the first time. I was playing at Fuji Rock, an annual music festival in the mountains near Tokyo, and after the last show, Ryan and I stayed for an additional ten days, touring around the beautiful country and sampling all the vegetarian cuisine we could find. We explored ancient temples, wandered through pristine Japanese gardens, and ate some of the most memorable bowls of ramen and udon along the way. Inspired by our journeys in Japan, this simple one-pot soup with mushrooms and tofu is here to transport your taste buds to Tokyo. Made with a savory miso broth—seasoned with minced garlic, ginger, fresh cilantro, chopped scallions, and lime—this spicy soup will have everyone saying *oishi* after every bite!   **—Adam**

1 tablespoon vegetable oil
2 cups (157 g) thinly sliced mushrooms
4 cups (946 ml) vegetable broth (page 46)
1 tablespoon (12 g) minced ginger
2 tablespoons tamari or soy sauce
2 large garlic cloves (10 g), minced
1 serrano chili pepper, seeded and minced
1 to 2 tablespoons lime juice
1 teaspoon sambal oelek (see note)
6 ounces (170 g) firm tofu, cubed
12 ounces (340 g) fresh udon noodles
½ cup (40 g) finely chopped scallions, plus more
    for garnish
¼ cup (12 g) coarsely chopped cilantro
2 sheets of nori seaweed (5 g), cut into strips,
    plus more for garnish
1 tablespoon red miso paste

Heat the oil in a large saucepan over medium heat. When hot, add the mushrooms and sauté for 3 minutes. Add the broth, ginger, tamari, garlic, and chili pepper. Cover pan, raise heat, and bring to a boil. Lower heat to a simmer and cook for 4 minutes. Add the lime juice and sambal oelek, and simmer for 5 minutes. Add the tofu cubes, return to a simmer, and cook 5 minutes. Add the noodles and cook 3 minutes. Add the scallions, cilantro, seaweed, and miso paste, stir to combine, and remove from heat. Let cool for 5 minutes, then taste for salt and lime and adjust as needed. Serve topped with additional scallions and seaweed, if desired, and enjoy!

Notes

- Seeding the serrano pepper will lower the heat level significantly. Remove all the seeds and white ribs for a mild soup, leave half of them in for medium, and leave all of them in for a spicy version.

- For the lime juice, start with 1 tablespoon of juice, and add more to taste if needed.

- Sambal oelek is a spicy chili paste from Indonesia. You can find it in the Asian section of many grocery stores, near the sriracha.

- To make this Gluten-Free: use gluten-free noodles, and use tamari instead of soy sauce.

Locro de Papa

Serves 8 to 10 • Gluten-Free

Special Tools: Immersion Blender or Standard Blender

In 2015, we traveled to the Galapagos, and as nature lovers, we were in heaven; since the wildlife on these isolated islands has never been hunted, the animals are completely unafraid of humans, allowing us to get so close we could reach out and touch them. When we hiked into the jungle to visit the legendary giant tortoises, we could hear them breathing, and every time we snorkeled in the ocean, curious sea lions would swim right up to us, blowing bubbles and swirling around in the water like aquatic acrobats. Our ship carried fewer than fifty passengers, and each day, the chefs prepared meals inspired by local Ecuadorian cuisine. World-famous for their soups, this Latin-American country is especially known for *locro de papa*. Made with creamy russet potatoes, loads of melted cheese, and cubes of soft avocado, this smooth and satisfying soup is the culinary equivalent of a warm, cozy sweater.

FOR THE SOUP
- 3 tablespoons extra-virgin olive oil
- 1 large onion (400 g), coarsely chopped
- 2 teaspoons ground cumin
- 1 teaspoon ground annatto (see note)
- 4 large garlic cloves (20 g), minced
- 3½ pounds (1.6 kg) russet potatoes, peeled and cut into ½-inch cubes
- 7 cups (1.6 L) vegetable broth (page 46)
- ½ cup (118 ml) milk
- ½ cup (118 ml) heavy cream
- 1½ cups (170 g) shredded monterey jack cheese
- 1½ teaspoons salt

FOR GARNISH
- cubed avocado
- shredded monterey jack cheese
- thinly sliced green onions
- freshly ground black pepper

Heat the oil in a large pot over medium heat. When hot, add the onion, cumin, and annatto, and sauté until softened, 7 to 10 minutes. Add the garlic, and cook for an additional minute. Add the diced potatoes, and cook for 5 minutes, stirring occasionally. Add the broth, stirring to deglaze the bottom of the pan. Raise the heat, cover, and bring to a boil, then lower heat and simmer until the potatoes are tender, about 20 minutes. Blend until smooth using an immersion blender or by transferring the soup to a regular blender in batches. Add the milk, cream, cheese, and salt, and stir until blended. Serve hot, topped with cubed avocado, shredded cheese, green onions, and ground black pepper. Enjoy!

Notes

- Annatto is a seed with a bright orange color and mild flavor, commonly used in Latin American cooking. It is sold ground and whole, usually near the dried peppers and spices in the Latin section of your local market. Also look for it by its Spanish name, achiote.

Spinach and Orzo Soup

Serves 4 to 6 • Vegan

We are champions of the date night in. Eating out can quickly eat up your wallet, so we are all about staying home, making a romantic meal together, and setting the mood with low lighting, music, and flickering candles. Sometimes we'll even choose themed albums to match the cuisine we're cooking—the Buena Vista Social Club is the perfect soundtrack while you're chopping vegetables for Cuban Black Beans and Rice (page 127). Or maybe you've had a long, stressful day, and rather than lively music, the comforting sounds of a bubbling pot on the stove is your calming antidote. Either way, this colorful soup can be enjoyed as a zesty appetizer and is hearty enough to be the main course. With chopped spinach, bell peppers, diced tomatoes, freshly squeezed lemon juice, and orzo pasta, pick out something sweet from the dessert chapter, a classic movie you have never seen before, and soft blankets for snuggling on the couch, and let the date night in begin!

FOR THE SOUP

- 2 tablespoons extra-virgin olive oil
- 1 medium onion (350 g), finely chopped
- 1 red bell pepper (200 g), finely chopped
- 3 large garlic cloves (15 g), minced
- 5 cups (1.1 L) vegetable broth (page 46)
- 1 14.5-ounce (411 g) can diced tomatoes
- 6 ounces (170 g) fresh spinach, roughly chopped
- ½ cup (28 g) coarsely chopped italian parsley
- ½ cup (100 g) dry orzo pasta
- ½ teaspoon salt
- ½ teaspoon freshly ground black pepper
- ¼ to ½ cup (60 to 120 ml) freshly squeezed lemon juice

FOR THE CRISPY CROUTONS

- 4 cups (215 g) crusty bread cut into 1-inch cubes
- 1 tablespoon extra-virgin olive oil
- ⅛ teaspoon salt
- ⅛ teaspoon freshly ground black pepper

TO MAKE THE SOUP

In a large saucepan, heat the oil over medium heat. Add the onion and sauté until softened, 5 to 7 minutes. Add the red pepper and garlic, and cook for another 5 minutes. Add the broth and tomatoes, cover, raise heat and bring to a boil. Add the spinach, parsley, and orzo, bring back to a boil, then cover, lower heat to a simmer, and cook until the orzo is done, about 10 minutes. Remove from heat and add the salt, pepper, and lemon juice. Taste for salt and lemon and adjust as needed. Let cool 5 minutes before serving, and enjoy!

TO MAKE THE CROUTONS

Preheat oven to 350°F/177°C, and line a baking sheet with parchment or a silicone mat. Place the bread cubes in a large mixing bowl, then drizzle over the oil, salt, and pepper, tossing to coat the cubes evenly. Transfer the croutons to the baking sheet and spread in a single layer. Bake until crispy, about 15 minutes.

Husbands' Penicillin Matzo Ball Soup

Serves 6 to 8

The next time you come down with a cold or flu, before running to the pharmacy to purchase over-priced medications, open our book to this page and discover why this traditional soup, also known as Jewish penicillin, has been a go-to family remedy for generations. My grandma loved preparing it for us, especially when anyone was sick, and now I make it for my husband anytime he's feeling under the weather. Maybe it's the simple combination of ingredients that makes this recipe so comforting, or perhaps it's infused with the spirit of millions of grandmas all over the world who have ever made it for their loved ones. Perfect for a rainy day—or a runny nose—relax, get some rest, and let the Husbands take care of you. —*Adam*

FOR THE MATZO BALLS

4 large eggs
2 teaspoons finely minced onion
1 teaspoon salt
pinch of ground cayenne pepper
2 tablespoons (28 g) unsalted butter, melted
¾ cup (95 g) matzo meal

FOR THE SOUP

3 tablespoons extra-virgin olive oil
1 medium onion (350 g), coarsely chopped
6 carrots (540 g), sliced into ¼-inch rounds,
    divided
4 celery ribs (240 g), coarsely chopped
½ cup (118 ml) white wine
2 quarts (1.9 L) vegetable broth (page 46)
4 large garlic cloves (20 g), minced
2 bay leaves
1 teaspoon dried dill
1½ teaspoons salt
fresh dill, for garnish

Notes

- For the 2 teaspoons of finely minced onion, first chop the whole onion for the soup, then set aside 2 teaspoons of that to mince for the matzo balls.

TO MAKE THE MATZO BALLS

First, separate the eggs: place the yolks in a large bowl and the whites in a medium bowl. To the yolks, add the onion, salt, and cayenne pepper, and whisk to combine. Add the melted butter, and whisk until smooth, then set aside. Using an electric mixer, beat the egg whites until they hold stiff peaks when the beaters are lifted. Add the fluffy egg whites to the yolk mixture, and gently fold with a rubber spatula until blended, taking care not to deflate the whites too much. Add the matzo meal in three additions, folding gently after each one. Cover the bowl with plastic wrap and refrigerate for 1 hour.

Line a baking sheet with parchment. Using your hands, form the mixture into balls about 1 to 1½ inches wide, using about 2 tablespoons of dough per ball. Place the balls on the parchment until ready to cook.

TO MAKE THE SOUP

Heat the oil in a large pot over medium heat. When hot, add the onion, 4 carrots, and celery, and sauté for 10 minutes until the vegetables are tender. Add the wine, and cook for another 2 minutes. Add the broth, garlic, bay leaves, dried dill, and salt, and stir to combine. Cover the pot, raise the heat, and bring to a boil. When boiling, lower heat and simmer for 30 minutes, covered. Carefully pour the soup through a fine-mesh strainer, then return the broth to the pot, discarding the solids.

Bring the soup back to a boil. Add the remaining 2 carrots, then drop the matzo balls in one at a time, spacing them evenly around the pot. Cover the pot and lower heat to a simmer, cooking for 30 minutes without opening the lid. Serve a few ladlefuls of broth in each bowl, along with 2 to 3 matzo balls per person, garnish with fresh dill, if desired, and enjoy!

Mulligatawny Soup

Serves 6 to 8 • Gluten-Free, Vegan Option

One of our favorite local Indian restaurants makes the best mulligatawny soup, and it was our goal to duplicate it for this book. Ryan and I spent time researching techniques and ingredients, and even dined at the restaurant like undercover detectives to compare our results. At first, I doubted whether we could pull it off, but after hard work, dedication, and a bit of luck in the kitchen, our version surpassed the original! Pair it with our Indian Curry with Chickpeas and Cauliflower (page 109) and Samosas with Mango Chutney (page 143), and set the table for an authentic Indian feast!

—Adam

---

2 tablespoons unsalted butter
1 large onion (400 g), finely chopped
4 carrots (315 g), coarsely chopped
4 large celery ribs (300 g), coarsely chopped
4 large garlic cloves (20 g), minced
1 serrano pepper, seeded and finely chopped
½ Granny Smith apple (115 g), cored, peeled, and grated
1 tablespoon curry powder
1 teaspoon ground coriander
½ teaspoon ground turmeric
1 teaspoon ground ginger
8 cups (1.9 L) vegetable broth (page 46)
1 cup (210 g) red lentils, rinsed and drained
1½ to 2 teaspoons salt
chopped cilantro, for garnish

In a large pot, melt the butter over medium heat. When hot, add the onion, carrots, and celery, and cook until softened, 7 to 10 minutes. Add the garlic, serrano pepper, grated apple, curry powder, coriander, turmeric, and ginger, and sauté for 2 minutes. Add the broth, cover, raise heat, and bring to a boil. Add the lentils, return to a boil, then lower heat and simmer, covered, for 60 minutes. Let the soup rest, covered, for 5 minutes. Add the salt and adjust to taste. Serve hot, with generous amounts of chopped cilantro at the table. Enjoy!

Notes

- To make this Vegan: substitute vegan butter instead of unsalted butter.

Thai Coconut Curry Soup

Serves 5 to 7 • Gluten-Free Option, Vegan

When we first started dating, we were living in Hollywood, and the restaurants by our apartment were truly international: all within one block, we could choose from Mexican, Greek, French, Italian, and Indian, but our favorite was a quirky, family-owned Thai place complete with karaoke, just steps away from our front door. We were inspired by their spicy, aromatic curries, and this soup takes us back to the early days of our relationship. In our version, tofu and marinated vegetables are roasted until toasty and golden, then simmered in an intensely flavorful broth made with garlic, ginger, lemongrass, fresh cilantro, red curry paste, and coconut milk. Served with a scoop of rice, it can be a meal in itself, or the first course of a Southeast Asian dinner party—just don't forget the Thai Iced Tea Popsicles (page 198) for dessert!

FOR THE ROASTED VEGETABLES
1 red bell pepper (100 g), coarsely chopped
5 white or brown mushrooms (80 g), thinly sliced
1 head broccoli (120 g), cut into bite-size pieces
1 large carrot (100 g), coarsely chopped
1 Yukon Gold potato (190 g), chopped into
     ½-inch cubes
1 zucchini (140 g), coarsely chopped
10 ounces (284 g) firm tofu, cubed
¼ cup (59 ml) tamari or soy sauce
1 teaspoon red curry paste
2 tablespoons toasted sesame oil

FOR THE SOUP
2 tablespoons coconut oil
2 tablespoons (32 g) grated ginger
3 large garlic cloves (15 g), minced or pressed
1 stalk lemongrass, cut into 3-inch pieces
4 tablespoons red curry paste
4 cups (946 ml) vegetable broth (page 46)
3 tablespoons tamari or soy sauce
3 13.5-ounce (403 ml each) cans coconut milk
1 tablespoon freshly squeezed lime juice
¼ cup (12 g) coarsely chopped cilantro

FOR SERVING
white or brown rice

TO MAKE THE ROASTED VEGETABLES
Preheat oven to 350°F/177°C, and line a rimmed baking sheet with parchment or a silicone baking mat. In a mixing bowl, combine the bell pepper, mushrooms, broccoli, carrot, potato, zucchini, and tofu, and toss to combine. In a small bowl or glass measuring cup, whisk together the tamari, curry paste, and sesame oil, then drizzle the mixture over the bowl of veggies. Toss to coat everything evenly, then spread the mixture on the baking sheet in a single layer. Roast in the oven for 40 minutes.

TO MAKE THE SOUP
In a large pot, melt the coconut oil over medium heat. When hot, add the ginger, garlic, lemongrass, and curry paste, and sauté for 2 minutes. Add the broth, tamari, and coconut milk, and stir to dissolve any lumps. Add the roasted vegetables along with any juices on the baking sheet, and stir to combine. Bring to a simmer, then add the lime juice and cilantro and remove from heat. Serve warm, in bowls with a few scoops of rice, if desired, and enjoy!

Notes

- Red curry paste and toasted sesame oil are available in the Asian section of many grocery stores.

- Once the coconut milk is added, do not allow the soup to boil, as that can cause the coconut milk to separate and curdle.

- Canned coconut milk is available in the Asian section of many grocery stores, or online.

- To make this Gluten-Free: use tamari instead of soy sauce.

Roasted Butternut Squash Soup

Serves 6 to 8 • Gluten-Free, Vegan Option

Special Tools: Immersion Blender or Standard Blender

When I was growing up, I hated squash more than going to the dentist. I did everything I could to avoid it, hiding pieces in my napkin and hoping no one would notice. I would wait for the right moment when the adults were deep in conversation, then silently sneak away, making a beeline for the bathroom, where I would surreptitiously flush away the mushy orange contents in my crumpled napkin. But one glorious day, I was introduced to the power of roasting vegetables, and my life completely changed. In the oven, butternut squash transforms from bland and boring to soft and sweet in a matter of minutes. In this simple recipe, it is deeply roasted and caramelized, and blended with golden carrots, fresh sage leaves, and a charred serrano pepper for a hint of heat. Garnished with a dollop of greek yogurt and a squeeze of lime, this soup is so soothing, you'll certainly want to save some space for seconds.

—Ryan

FOR THE SOUP

1 butternut squash (about 2.2 lbs / 1 kg), peeled, seeded, and chopped into ½-inch cubes
3 carrots (150 g), chopped into ½-inch cubes
1 serrano pepper, cut in half lengthwise and seeded
4 tablespoons extra-virgin olive oil, divided
1 large onion (400 g), coarsely chopped
3 large celery ribs (160 g), coarsely chopped
4 large garlic cloves (20 g), minced
4 sage leaves, minced
¾ teaspoon salt
6 cups (1.4 L) vegetable broth (page 46)

FOR GARNISH

greek yogurt
sage leaves
cilantro
lime wedges

Preheat the oven to 425°F/218°C, and line a baking sheet with parchment or a silicone baking mat. Arrange the cubed squash, carrots, and serrano pepper on the sheet, and drizzle 2 tablespoons of olive oil over the top. Toss to coat, then bake until tender and roasted, about 40 minutes.

In a large pot, heat the remaining 2 tablespoons of olive oil over medium heat. When hot, add the onion and celery, and cook until softened, 7 to 10 minutes. Add the garlic, sage, and salt, and cook for 1 minute. Add the roasted vegetables, toss to coat, then add the broth. Stir to combine, cover, raise heat, and bring to a boil, then lower heat and simmer for 15 minutes. Purée using an immersion blender or by transferring to a regular blender in batches. Serve warm with a dollop of greek yogurt, sage leaves, cilantro, and lime wedges at the table. Enjoy!

Notes

- To make this Vegan: substitute vegan yogurt or sour cream for the greek yogurt.

Salads

This is a wild guess, but we're assuming the holidays just ended, your bathroom scale gave you some unpleasant news, and you are looking for a few lighter recipes to start the year off right. Welcome! Pat yourself on the back for being here—even if it is for just a few weeks. There are fourteen nutritious salads in this chapter to help fulfill your well-intentioned New Year's resolutions and balance out the pie brigade that took place over Christmas. Or perhaps it's the middle of summer, and you are simply looking for a wholesome main course or a healthy meal to pack up and show off at work. Throughout these next few pages, you will find everything from hearty dinner salads to exotic international sides. Perfect for picnics, outdoor gatherings, or a low-cal lunch, these versatile recipes are here for every occasion . . . and we promise not to tell if you sneak over to page 176 to make a batch of our Dark Chocolate Florentine Cookies—your secret is safe with us.

Kale Caesar Salad with Crispy Garlic Croutons

Serves 4 to 6 • Gluten-Free Option

Vegetarians rejoice! The day has come, and you can finally enjoy Caesar salad once again. With crisp green kale leaves and a zesty dressing that doesn't require the traditional anchovies, let us say hallelujah to this saintly substitute. Topped with crispy garlic croutons and shaved Parmesan, please rise as we welcome this delicious meat-free alternative.

FOR THE CRISPY GARLIC CROUTONS
1 small baguette (120 g), cut into 1-inch cubes
  (about 4 cups)
2 tablespoons extra-virgin olive oil
⅛ teaspoon salt
⅛ teaspoon freshly ground black pepper
½ teaspoon garlic powder

FOR THE DRESSING (MAKES Đ CUP)
½ cup (112 g) greek yogurt
¼ cup (28 g) grated Parmesan cheese
1 tablespoon dijon mustard
2 teaspoons apple cider vinegar
1 tablespoon lemon juice
1 tablespoon extra-virgin olive oil
¼ teaspoon salt
½ teaspoon freshly ground black pepper
1 large garlic clove (5 g), minced or pressed

FOR THE SALAD
1 large handful of washed, trimmed, and roughly
  chopped kale per person
grated or shaved Parmesan
freshly ground black pepper

OPTIONAL TOPPINGS
thinly sliced tomato
thinly sliced red onion
crispy tofu (see page 128)

MAKE THE CRISPY GARLIC CROUTONS
Preheat oven to 350°F/177°C, and line a baking sheet with parchment or a silicone mat. Place the bread cubes in a large bowl, then drizzle over the olive oil as you toss them gently. Add the salt, pepper, and garlic powder, and continue tossing to coat evenly. Spread the cubes in a single layer on the prepared baking sheet, and bake until crispy, about 15 minutes. Use while warm, or let cool completely before storing in an airtight container at room temperature for up to a week.

MAKE THE DRESSING
Combine all ingredients in a small bowl, and stir to combine. Transfer to a storage container and keep refrigerated until use. The dressing will stay fresh for up to a week.

ASSEMBLE THE SALAD
Place a large handful of kale per person in a large bowl. Add a few tablespoons of the dressing, and toss to combine. Taste and add more dressing to your liking, tossing to coat the kale evenly. Top with croutons, Parmesan, and black pepper. Enjoy!

Notes

- To make this Gluten-Free: use a gluten-free bread instead of a baguette.

Summer Caprese with Grilled Peaches

Serves 4 to 5　•　Gluten-Free

Special Tools: Grill or Grill Pan

A fresh caprese salad is a work of art. The classic combination of tomatoes, basil, and mozzarella makes a mouthwatering masterpiece, and its vibrant hues of red, green, and white represent this dish's traditional Italian heritage. While these colorful ingredients can be found throughout the year, it shines in the summer, when heirloom tomatoes are at the peak of their season—tender, sweet, and bursting with flavor. Here we add sliced peaches that have been grilled to perfection, lightly caramelized, and are still warm from the flame. Drizzled with olive oil, balsamic vinegar, and a pinch of flaky sea salt, this crowd-pleasing salad comes together in under ten minutes and is best enjoyed outdoors with friends on a sunny summer day.

½ cup (118 ml) balsamic vinegar
2 peaches, pits removed, sliced ¼-inch thick
3 to 4 large heirloom tomatoes in various colors, thinly sliced
8 ounces (227 g) mozzarella cheese, sliced into thin rounds
6 to 8 basil leaves
2 to 3 tablespoons extra-virgin olive oil
a few pinches of flaky sea salt
a few pinches of freshly ground black pepper

Pour the balsamic vinegar in a small saucepan, and place over medium-low heat. Bring to a simmer and cook until the vinegar reduces to a few tablespoons and thickens to a syrup, 8 to 9 minutes. Set aside to cool.

Heat a grill pan (or outdoor charcoal grill) over high heat until hot. Lay the peach slices on the grill and cook without moving the slices until the peaches are tender with black grill marks underneath, 2 to 3 minutes. Remove from heat and set aside.

To assemble, lay a slice of peach on a serving plate, then place a tomato slice on top, overlapping slightly, followed by a slice of cheese and a basil leaf. Repeat with the remaining peaches, tomatoes, cheese, and basil, fanning out the slices decoratively. Drizzle the reduced balsamic over the stack, followed by the olive oil. Sprinkle salt and pepper generously over the top, and serve immediately. Enjoy!

Caribbean Black Bean Salad

Serves 8 to 10　•　Gluten-Free, Vegan

Have you ever been invited to a potluck but had no idea what to bring? Your search ends here. This bright Caribbean-inspired salad will bring a splash of color to every plate. Filled with black beans and rice, sweet bell peppers, and a zesty dressing made from fresh garlic, cumin, dijon mustard, and apple cider vinegar, this rainbow-colored salad is the answer to all your potluck prayers. Assemble it the night before so the day of the party is spent doing more important things—like picking out the right tiki shirt.

2 cups (473 ml) water
1 cup (195 g) uncooked long-grain rice
1 15-ounce (425 g) can black beans, rinsed and drained
1 red bell pepper (about 200 g), seeded and finely chopped
1 yellow bell pepper (about 200 g), seeded and finely chopped
1 bunch (115 g) scallions, thinly sliced
¼ cup (60 ml) extra-virgin olive oil
½ cup (118 ml) apple cider vinegar
1 tablespoon dijon mustard
1 teaspoon ground cumin
1 large garlic clove (5 g), minced or pressed
¾ teaspoon salt
¼ teaspoon freshly ground black pepper

Pour 2 cups of water into a medium saucepan. Bring to a boil, then add the uncooked rice, stir to combine, and return to a boil. Cover pan, and reduce heat as low as possible. Simmer without opening the lid for 15 minutes, until the rice is tender and the water is absorbed.

In a large mixing bowl, combine the cooked rice, black beans, chopped red and yellow peppers, and scallions, and toss to combine. In a small bowl or measuring cup, combine the olive oil, apple cider vinegar, mustard, cumin, garlic, salt, and black pepper. Whisk thoroughly to combine, then pour over the rice mixture. Toss gently to coat, then either serve immediately or keep refrigerated for up to three days.

Spinach Salad with Toasted Pine Nuts, Warm Goat Cheese, and Pomegranate Vinaigrette

Serves 4 to 6 • Gluten-Free Option

Looking for a salad to dazzle your dinner guests? Want to make a good impression on that special someone you're having over for the first time? Do not turn the page, do not pass go, and do not collect $200. Head directly to the store, pick up some ingredients, and let this salad work its magic. With a few quick steps, you can transform basic green leaves into something memorable. Here, fresh spinach is topped with toasted pine nuts and crispy rounds of warm goat cheese. If you're a fan of chèvre, wait until you try it coated in bread crumbs and sautéed till golden and melty. Dressed in an elegant pomegranate vinaigrette and sparkling with ruby-red pomegranate arils, don't be surprised when your date proposes to you before the main course.

FOR THE POMEGRANATE VINAIGRETTE
(MAKES ABOUT 1½ CUPS)
2 tablespoons pomegranate molasses
¼ cup (60 ml) white wine vinegar
3 tablespoons dijon mustard
1 teaspoon honey
½ teaspoon salt
¼ teaspoon freshly ground black pepper
2 large garlic cloves (10 g), minced or pressed
¾ cup (177 ml) extra-virgin olive oil

FOR THE TOASTED PINE NUTS
½ cup (70 g) pine nuts

FOR THE CRISPY GOAT CHEESE
1 log of goat cheese, chilled
½ cup (60 g) all-purpose flour
1 large egg
½ cup (30 g) panko bread crumbs
vegetable oil, for sautéing

FOR ASSEMBLY
1 large handful of spinach leaves per person
pomegranate arils

TO MAKE THE POMEGRANATE VINAIGRETTE
Combine all the ingredients except the olive oil in a small bowl. Whisk to combine, then while continuing to whisk, slowly add the olive oil until the mixture is smooth and blended. Transfer to a storage bottle, and keep refrigerated for up to a week. Shake well before using.

TO MAKE THE TOASTED PINE NUTS
Place the pine nuts in a dry skillet over medium heat, and stir occasionally until the nuts are fragrant and beginning to turn golden brown, about 3 to 5 minutes. Remove the skillet from heat and transfer the nuts to a bowl or plate to stop them from cooking further. Cool completely, then keep in an airtight container at room temperature for up to a week.

TO MAKE THE CRISPY GOAT CHEESE
Cut the log of goat cheese into ½-inch slices. Place three shallow bowls on the counter, filling the first with the flour, the second with a whisked egg, and the third with the bread crumbs. Dip each slice in the flour to coat, then the egg (making sure to thoroughly coat all sides), then the bread crumbs. Let the slices rest on a plate or wire rack while you place a large heavy skillet over medium heat. Pour enough vegetable oil in the pan to make a layer ⅛-inch deep. When hot, add the goat cheese slices in batches, making sure to not crowd the pan. Cook until the bottom of each slice is golden brown, about 2 minutes, then flip and repeat on the second side. Transfer to a plate lined with paper towels to drain briefly, then serve while hot.

TO ASSEMBLE
Place a large handful of spinach leaves on a plate. Drizzle with the pomegranate vinaigrette, then top with a few slices of crispy goat cheese, a sprinkle of toasted pine nuts, and pomegranate arils.

Notes

- To make this Gluten-Free: use gluten-free bread crumbs instead of panko bread crumbs.

Classic Italian Pasta Salad with Parmesan

Serves 8 to 10 • Gluten-Free Option

Our neighborhood of Eagle Rock feels like a small country town, even though it is just fifteen minutes from the skyscrapers of Los Angeles. Blissfully hidden from the bustle of the city, the tree-lined streets are filled with mom-and-pop businesses—many of which have been here for generations, like our local Italian bakery. Anytime we pass by, the aroma of freshly baked bread lures us inside, and we always leave with a warm baguette—and a container of their famous pasta salad. While their recipe remains a family secret, we created our own version to enjoy anytime the craving strikes. Dressed in a tangy vinaigrette made with minced garlic, white wine vinegar, and dried herbs, fusilli pasta is tossed with tender carrots, black olives, and capers. Served chilled and topped with freshly shaved Parmesan, this classic salad is a little taste of Italy . . . and our very own neighborhood!

1 pound (454 g) dried fusilli pasta
1 cup (140 g) finely chopped carrots (about
   2 medium carrots)
1 cup (140 g) peas, frozen or fresh
1¼ cups (142 g) grated Parmesan
¾ cup (100 g) pitted and sliced black olives
2 teaspoons capers
¼ cup (60 ml) white wine vinegar
2 tablespoons water
¾ teaspoon salt
1 teaspoon freshly ground black pepper
1 teaspoon granulated sugar
1 teaspoon dried oregano
1 teaspoon dried basil
2 large garlic cloves (10 g), minced or pressed
¾ cup (177 ml) extra-virgin olive oil

Bring a large pot of salted water (use 1 teaspoon of salt for each quart of water) to a boil over high heat. Add the fusilli, return to a boil, and set a timer as indicated on the package (usually about 12 minutes). When 8 minutes remain on the timer, add the chopped carrots, and stir to combine. When 3 minutes remain, add the peas. When the timer rings and the pasta is al dente, drain the pasta and vegetables into a colander, and rinse with cold water until room temperature. Transfer to a large mixing bowl, and add the Parmesan, olives, and capers, tossing to combine.

In a small bowl, combine the white wine vinegar, water, salt, black pepper, sugar, oregano, basil, and garlic, and whisk to combine. While continuing to whisk, slowly add the olive oil. Pour the mixture over the pasta, and toss to combine. Keep refrigerated until ready to serve, up to a week. Serve chilled, and enjoy!

Notes

- To make this Gluten-Free: use gluten-free pasta.

Tangy Potato Salad with Lemon and Capers

Serves 8 to 10 • Gluten-Free, Vegan

This is no ordinary potato salad. Quite the contrary—in this light recipe, the potatoes are actually visible and not hidden beneath a river of excess mayonnaise. In fact, there is no mayo to be found in the ingredient list. Instead, this zippy rendition uses dijon mustard and freshly squeezed lemon juice as a tangy replacement. Mixed with capers, homemade pickled red onions, and fresh herbs, there will never be abandoned potato salad left on anyone's plate again.

FOR THE PICKLED RED ONIONS
- 1 large (350 g) red onion, thinly sliced
- 2 teaspoons granulated sugar
- 3 teaspoons salt
- 1½ cups (355 ml) apple cider vinegar

FOR THE POTATO SALAD
- 2 pounds (907 g) red potatoes, cut into ¾-inch pieces
- ¼ cup (44 g) capers
- ¾ cup (100 g) pickled red onions, coarsely chopped
- 1½ tablespoons dijon mustard
- 3 tablespoons extra-virgin olive oil
- 2 tablespoons (8 g) finely chopped parsley
- 2 tablespoons (6 g) finely chopped fresh dill
- 1 teaspoon lemon juice
- 1 teaspoon salt
- 1 teaspoon freshly ground black pepper

TO MAKE THE PICKLED RED ONIONS
Place the sliced onion in a jar with a tight-fitting lid, such as a Mason jar. Add the sugar, salt, and apple cider vinegar, then cover tightly and shake vigorously until the salt and sugar are dissolved. Refrigerate 45 minutes, shaking occasionally. Keep refrigerated until ready to use, up to 2 weeks.

TO MAKE THE POTATO SALAD
Place the cubed potatoes in a large, deep saucepan. Pour in enough water to cover the potatoes by several inches, about 2 quarts. Add a tablespoon of salt, and bring to a boil, stirring occasionally. Lower heat and simmer until the potatoes are tender when pierced with a fork, but not falling apart, 8 to 10 minutes. Drain into a colander, then transfer the potatoes to a large mixing bowl. Add the remaining ingredients and toss gently to combine. Cover and refrigerate until chilled, at least 2 hours. The salad will stay fresh for up to a week.

Notes

- You will have onions left over, so try them in salads, sandwiches, or pizza, and enjoy!

Lebanese Cabbage Salad

Serves 6 to 8 • Gluten-Free, Vegan

I don't consider myself a picky eater, but I draw the line at coleslaw. After courageously sampling the stuff at summer barbecues over the years, I'm beginning to wonder if a good recipe even exists. Does it serve any purpose other than impolitely leaking sweet juice from soggy cabbage onto all the other food just sitting there on the plate, so dry and innocent? The first time I saw this cabbage salad at our local Lebanese restaurant, I almost leaped from my chair, mistaking this similar-looking side for coleslaw, but once the kind waitress explained they were nothing alike, I took a bite and fell in love. Made with crisp shredded cabbage, roma tomatoes, and cucumbers, this tangy Middle Eastern specialty is tossed with fresh mint, lemon juice, minced garlic, and lots of black pepper. It is a neighborly accompaniment to a *mezze* platter complete with warm pita, hummus (page 262), and tabbouleh (page 81), and while it may look like a distant coleslaw cousin, it is welcome on my plate anytime!

—Adam

---

1 pound (454 g) cabbage, shredded (about 4 packed cups)
1 cucumber (198 g), sliced into ¼-inch rounds, then cut into quarters
2 roma tomatoes (165 g), coarsely chopped
1 tablespoon (3 g) fresh mint leaves, finely chopped
3 tablespoons extra-virgin olive oil
4 to 5 tablespoons lemon juice
2 large garlic cloves (10 g), minced or pressed
1 teaspoon salt
¾ teaspoon freshly ground black pepper

Combine all ingredients in a large salad bowl, and toss to combine. Chill at least 1 hour before serving, and enjoy! The salad will stay fresh for up to 3 days.

Kale Quinoa Tabbouleh with Crunchy Spiced Chickpeas

Serves 6 to 8 • Gluten-Free, Vegan

This tabbouleh is fantastic, but can we please talk about these chickpeas? You'll want to make as many batches as your oven can handle, because if you like them as much as we do, you will be devouring this addicting topping by the handful before you even have the chance to add it to the salad. Baked with spicy cayenne, paprika, garlic powder, and cumin, this crunchy snack is sprinkled over the top of fresh kale and quinoa, mixed with plenty of parsley, chopped tomatoes, scallions, loads of mint, pressed garlic, and lemon juice. Pair this with our Hummus Four Ways (page 262) and a Spanakopita Quiche (page 26), and we'll see you in chickpea rehab!

FOR THE CRUNCHY SPICED CHICKPEAS
- 1 15-ounce (425 g) can chickpeas
- 1 teaspoon extra-virgin olive oil
- ½ teaspoon salt
- ⅛ teaspoon ground cayenne pepper
- ½ teaspoon ground cumin
- ¼ teaspoon garlic powder
- ¼ teaspoon smoked paprika

FOR THE TABBOULEH
- ⅔ cup (123 g) uncooked quinoa
- 1⅓ cups (315 ml) water
- 1 teaspoon salt, divided
- 1 cup (44 g) kale, stem removed, and roughly chopped
- ½ cup (22 g) parsley, coarsely chopped
- ½ cup (40 g) scallions, thinly sliced
- 1 tablespoon (3 g) fresh mint, coarsely chopped
- 2 medium tomatoes (280 g), finely chopped
- 1 large garlic clove (5 g), minced or pressed
- 4 to 5 tablespoons fresh lemon juice
- 3 tablespoons extra-virgin olive oil
- ¼ teaspoon freshly ground black pepper

MAKE THE CRUNCHY SPICED CHICKPEAS
Preheat oven to 400°F/204°C, and line a baking sheet with parchment or a silicone mat. Place the chickpeas into a colander, rinse well, then drain. Spread them on the baking sheet, and let air-dry for 30 minutes.

In a large bowl, combine the fully dried chickpeas with the oil, salt, and spices, and toss to coat evenly. Spread the chickpeas on the prepared baking sheet, and bake until golden and crispy, 40 to 45 minutes, shaking the pan every 10 minutes to roll the chickpeas around. Let cool 5 minutes, then use immediately or cool completely and keep in a dry airtight container at room temperature for up to a week.

MAKE THE TABBOULEH
Rinse the quinoa in a fine-mesh strainer under cold water until the water runs clear. Transfer the quinoa to a small saucepan, add the water and ½ teaspoon of the salt, and bring to a boil over medium-high heat. Lower heat to a simmer, cover, and cook for 15 minutes, until the water is absorbed and the quinoa is fluffy. Remove from heat and let the pan rest without opening the lid for 5 minutes.

In a large mixing bowl, combine the cooked quinoa with ½ teaspoon salt and the remaining ingredients, and toss to combine. Serve immediately, or keep refrigerated for a few hours to chill. Top with the baked chickpeas at the table just before serving so they stay crisp.

Summer Corn and Zucchini Salad
with Cherry Tomatoes

Serves 6 to 8 • Gluten-Free, Vegan

Each spring, our local community garden holds a neighborhood plant sale. We make sure to arrive early to beat the crowds, stocking up on tomato cuttings to fill the planter beds in our backyard. Throughout the summer months, you will find us outside picking basil leaves and sampling them together with plump cherry tomatoes and sun golds still warm on the vine. Every year, we plant a rainbow of varieties and cook with them all season long—if we don't end up eating them first. Here, they are tossed in a bowl with all the stars of summer: diced zucchini, sweet corn, juicy nectarines, and handfuls of fresh basil. Garnished with red onions, balsamic vinegar, salt, and pepper, this quintessential summer salad is begging to be paired with a Meatless Western Bacon Cheeseburger (page 106) and a glass of our Strawberry Sangria Sparkler (page 222) at your next summer soirée.

FOR THE SALAD
6 ears of corn, husk and silk removed
½ zucchini, diced into ½-inch pieces (about 1 cup / 143 g)
1¾ cups (290 g) cherry tomatoes, quartered
½ cup (70 g) coarsely chopped red onion
2 nectarines, diced into ½-inch pieces and pit removed (about 1½ cups / 225 g)
2 large handfuls of basil, finely chopped (about 22 g)
2 tablespoons extra-virgin olive oil
2½ teaspoons balsamic vinegar
1½ teaspoons salt
½ teaspoon freshly ground black pepper

FOR GARNISH
halved cherry tomatoes
nectarine slices
basil leaves

Fill a large pot with 3 inches of water, cover, and bring to a boil. Add the corn, then cover, reduce heat to a simmer, and cook for 5 minutes. Transfer the corn to a cutting board and let rest until cool enough to handle comfortably, 3 to 4 minutes. Once cool, stand each ear vertically on the cutting board and use a sharp knife to slice down the sides of the corn, removing the kernels.

Transfer the kernels to a large bowl, then add all the remaining ingredients. Toss to combine, then refrigerate until chilled, about 1 hour. Garnish with cherry tomatoes, nectarine slices, and basil leaves, if desired, and serve.

Moroccan Bread Fattoush Salad

Serves 6 to 8 • Gluten-Free Option, Vegan

Special Tools: Thermometer

Los Angeles attracts visitors from all over the world, and for good reason: you can spend a winter's day at the beach, soaking up 80 degrees of golden sunshine while sipping on a Tropical Rum Punch (page 227) in the middle of December, then pack your belongings, head to the mountains, and go skiing for the rest of the afternoon. When the global cuisines from LA's immigrants begin mixing together, the result is something entirely new and unique—like the Korean taco truck that visits our neighborhood every Tuesday night, offering a fusion menu of Mexican dishes filled with traditional Korean ingredients, including their legendary kimchi quesadillas. Inspired by our international city, we wanted to create a Mediterranean mash-up of our own. If Italy, Morocco, and the Middle East had a baby, this would be their love child. Featuring the crusty Moroccan bread known as *khobz,* this salad is part Italian *panzanella* and part Middle-Eastern *fattoush,* combining the best of all three worlds. Loaded with chopped tomatoes, cucumbers, radishes, and fresh mint, this cool medley is topped with toasted bread cubes still warm from the oven and tossed in a zesty *fattoush* dressing with sumac, lemon juice, and minced garlic. This is a delicious celebration of cultures, and we are proud to welcome it into our home.

FOR THE *KHOBZ* BREAD
½ cup (118 ml) water
1 teaspoon granulated sugar
1½ teaspoons active dry yeast
2 cups (240 g) bread flour (see note)
1 teaspoon salt
1 tablespoon extra-virgin olive oil

FOR THE DRESSING
1 teaspoon sumac powder (see note)
3 tablespoons fresh lemon juice
2 large garlic cloves (10 g), minced or pressed
½ teaspoon salt
½ teaspoon freshly ground black pepper
¼ cup (59 ml) extra-virgin olive oil

FOR THE SALAD AND ASSEMBLY
3 tablespoons extra-virgin olive oil
¼ teaspoon salt
3 large tomatoes (470 g total), coarsely chopped
1 cucumber (195 g), thinly sliced
½ cup (30 g) scallions, thinly sliced
4 cups (120 g) lettuce, coarsely chopped
½ cup (15 g) parsley, finely chopped
½ cup (15 g) mint leaves, finely chopped
4 large radishes (50 g), thinly sliced

TO MAKE THE *KHOBZ* BREAD

In a microwave-safe measuring cup, combine the water and sugar and stir to dissolve. Heat until the water reaches 115°F/46°C, then stir in the yeast and let rest for a few minutes until foamy.

While the yeast is proofing, combine the flour and salt in a mixing bowl, and whisk to combine. Once the yeast is foamy on top, pour the yeast mixture into the bowl with the flour, add the olive oil, and stir until the dough comes together. If the dough seems too dry, add a few drops of water, or if it is too wet, add a few spoonfuls of flour. Transfer the dough to a lightly floured work surface, and knead by hand until it is smooth and elastic, about 10 minutes. Alternatively, the dough can be kneaded in a stand mixer on medium speed for about 5 minutes. Either way, once it is done being kneaded, form the dough into a 6-inch ball, and let it rest on the work surface for 15 minutes.

Line a baking sheet with parchment or a silicone mat. Flatten the ball of dough into a circle about 8 inches (20 cm) wide, and place it on the prepared baking sheet. Let rest at room temperature for 1 hour.

Preheat the oven to 400°F/204°C. Use a sharp knife to cut an *X* on the top of the loaf. Bake until the outside is golden brown and the loaf sounds hollow when tapped, about 20 to 25 minutes. Let cool while you make the dressing.

TO MAKE THE DRESSING

In a small bowl, combine the sumac, lemon juice, garlic, salt, and pepper, and whisk to combine. Add the olive oil slowly to prevent separation, whisking until smooth and blended.

TO MAKE THE SALAD

Cut the bread into 1-inch cubes. You will end up with about 7 cups. Heat a large, deep skillet over medium-low heat. Add 3 tablespoons of olive oil, and when hot, add the bread cubes and sprinkle ¼ teaspoon of salt over the top. Stirring occasionally, cook until the bread is toasty and beginning to brown, about 10 minutes.

While the bread is toasting, combine the tomatoes, cucumber, scallions, lettuce, parsley, mint, and radishes in a large salad bowl, and toss to combine. Add the dressing, and toss to coat the vegetables evenly. Once the bread is toasted, add the cubes to the salad bowl, and toss to combine. The salad can be served immediately (for crispy, warm bread) or refrigerated for up to a day before serving (for soft bread that has absorbed the flavors from the salad). Both ways are delicious!

Notes

- If you do not have bread flour, you can substitute all-purpose flour in the bread recipe.

- Sumac is a tangy, lemony spice that can be found in natural food stores as well as markets that carry Middle Eastern products. It can also be bought online.

- If you want to enjoy this salad but don't have time to bake a loaf of bread, you can substitute store-bought bread instead. Choose a loaf that weighs about 13 ounces and is fairly dense and chewy. When cut into cubes, you should have about 7 cups of bread.

- To make this Gluten-Free: substitute a loaf of gluten-free bread for the *khobz*.

Roasted Rainbow Beet Salad

Serves 4 to 6 • Gluten-Free

I grew up despising beets. The worst was the dreaded borscht that would make its ominous appearance on holidays and special occasions. I haven't tried it in years, but perhaps for our next book, I'll overcome my phobia and work some kitchen magic with that traumatizing cold pink soup. Borscht aside, my fear of beets has blossomed into a deep-rooted love, as over the years, they began surreptitiously presenting themselves on salads and pizzas at trendy restaurants around town. Here, they are roasted in the oven until tender and tossed with freshly squeezed lime juice and smoky paprika. Topped with creamy goat cheese, chopped thyme leaves, and a pinch of cayenne, this spirited salad is a delicious and colorful way to start any meal.

—Adam

2 to 3 red beets (283 g total), peeled and diced into ½-inch pieces
2 to 3 golden beets (226 g total), peeled and diced into ½-inch pieces
6 to 8 small Easter egg radishes (226 g total), diced into ½-inch pieces
2 tablespoons extra-virgin olive oil
½ teaspoon salt
½ teaspoon freshly ground black pepper
1 tablespoon fresh lime juice
pinch of ground cayenne pepper (optional)
a few pinches of smoked paprika
¼ teaspoon chopped fresh thyme leaves
2 ounces (57 g) goat cheese, crumbled
lime zest, for garnish
lemon zest, for garnish
a few pinches of flaky sea salt, for garnish

Preheat oven to 400°F/205°C, and line a baking sheet with parchment paper or a silicone mat. Scatter the diced beets and radishes on the baking sheet, and drizzle the olive oil over the top. Sprinkle the salt and pepper over the vegetables, then use a spatula to toss, coating them lightly with olive oil. Roast in the oven until the beets and radishes are tender when pierced with a fork, 35 to 45 minutes. Transfer the cooked vegetables to a medium bowl, then add the lime juice, cayenne pepper, paprika, and thyme, tossing to combine evenly. Top with goat cheese crumbles, lime and lemon zest, and a pinch or two of flaky sea salt. Serve hot, and enjoy!

Tropical Fruit Salad with Fresh Ginger

Serves 8 to 10   •   Gluten-Free, Vegan

Many summers ago, Ryan was under the weather on the day we were supposed to leave for our big trip to Hawaii. It seemed like sipping piña coladas on Poipu Beach might not be in the cards for us, but at the last minute he gathered enough strength to stumble to the car and ride to the airport. We barely caught our flight, and his entire first day on Kauai was spent recovering in a hotel bed. Thankfully, the Hawaiian air helped quickly cure his ailments, he was able to enjoy the rest of the vacation, and we sipped piña coladas on the beach the very next day. This light tropical fruit salad has some of that same healing magic from the islands that Ryan experienced. Packed with sweet pineapple, mango, banana, kiwi, strawberry, and blueberry, and tossed in a lemon-mint-ginger dressing sprinkled with flakes of coconut, say aloha to this tropical bowl of paradise.   —*Adam*

1 pineapple, cored, skin removed, fruit cut into chunks (about 570 g of fruit)
2 mangoes (460 g), peeled and diced into ½-inch pieces
6 bananas (425 g), sliced ½-inch thick
2 kiwis (160 g), peeled and diced into ½-inch pieces
10 strawberries (220 g), trimmed and cut into quarters
1 cup (160 g) blueberries
1 packed tablespoon (3 g) fresh mint, finely chopped
1 tablespoon fresh lemon juice
1½ teaspoons (8 g) grated fresh ginger
3 tablespoons (10 g) unsweetened coconut chips or flakes

Combine all the ingredients in a large bowl, and toss to combine. Serve immediately, and enjoy!

Notes

- Bananas turn brown quickly, so if making this salad ahead of time, combine all ingredients except the bananas, and keep the salad refrigerated for up to 24 hours. When ready to serve, slice and add the bananas, and toss to combine.

Romantic Picnic Salad with Arugula, Hearts of Palm, Artichoke Hearts, and Watermelon Radish Hearts

Serves 4 • Gluten-Free, Vegan Option

Why wait for a special occasion to express affection to your loved one? Yes, this adorable salad would bring tears to their eyes when you present it to them on Valentine's Day at a quiet picnic spot with a bottle of bubbly, and of course, you would receive lots of extra kisses if you delivered this enchanting work of art to the bedroom for a fairy-tale breakfast-in-bed birthday brunch. But why not surprise your sweetie with an intimate love salad on a typical Tuesday work night when they least expect it? Made with fresh arugula, hearts of palm, artichoke hearts, and thin slices of heart-shaped watermelon radishes and passionately dressed in a tangy balsamic vinaigrette, this charming salad is sure to stir up some love, whatever the occasion.

FOR THE BALSAMIC VINAIGRETTE
¼ cup (59 ml) balsamic vinegar
1½ teaspoons dijon mustard
3 tablespoons (25 g) minced shallots
1 large garlic clove (5 g), minced or pressed
½ teaspoon salt
½ teaspoon freshly ground black pepper
½ cup (118 ml) extra-virgin olive oil

FOR THE SALAD
6 cups (240 g) arugula (about 1½ cups per serving)
8 hearts of palm, cut into ½-inch slices
12 to 14 canned artichoke hearts, quartered
2 watermelon radishes, thinly sliced and cut into heart shapes using a cookie cutter
shaved pecorino romano cheese, for garnish
flaky sea salt, for garnish
freshly ground black pepper, for garnish

TO MAKE THE BALSAMIC VINAIGRETTE
In a small bowl or glass measuring cup, combine the vinegar, mustard, shallots, garlic, salt, and pepper. While whisking, slowly add the olive oil, and continue whisking to combine.

TO ASSEMBLE THE SALAD
Place a large handful of arugula on each serving plate. Drizzle a small amount (about 1 tablespoon, or to taste) of the dressing over the arugula, then top with palm slices, artichoke hearts, and the radish hearts. Add a few pieces of shaved pecorino, then sprinkle the top with a few pinches of flaky salt and pepper. Serve and enjoy!

Notes

- To make this Vegan: omit the pecorino romano cheese garnish.

Sentimental Citrus Salad

Serves 4 to 6 • Gluten-Free, Vegan Option

When we moved into our home, we had a fruitful vision for a long, narrow stretch of land behind our house that was neck-high in weeds. We cleared the brush, covered the soil with truckloads of mulch, and lined the path with orange, lemon, grapefruit, avocado, lime, nectarine, loquat, plum, and pomegranate trees to accompany the tangerine tree on the patio that has been here for over fifty years. Living in Los Angeles has pros and cons with its large crowds and endless traffic, but winter makes me sentimental, walking down our mini orchard in shorts and a T-shirt, harvesting bagfuls of sweet citrus while in other parts of the country, people are shoveling snow and ice from their driveways every morning. Even in January, this vibrant salad is a ray of California sunshine. With four kinds of citrus, paper-thin slices of red onion, shaved fennel, and topped with crumbled feta, pomegranate arils, and fresh mint leaves, this salad will brighten your day—and your dinner table—no matter where you are!

—Adam

4 blood oranges
2 navel oranges
1 pink grapefruit
1 pomelo
25 grams fennel root, shaved or sliced as thinly as possible
20 grams red onion, shaved or sliced as thinly as possible
¼ cup (60 g) crumbled feta
2 tablespoons (5 g) chopped mint leaves
2 to 3 tablespoons pomegranate arils
1 to 2 tablespoons extra-virgin olive oil

Peel all of the citrus, then cut each fruit into ¼-inch slices. Arrange the sliced fruit on a serving plate, then top with the shaved fennel and onion, followed by the crumbled feta, mint leaves, pomegranate arils, and a drizzle of olive oil. Serve immediately and enjoy!

Notes

- To make this Vegan: omit the feta cheese.

Entrées

We've been asked every vegetarian question on the planet: How do we get our protein? Do we eat anything besides vegetables? Isn't all vegetarian food bland, boring sticks and leaves? Do we ever miss meat? How do we even live? These are all excellent questions, and we understand why people are curious, since sitting down to a home-cooked meal at the end of a long day is a special and sacred moment. Whether you are enjoying a quick weeknight dinner on your own, planning an elegant date night for two, or hosting a party for a large group of friends, there are twenty-one original meatless entrées in this chapter that will have everyone at the table licking their plates and asking for seconds. These protein-packed main courses will pleasantly fill you up, and nothing here is made with boring sticks and leaves. Get ready to add more stamps to your international passport as we sample delicious vegetarian cuisine from across the globe. Bring your appetite, and join us as we travel on an exotic, all-expenses-paid trip to Cuba, Thailand, Spain, Korea, Morocco, Italy, Vietnam, India, and Mexico, and pack some plutonium, since we'll be going back in time to sample a few of our childhood favorites, and vegetarianize entrées we thought we could never enjoy again.

Spicy Five-Bean Chili

Serves 6 to 8 • Gluten-Free, Vegan Option

This recipe is here to give any nonvegetarian chili a run for its money. Enter it in a cook-off contest and be prepared to walk away with the first-place ribbon. Using five colorful varieties of beans, our prizewinner includes an assortment of cannellini, red kidney, white navy, black, and pinto. Simmered with hearty vegetables and loads of garlic and herbs, this spicy chili is ready to take home the trophy at next summer's outdoor barbecue.

FOR THE CHILI
3 tablespoons extra-virgin olive oil
1 medium onion (300 g), finely chopped
1 green bell pepper (200 g), finely chopped
1 red bell pepper (200 g), finely chopped
1 jalapeño pepper, seeded and finely chopped
1 medium carrot (115 g), finely chopped
1 large celery rib (55 g), finely chopped
4 large garlic cloves (20 g), finely chopped
2 medium zucchini (350 g), coarsely chopped
2 tablespoons chili powder
2 teaspoons ground cumin
1½ teaspoons salt
½ teaspoon freshly ground black pepper
1 teaspoon smoked paprika
⅛ teaspoon ground cayenne pepper
½ teaspoon dried oregano
2 bay leaves
1 15-ounce (425 g) can red kidney beans,
  rinsed and drained
1 15-ounce (425 g) can black beans, rinsed
  and drained
1 15-ounce (425 g) can pinto beans, rinsed
  and drained
1 15-ounce (425 g) can white navy beans,
  rinsed and drained
1 15-ounce (425 g) can cannellini beans,
  rinsed and drained
1 28-ounce (794 g) can diced tomatoes
2 cups (473 ml) vegetable broth (page 46)
¼ cup (12 g) cilantro, finely chopped

FOR GARNISH
plain yogurt or sour cream
grated cheddar cheese
tortilla chips
corn bread (see page 152)
thinly sliced green onions

In a large pot, heat the oil over medium heat. When hot, add the onion, all three peppers, carrot, and celery, and stir to combine. Sauté for 10 to 12 minutes, stirring occasionally, until all the vegetables are softened. Add the garlic, zucchini, chili powder, cumin, salt, black pepper, paprika, cayenne pepper, oregano, and bay leaves, then stir to combine and cook for 4 minutes. Add all the beans, tomatoes, and broth, raise heat to high, and bring to a boil. Cover pot, lower heat to a simmer, and cook for 30 minutes. Add the cilantro, stir to combine, and remove from heat. Serve hot and enjoy!

Notes

- To make this Vegan: use nondairy sour cream and vegan cheese.

Date Night Risotto with Asparagus and Lemon

Serves 4 • Gluten-Free

Since the odds of rainfall in Los Angeles are about as slim as winning the lottery, whenever water finally does emerge from those unfamiliar gray, puffy things hanging in the sky, we like to celebrate. Our goal on those unusual wet days is to stay home wearing soft robes and comfy slippers with a cup of Soothing Ginger-Honey Tea (page 239) in hand, clearing our schedule so the only plans for the evening are to cook a romantic meal and enjoy the relaxing sounds of rain hitting our roof. Add a creamy risotto to the equation, pour a glass of your favorite wine, and you have a perfect date night without ever leaving home—and even better, this easy dinner comes together in under thirty minutes, leaving you more time to spend with your honey.

1 pound (454 g) asparagus (about 1 bunch)
6 cups (1.4 L) vegetable broth (page 46)
2 tablespoons extra-virgin olive oil, divided
2 tablespoons unsalted butter, divided
1 large onion (420 g), finely chopped
3 large garlic cloves (15 g), minced
zest from one lemon, plus more for garnish, if desired
1½ cups (290 g) uncooked arborio rice
½ cup (118 ml) white wine
2 ounces (about ½ cup / 57 g) pecorino romano cheese, grated
3 tablespoons lemon juice
¼ teaspoon freshly ground black pepper

Remove and discard the tough ends of the asparagus, then cut off the tips and set them aside. Cut the remaining asparagus into ½-inch pieces.

Pour the broth into a medium saucepan, cover, and bring to a boil over high heat. Once boiling, lower heat to a bare simmer, and keep covered.

While the broth is warming up, place another medium saucepan over medium heat, and add 1 tablespoon of the olive oil. When hot, add the reserved asparagus tips and cook until bright green and crisp, 2 to 3 minutes. Remove the tips, and set aside in a small bowl. To the pan, add the remaining tablespoon of olive oil and 1 tablespoon of butter. Once the butter melts, add the onion and cook until softened and beginning to turn golden, 7 to 10 minutes, stirring occasionally. Add the garlic, lemon zest, and rice, and cook for 3 minutes, stirring constantly. Add the wine, and stir until the liquid is absorbed. Start a timer for 5 minutes, then begin adding the broth, about ½ cup at a time, stirring constantly, and waiting to add more broth until the previous addition has been completely absorbed.

Once the timer rings, add the chopped asparagus spears and continue adding broth while you stir, until all the broth has been added and the rice is creamy and al dente. Remove the pan from heat, then add the grated cheese, remaining 1 tablespoon of butter, lemon juice, and pepper. Stir well to combine, then taste for salt and adjust as needed. Let the pan rest for 10 minutes, covered. Stir one more time, then serve hot, topped with the crispy asparagus tips and lemon zest, if desired.

Sweet Potato Gnocchi in a Browned Butter Sage Sauce

Serves 4

When we were in New York for the Saveur Blog Awards, there were two days of culinary activities for all the finalists, including photography workshops, panel discussions, and test kitchen tours. Our favorite was the pasta-making class, where a small group of us learned authentic Italian secrets, tucked away in a restaurant basement in the heart of Manhattan. We had always felt intimidated by the process, but after seeing how easy it was, we've been whipping up homemade pasta dinners ever since. If this is your first time, gnocchi is a great place to start; you don't need a pasta machine, and since the noodles are shaped by hand, there is no pressure to make them look perfect. Made with roasted sweet potatoes, these golden gnocchi use masa harina—the same Mexican corn flour in tortillas and tamales—for a flavorful Southwest twist. Pan-fried until crispy and tossed in a savory browned butter and sage sauce, these pasta pillows are so soft, you can practically sleep on them.

FOR THE GNOCCHI
- 1 tablespoon extra-virgin olive oil
- 1 pound (454 g) sweet potatoes
- 6 tablespoons (44 g) masa harina (see note)
- 1 large egg
- ¾ teaspoon salt
- 1 ounce (¼ cup/28 g) grated Parmesan cheese, plus more for garnish
- 2 teaspoons brown sugar
- 1¾ cups plus 2 tablespoons (225 g) all-purpose flour, plus more as needed

FOR THE SAUCE
- 20 fresh sage leaves, chopped (about 2 tablespoons), plus more for garnish
- 8 tablespoons (1 stick/113 g) unsalted butter
- 1 teaspoon salt
- 2 tablespoons extra-virgin olive oil

Preheat the oven to 425°F/218°C, and line a baking sheet with parchment or a silicone mat. Drizzle the olive oil over the center of the baking sheet. Cut the sweet potatoes in half lengthwise, and lay them cut-side-down on the prepared baking sheet, moving them around to coat the bottoms evenly in oil. Poke the skins of the potatoes several times with the tip of a sharp knife to create vents, then bake until completely soft when pierced with a knife, 30 to 40 minutes. Let them cool enough to handle safely, then scoop the insides into a large mixing bowl and cool to lukewarm, discarding the skins.

Once the potatoes have cooled, add the masa harina, egg, salt, Parmesan, and brown sugar, and stir to combine. Add the flour, and stir until the dough comes together. Transfer the dough to a floured countertop and knead briefly, just enough to form the dough, adding additional flour if it is too sticky. Form the dough into a ball, wrap in plastic, and let rest for 15 minutes at room temperature. Unwrap and divide into 4 smaller pieces, placing one of the pieces on the work surface and keeping the remaining dough wrapped in plastic. Use your hands to roll the ball of dough into a long rope about ¾-inch wide. Cut the rope into 1-inch lengths, and move the pieces

aside, keeping them well floured to prevent sticking. If desired, add ridges on the gnocchi by rolling them on a gnocchi board or the back of a fork. Repeat with the remaining dough, yielding 75 to 80 gnocchi. They can be used immediately or frozen for future use (see note).

Bring a large covered pot of salted water to a boil, using 1 teaspoon of salt per 1 quart of water.

While the water is heating up, place the chopped sage leaves in a medium heatproof bowl and set aside. Place the butter and salt in a small saucepan, and set the pan over medium-low heat. Melt the butter, stirring often, then continue stirring as the butter gets foamy and the solids at the bottom of the pan begin to turn golden brown. When the butter solids are dark brown—but not burned—immediately remove the pan from heat and pour the butter into the bowl with the sage leaves. Do this carefully, as

the mixture will steam and sputter vigorously. Stir to combine, then set aside.

When the water is boiling, add the gnocchi, stirring to prevent them from sticking together. Bring back to a boil, then lower heat to a simmer and cook until all the gnocchi are floating. Wait another 30 seconds, then drain into a colander and set aside.

Set a large nonstick skillet over medium-high heat. When hot, add the olive oil, then add enough gnocchi to fill the skillet in a single layer. Cook until the undersides are golden brown and crispy, about 4 minutes, then flip them using a spatula or tongs, and cook the second side until golden brown, another 4 minutes. Transfer to a heatproof serving bowl, repeating the process with any remaining gnocchi, then pour over the sage butter, tossing to combine. Serve hot, topped with fresh sage leaves, and enjoy!

Notes

- Masa harina is a special type of corn flour used to make tamales and tortillas. It is different from cornmeal—which will not work as a substitute—and is available in the Latin American section of many grocery stores.

- To freeze the gnocchi: cover a tray with parchment paper, and arrange the gnocchi on the paper in a single layer without touching. Place the tray in the freezer until the gnocchi are frozen, 2 to 3 hours, then transfer the gnocchi to a ziplock plastic bag or sealed container for storage, up to two months.

- If the gnocchi will not fit in your skillet in one single layer, you can sauté them in batches. Set the oven to 200°F/93°C, and place the empty serving bowl inside. When the first batch of gnocchi is done, transfer it to the heated serving bowl, then return it to the oven to keep them warm while you make the remainder.

Calzones with Broccoli, Pesto, Artichoke Hearts, and Sun-Dried Tomatoes

Makes 4

Special Tools: Thermometer

Trader Joe's used to sell frozen calzones similar to this recipe, and we were nearly in tears when the store stopped carrying them. For those lucky few who fondly remember this quick packaged dinner, you will be thrilled to learn that you can now enjoy them once again. Fresher than any frozen version, these crispy homemade calzones are better than the original. Oozing with creamy mozzarella and filled with chopped broccoli florets, sun-dried tomatoes, and tangy artichoke hearts in a creamy pesto sauce, make them for dinner tonight and you will understand why we are celebrating their glorious return.

FOR THE CRUST (SEE NOTE)
¾ cup (177 ml) water
1 teaspoon granulated sugar
2¼ teaspoons (1 packet) active dry yeast
2 cups (240 g) all-purpose flour
¾ teaspoon salt
3 tablespoons extra-virgin olive oil

FOR THE PESTO (SEE NOTE)
2 tablespoons pine nuts
2 large garlic cloves (10 g), minced or pressed
1 large handful (12 g) fresh basil leaves
1 ounce (¼ cup / 28 g) Parmesan cheese, grated
¼ teaspoon salt
1 tablespoon extra-virgin olive oil
1½ tablespoons heavy cream

FOR THE FILLING AND ASSEMBLY
4¾ ounces (135 g) broccoli florets, cut into bite-size pieces
½ cup (65 g) coarsely chopped sun-dried tomatoes
½ cup (65 g) coarsely chopped canned artichoke hearts (not packed in oil)
4¾ ounces (135 g) mozzarella cheese, cubed
a few tablespoons of cornmeal or farina (Cream of Wheat) for the pan
a drizzle of extra-virgin olive oil to brush the calzones

TO MAKE THE CRUST

Combine the water and sugar in a heatproof measuring cup, and stir to dissolve. Microwave the mixture in 15-second bursts, until the water reaches 115°F/46°C (alternatively, this can be done in a small pan on the stove instead of the microwave). When the mixture is at the correct temperature, add the yeast and stir with a fork to break up any clumps. Let the mixture rest (proof) until foamy on top, about 10 minutes.

While the yeast is proofing, place the flour and salt in a large mixing bowl and whisk to combine. Once the yeast mixture is foamy, pour it into the bowl with the flour, and add the olive oil. Stir to combine until the dough comes together into one clump. If too sticky, add more flour a spoonful at a time. Transfer the dough to a floured work surface and knead until smooth and elastic, about 10 minutes, adding more flour as needed if the dough becomes sticky. Cover the dough with a clean kitchen towel and let rise for 1 hour at room temperature.

TO MAKE THE PESTO

Place the pine nuts in a small, dry skillet and set over medium-low heat. Stirring or shaking the pan occasionally, cook until fragrant and golden brown, 5 to 7 minutes. When toasted, immediately transfer them to a plate to prevent overcooking. Let cool briefly, then place in a food processor or blender. Add the garlic, basil, Parmesan, and salt, and process until smooth, stopping to scrape down the sides as needed. With the machine running, add the olive oil. Transfer the pesto to a bowl, then add the cream and stir to combine.

TO MAKE THE FILLING AND
ASSEMBLE THE CALZONES

Place a steamer basket in a pot, and add a few inches of water. Cover pan and bring to a boil, then add the broccoli florets and steam until tender, about 4 minutes. Transfer the broccoli to a medium mixing bowl to cool briefly, then add the sun-dried tomatoes, artichoke hearts, cubed mozzarella, and pesto, and toss to combine.

Preheat the oven to 500°F/260°C. Sprinkle a few tablespoons of cornmeal or farina over a baking sheet, and spread it around with your hands.

When the dough has risen, divide it into 4 equal portions. Roll each one out to a square about ⅛-inch thick and 6 to 8 inches on each side. Lay the squares with one of the corners facing you. Divide the filling equally between the four calzones, spooning it onto the bottom half of each square, leaving a ½-inch space between the filling and the edge of the dough. Fold the top corner of the dough over the filling, creating a triangle shape with the filling completely enclosed inside. Starting at one end, roll and pinch the edges together to seal them closed. Gently lift the calzones and transfer them to the prepared baking sheet, leaving at least 1 inch between each one. Brush the tops lightly with olive oil, then use a sharp knife to cut 2 to 3 small vents in the top middle of each calzone. Bake for 13 to 15 minutes, until golden brown and bubbly. Let rest for 10 minutes, then serve and enjoy!

Notes

- You can easily use store-bought pizza dough to save time.

- The pesto can be made up to a week ahead of time, kept in a sealed container in the fridge.

Meatless Western Bacon Cheeseburgers

Makes 4 to 5

Special Tools: Thermometer

This masterpiece is a vegetarian take on a childhood fast-food favorite. While it may involve a bit more effort than just leisurely pulling into a drive-through, these juicy burgers are so tasty they may even convert some of your meat-eating friends. With crunchy golden onion rings, a tangy homemade tamarind barbecue sauce (page 286), a savory patty made from quinoa, cannellini beans, Parmesan, and spices, and finished with a slice of melted American cheese and crispy shiitake bacon (page 40), just add an affogato shake (page 244) to the equation, and let the games begin!

FOR THE BURGERS
- ¼ cup (45 g) uncooked quinoa
- ½ cup (118 ml) water
- 1 15-ounce (425 g) can cannellini beans, drained and rinsed
- 1 large egg
- ½ teaspoon garlic powder
- ½ teaspoon smoked paprika
- ¼ teaspoon onion powder
- ½ teaspoon ground cumin
- ½ teaspoon chili powder
- ½ teaspoon salt
- ½ teaspoon freshly ground black pepper
- 1 scallion, finely chopped
- ½ ounce (2 tablespoons / 14 g) grated Parmesan
- ¾ cup (83 g) fine bread crumbs
- 4 tablespoons extra-virgin olive oil
- 4 to 5 slices of American cheese

FOR THE ONION RINGS
- vegetable oil, for frying (about 1 to 2 quarts)
- 1 large yellow onion (420 g)
- 1 cup (120 g) all-purpose flour
- 1 teaspoon baking powder
- 1 teaspoon salt
- 1 large egg
- ¾ cup (177 ml) milk of your choice
- ¾ cup (38 g) panko bread crumbs
- a few sprinkles of salt, for garnish

FOR ASSEMBLY
- 4 to 5 hamburger buns
- smoky tamarind barbecue sauce (see page 286)
- shiitake bacon (see page 40)

TO MAKE THE BURGERS

Preheat oven to 200°F/93°C, and put an oven-safe dinner plate in the oven. Place the quinoa in a dry skillet, and set over medium heat. Stirring often, cook the quinoa until browned and deeply toasted, 10 to 15 minutes. Remove from heat, transfer the quinoa to a fine-mesh strainer, and rinse under cold water to remove the bitter coating from the quinoa—do this carefully, as it will steam vigorously. Let drain, then transfer the quinoa to a small saucepan. Add ½ cup water, and stir to combine. Cover, bring to a boil, then lower heat and simmer gently without opening the lid for 15 minutes. Turn off the heat and continue to leave the pan covered for 5 minutes, then uncover and fluff the quinoa with a fork.

In a large bowl, mash the beans until smooth. Add the cooked quinoa, egg, spices, scallion, Parmesan, and bread crumbs, and stir until evenly blended. Let the mixture rest for 10 minutes.

Heat the olive oil in a large skillet over medium-high heat. Form the mixture into patties, and place them in the skillet. Cook each patty until the

underside is golden brown, 5 to 7 minutes. Flip and repeat with the second side. Top each burger with a slice of American cheese, then transfer them to the plate in the oven to keep warm.

TO MAKE THE ONION RINGS

Fill a large, deep skillet (preferably cast iron) or saucepan with 2 to 3 inches of neutral vegetable oil. Clip a cooking thermometer on the side of the pan, and set heat to medium-high. Bring the oil to a temperature of 365°F/185°C, then adjust the heat as needed to maintain the oil at that temperature. Near the stove, set a plate covered with a few layers of paper towels.

While the oil is heating, peel the onion, then slice it into ¼-inch-thick circles and separate them into individual rings. In a medium bowl, combine the flour, baking powder, and salt, and whisk to blend. Place a wire rack on a baking sheet, and set it next to the bowl. Dip each onion ring in the flour mixture, coating all sides evenly, then lay it on the rack. Once the rack is filled with floured onions (you may have onion slices left over, which you can reserve for another use), add the egg and milk to the bowl

of flour. Whisk to combine, making a batter. Dip each onion ring in the batter, coating all sides, then place back on the wire rack to drain until no longer dripping. Place the panko bread crumbs in a shallow bowl or plate, and dip the battered onion rings in the bread crumbs, coating them evenly on all sides. Place the coated ring back on the rack to dry briefly while the oil heats up.

Carefully place several rings in the hot oil, without crowding the pan, and cook until the undersides are golden, then flip and repeat, about 3 minutes total. Remove the rings from the oil using a spider strainer or slotted spoon, and place on the paper towels to drain. Sprinkle with salt, and let cool while you fry the remaining onion rings. Serve immediately while still warm.

TO ASSEMBLE

Spread barbecue sauce on both sides of the hamburger bun, and place one or two onion rings on the bottom half. Then top with a patty, shiitake bacon, and the top half of the bun. Serve immediately, and enjoy!

Indian Curry with Chickpeas and Cauliflower

Serves 4 to 6 as a main, 6 to 8 as a side   •   Gluten-Free, Vegan

Our first date was at a shopping mall food court eating from Styrofoam containers, but I promise it was better than it sounds. Across the street from the campus of USC was an aging outdoor mall with a cafeteria that was often crowded and noisy, especially during lunchtime when it filled with hordes of hungry students. But hidden within the chaos, a surprisingly authentic Indian restaurant served traditional dishes at student-friendly prices. It may not have earned a Michelin star for ambience, but the food was always a hit. Adam was on campus for a piano lesson that day, so I ironed my nicest shirt and swapped my glasses for contact lenses, hoping to make a good impression—only to find out much later that he preferred me with glasses and was somewhat disappointed when I showed up without them. While we have long forgotten the exact dishes we enjoyed that afternoon, and the mall itself was demolished several years ago, the memory of that meal remains with us, and Indian food has been a part of our culinary lives ever since. There is something intensely comforting about a coconut curry, and when tender chickpeas and fresh cauliflower are the centerpiece, it is bound to light a spark, even if eaten from a plastic tray in a food court.

—Ryan

2 tablespoons extra-virgin olive oil
1 large onion (450 g), coarsely chopped
2 large garlic cloves (10 g), minced
1-inch piece of ginger (about 2 tablespoons / 24 g), minced
1 serrano pepper, seeds and white ribs removed, finely chopped
1 to 2 teaspoons salt
1½ tablespoons curry powder
1 teaspoon ground coriander
1 teaspoon ground turmeric
2 15-ounce (425 g each) cans chickpeas, drained and rinsed
2 13.5-ounce (403 ml each) cans coconut milk (see note)
1 medium head cauliflower, center stem removed, florets cut into bite-size pieces
½ teaspoon freshly ground black pepper
¼ cup (12 g) cilantro, finely chopped
1 to 2 tablespoons lemon juice
prepared basmati rice, to serve

Pour the olive oil into a large, deep skillet over medium heat. Add the onion and cook until softened, 7 to 9 minutes. Add the garlic, ginger, and serrano pepper, and cook for 1 minute. Then add 1 teaspoon of the salt, curry, coriander, and turmeric, and cook for 1 more minute. Add the chickpeas, coconut milk, and cauliflower, then cover the pan, bring almost to a boil, and cook at a bare simmer for 15 minutes. Add the pepper, cilantro, and lemon, then taste for salt and lemon and adjust as needed. Serve hot, with rice, if desired, and enjoy!

Notes

- Canned coconut milk is available in the Asian section of many grocery stores or online.

One-Pan Pasta Primavera

Serves 4 • Vegan Option

A gourmet pasta dinner in less than 10 minutes? The first time I heard about one-pan pasta, I was skeptical. I've always cooked it in the traditional way—in a large pot of boiling salted water—but in this unorthodox method, all the ingredients are combined in one pan, and by the time the table is set and the candles are lit, dinner will be ready to serve. It seems to go against everything an Italian grandmother would teach you, yet it results in perfectly al dente noodles and a silky sauce every time. This innovative take on classic pasta primavera includes a rainbow of cherry tomatoes, chopped broccoli florets, asparagus spears, mushrooms, and handfuls of spinach, with an elegant sauce seasoned with fresh basil, garlic, and a serrano pepper for a gentle heat. This simple spaghetti is a weeknight dinner savior.

—Ryan

12 ounces (340 g) dry spaghetti
3 large garlic cloves (15 g), thinly sliced
1 serrano pepper, seeds and white ribs removed, finely chopped
12 ounces (340 g) cherry tomatoes
½ cup (75 g) finely chopped red bell pepper (about ½ of a medium pepper)
1 medium head broccoli (about 2 cups / 115 g), coarsely chopped
6 asparagus spears (85 g), cut into ½-inch lengths
½ medium onion (165 g), finely chopped
6 cremini or white mushrooms (95 g), sliced
2 handfuls spinach (75 g), roughly chopped
2 teaspoons salt
¼ teaspoon freshly ground black pepper
4½ cups (1.06 L) water
1 handful (15 g) fresh basil leaves, cut into strips
1½ ounces (about ⅓ cup / 43 g) pecorino romano cheese, grated, plus more for garnish

Place everything except the basil and cheese in a large, deep saucepan. Bring to a boil over medium-high heat, using tongs to toss often. Once boiling, continue to toss and cook for 9 minutes, until the liquid reduces and thickens to a sauce and the pasta is al dente. Add the basil and cheese, and continue tossing to combine. Serve immediately, topped with additional cheese, if desired, and enjoy!

Notes

- To make this Vegan: omit the pecorino romano cheese.

Fingerling Potato, Gruyère, and Caramelized Onion Galette

Serves 4

If you have never tried a galette before, we need to fix this immediately. Easier to make than pie, this rustic dish comes in a variety of flavors, from baked sweet galettes topped with fresh berries and scoops of vanilla ice cream to delicious savory galettes like this one made with a wealth of caramelized onions and melted gruyère cheese. Resting in a golden rosemary crust—perfectly flaky, light, and buttery—your uncertain dinner plans for this evening are now finalized.

FOR THE ROSEMARY CRUST
- 1¼ cups plus 2 tablespoons (165 g) all-purpose flour
- ½ teaspoon salt
- 1 tablespoon fresh rosemary, very finely minced
- 8 tablespoons (113 g) unsalted butter, cubed and chilled
- ¼ cup (55 g) greek yogurt or sour cream
- 2 teaspoons lemon juice
- ¼ cup (59 ml) cold water

FOR THE FILLING AND ASSEMBLY
- 3 tablespoons extra-virgin olive oil, divided
- 1 large onion (420 g), cut in half and thinly sliced
- ¼ teaspoon salt
- 6 ounces (170 g) fingerling potatoes
- ¼ teaspoon flaky sea salt
- ¼ teaspoon freshly ground black pepper
- 4 ounces (about 1 cup / 113 g) gruyère cheese, grated
- 1 egg yolk
- 1 teaspoon water

TO MAKE THE CRUST

In a large bowl, whisk together the flour, salt, and rosemary. Scatter the butter pieces over the flour mixture, and use a pastry knife or your fingers to blend in the butter until the largest pieces are the size of peas.

In a small bowl, whisk together the yogurt, lemon juice, and water. Pour into the large bowl with the flour, and stir until the dough forms into one mass and no longer sticks to the sides of the bowl. Add a tablespoon or two of flour if the dough is too sticky. Gather the dough into a 6-inch ball, press into a disc about 3 inches thick, wrap tightly in plastic, and refrigerate for at least one hour, up to a day.

TO MAKE THE FILLING

Pour 2 tablespoons of oil into a large skillet, and place over low heat. When hot, add the onions and salt, and simmer until browned and deeply caramelized, about 20 minutes. Remove the onions from the pan and transfer to a plate to cool, then return the skillet to the stove—no need to rinse it out.

Thinly slice the potatoes lengthwise in ⅛-inch slices. Pour enough water in the skillet to cover the bottom by about ½ inch. Place the potato slices in the water, spreading them out so every slice is covered. Turn the heat to high, bring to a boil, then lower heat to a simmer and cook until the potatoes are tender when pierced with a fork, about 10 to 15 minutes. Remove the potatoes from the skillet, and place in a medium bowl. Add the remaining tablespoon of olive oil, salt, and pepper to the potatoes, and toss gently to combine.

TO ASSEMBLE

Preheat oven to 400°F/204°C. Line a baking sheet with parchment paper or a silicone baking mat, and set aside. Remove the dough from the fridge, unwrap it, and place it on a floured work surface. Roll it out to a 12-inch circle about ¼-inch thick.

Transfer the circle of dough to the prepared baking sheet. Sprinkle half the cheese over the center of the dough, leaving a 2-inch border around the sides. Then spread the onions over the cheese, leaving the same border. Sprinkle half the remaining cheese over the onions, then lay the potato slices on top. Sprinkle the remaining cheese over the potato slices, reserving a few pinches of cheese for the crust. Fold up the sides of the crust, pleating each one over the next as you work your way around the circle. In a small bowl, whisk together the egg yolk and teaspoon of water, then brush this mixture lightly over the crust. Sprinkle the crust with the reserved cheese. Bake until golden brown, 30 to 40 minutes. Let cool for 5 minutes, then serve while hot and enjoy!

Enchiladas with Chipotle-Marinated Tofu

Serves 6 • Vegan Option

Yes, plain tofu doesn't taste much better than a piece of paper, but when it is marinated with freshly squeezed lime and orange juice, minced garlic, chipotle chilies, and cumin, it can convert even a willful tofu critic into an avid fan. Mixed with sautéed mushrooms, green bell peppers, and handfuls of jack and cheddar cheese, this tasty Mexican-inspired meal is here to turn your typical weeknight dinner into a fun-filled flavor fiesta.

FOR THE MARINATED TOFU

14 ounces (397 g) firm tofu
2 tablespoons apple cider vinegar
3 tablespoons lime juice
4 tablespoons orange juice
3 large garlic cloves (15 g), minced or pressed
½ teaspoon onion powder
1 teaspoon ground cumin
2 tablespoons minced chipotle chilies in adobo sauce

FOR THE ENCHILADA SAUCE

3 tablespoons vegetable oil
3 tablespoons all-purpose flour
6 tablespoons chili powder
¾ teaspoon garlic powder
¾ teaspoon salt
½ teaspoon ground cumin
½ teaspoon dried oregano
3 cups (710 ml) vegetable broth (page 46)

FOR THE FILLING

3 tablespoons extra-virgin olive oil
1 large onion (415 g), finely chopped
1 green bell pepper (215 g), seeded and finely chopped
½ teaspoon salt
8 ounces (227 g) cremini or white mushrooms, sliced

FOR ASSEMBLY

5 ounces (1¼ cups / 142 g) cheddar cheese, grated
5 ounces (1¼ cups / 142 g) monterey jack cheese, grated
10 to 12 corn tortillas
sliced scallions, for garnish
sliced radishes, for garnish

TO MAKE THE TOFU

Place the tofu on a cutting board. Place another cutting board (or a plate) on top of the tofu and set a few heavy cans on top to weigh it down. Let the tofu drain for 15 minutes, then cut into ½-inch cubes and set aside. In a large bowl, combine the vinegar, lime and orange juice, garlic, onion powder, cumin, and chipotle chilies, and stir well. Add the tofu, and toss to coat. Refrigerate, stirring occasionally, for at least 1 hour, or up to overnight.

TO MAKE THE SAUCE

Pour the oil into a medium saucepan, and set over medium-high heat. When hot, add the flour and whisk for 1 minute. Add all the spices, and whisk to blend. Pour in the broth, whisk to combine, and simmer for 10 to 15 minutes until thickened sightly, stirring occasionally. Use immediately, or keep refrigerated in a sealed container for up to a week.

TO MAKE THE FILLING

Heat the oil in a large, deep skillet over medium heat. Add the onions, green pepper, and salt, and cook until softened, 7 to 10 minutes. Add the sliced mushrooms and cook, stirring occasionally, until tender, 4 minutes. Add the tofu and any remaining marinade in the bowl, and sauté until the tofu is warmed through. Use immediately, or keep refrigerated in a sealed container for up to 3 days.

TO ASSEMBLE

Preheat oven to 350°F/177°C. Pour about ½ cup of enchilada sauce in the bottom of a large baking dish (9×13-inch or larger) and spread it around with the back of a spoon.

In a medium bowl, mix together the two cheeses with your hands. Divide the cheese blend evenly between two bowls—half will be for the filling, and half will go on top. Then make an enchilada assembly line: place the bowls of cheese, the filling, a cutting board, and a stack of tortillas next to the baking dish.

Heat a tortilla until soft and pliable—either in the microwave or in a dry skillet over low heat—and place it on the cutting board. Spoon a line of filling down the middle, leaving a few inches of space on each side, then sprinkle cheese over the top of the filling. Roll the tortilla over the filling, creating a tube. Place the enchilada seam-side-down in the baking pan, starting in one corner. Continue rolling enchiladas and placing them snugly next to the previous one in the pan until the entire baking dish is packed and the filling is completely or nearly gone. Pour all the remaining sauce over the top, moistening all the tortillas if possible. Top evenly with the remaining cheese, then bake until bubbly, 25 to 30 minutes. Let rest for 5 minutes, then serve hot, garnished with sliced scallions and radishes, if desired, and enjoy!

Notes

- To make this Vegan: use vegan cheese instead of monterey jack and cheddar.

Cheesy Artichoke-Stuffed Ravioli

Serves 4 to 6

Special Tools: Food Processor; Pasta Maker

The first cooking blogger I ever followed was Deb Perelman from *Smitten Kitchen*. Since 2006, nearly ten years before we dreamed up *Husbands That Cook,* I have visited her blog obsessively, making recipes and reading all about the trials and tribulations of cooking in a tiny New York apartment. This comforting recipe is inspired by a spectacular casserole in her first cookbook, but here we transform it into homemade ravioli. Generously filled with caramelized onions and artichokes sautéed in white wine, these tender ravioli rest in a creamy Parmesan béchamel made with lemon and garlic. Garnished with a pinch of parsley, make this for your dinner guests and be prepared to accept the award for Best Host Ever.

—Ryan

FOR THE FILLING
- 1 tablespoon extra-virgin olive oil
- ½ onion (200 g), finely chopped
- 1 14-ounce (397 g) can artichoke hearts, drained and quartered
- 2 tablespoons white wine
- ¼ cup (28 g) grated pecorino romano cheese
- ¼ cup (28 g) grated Parmesan cheese
- 1 large egg yolk
- 2 teaspoons lemon juice
- ¼ teaspoon salt
- ¼ teaspoon freshly ground black pepper

FOR THE PASTA (SEE NOTE)
- 2 cups (240 g) all-purpose flour
- ½ teaspoon salt
- 3 large eggs
- 1 tablespoon extra-virgin olive oil

FOR THE SAUCE
- ¼ cup (57 g) unsalted butter
- ¼ cup (30 g) all-purpose flour
- 2 cups (473 ml) milk of your choice
- 1 large garlic clove (5 g), minced
- ¼ cup (59 ml) freshly squeezed lemon juice
- ¼ cup (28 g) grated Parmesan cheese
- ½ teaspoon salt
- ¼ teaspoon freshly ground black pepper
- a few pinches of chopped parsley, for garnish

TO MAKE THE FILLING
Heat the olive oil in a large skillet over medium heat. When hot, add the onion and cook until softened, 7 to 9 minutes. Add the artichokes and cook for 5 minutes. Add the white wine and stir until it is absorbed, less than a minute. Remove from heat and let cool briefly. Transfer the mixture to a food processor, and add the remaining ingredients. Pulse until chopped, but still slightly chunky—not puréed. Use immediately, or keep refrigerated in a sealed container for up to a week.

TO MAKE THE PASTA DOUGH
In a large bowl, combine the flour and salt. Make a well in the center of the flour and add the eggs and oil. Use a wooden spoon or your fingers to begin stirring the eggs in the well, slowly pulling in more flour as your stir. Continue stirring until the dough comes together, then begin kneading in the bowl, adding more flour if it seems too sticky. Transfer the dough onto a floured work surface, and knead until smooth and glossy, 5 to 10 minutes. Cover the dough with plastic and let rest at room temperature for 30 minutes.

Divide the ball of dough into 4 pieces, and place one of the pieces on the work surface, keeping the other three pieces covered. Roll the piece into a rectangle ¼-inch thick and about 4 inches wide, and pass it through the rollers of a pasta maker on the widest setting. Fold the sheet of pasta in thirds like a letter, forming a rectangle, and pass it through the rollers on the same setting. Repeat the process of folding and rolling several times, then set the rollers one notch thinner. Pass the pasta sheet through the rollers several times in a row without folding, creating a long, narrow sheet. Set the rollers one notch thinner and repeat the process, continuing until you have reached the second-thinnest setting on the machine.

Lay the pasta sheet horizontally on the work surface, and make one vertical cut in the middle to divide in half. Place rounded tablespoons of filling on one half of the pasta sheet, about an inch apart. Place the other pasta sheet on top, lining up the edges. Press the air bubbles out around each ball of filling, sealing the two pasta sheets together with your fingers. Use a pizza cutter or a pastry wheel and cut around the mounds of filling to make square ravioli. Set aside in a single layer until ready to cook. Repeat with the remaining dough and filling.

TO MAKE THE SAUCE

In a medium saucepan, melt the butter over medium heat. Once melted, add the flour and whisk to combine. Add the milk as you continue whisking—slowly at first, then in larger pours as the sauce begins to form. Once all the milk has been added, add the garlic and bring to a simmer. Cook for 2 to 3 minutes, until thickened sightly, then remove from heat and add the lemon juice, Parmesan, salt, and pepper, and whisk to combine. Keep warm until ready to use, or place in a sealed container in the fridge for up to a week.

TO ASSEMBLE

Bring a large pot of salted water (use 1 teaspoon of salt for each quart of water) to a boil over high heat. Carefully add the ravioli, returning to a boil before lowering heat to a simmer. Cook for 4 to 5 minutes, until the pasta is floating and al dente. Remove from the water with a spider strainer or slotted spoon, and place on the serving plates. Top with generous amounts of garlic béchamel sauce and a sprinkle of parsley, if desired.

Notes

- To save time, skip making the homemade pasta, and use wonton wrappers instead. Place one wrapper on a cutting board, and top with a rounded tablespoon of filling. Dip your finger in a small bowl of water, moisten the wrapper all around the filling, then lay a second wrapper on top, lining up the edges, and use your fingers to pinch and seal the edges closed. Repeat with additional wonton wrappers until all the filling is used. Add to a pot of boiling salted water and cook for 3 minutes.

California Gumbo

Serves 6 to 8 • Vegan

We are putting California on the map with this gumbo. Who would have thought that two vegetarian husbands from the West Coast could create something so authentic, so comforting, and so satisfying? Look out, Louisiana—we struck gold with this one-pot stew. In this hearty meal, fire-roasted tomatoes are simmered with green and red bell peppers, kidney beans, chopped celery, and okra. Seasoned with loads of garlic and spices, served over a steaming bowl of hot rice, and topped with our addictive shiitake bacon (page 40), this robust stew will have you California dreamin' on such a winter's day.

FOR THE GUMBO
¼ cup (59 ml) vegetable oil
¼ cup (30 g) all-purpose flour
1 large onion (475 g), finely chopped
3 large celery ribs (200 g), finely chopped
1 red bell pepper (200 g), seeded and finely chopped
1 green bell pepper (200 g), seeded and finely chopped
6 large garlic cloves (30 g), minced
1 14.5-ounce (411 g) can fire-roasted tomatoes
6 ounces (170 g) canned tomato sauce
16 ounces (454 g) okra, sliced into ½-inch pieces
4 cups (946 ml) vegetable broth (page 46)
2 bay leaves
1½ teaspoons granulated sugar
¼ teaspoon ground cayenne pepper
½ teaspoon dried thyme
1½ teaspoons chili powder
1 teaspoon salt
½ teaspoon freshly ground black pepper
1 teaspoon Cajun seasoning blend
1½ teaspoons smoked paprika
½ teaspoon dried oregano
2 teaspoons Cajun filé powder
1 tablespoon apple cider vinegar
1 tablespoon vegetarian worcestershire sauce
1½ teaspoons liquid smoke
1 tablespoon tamari or soy sauce
¼ cup (12 g) flat-leaf parsley, finely chopped
1 15-ounce (425 g) can red kidney beans, drained and rinsed

FOR GARNISH
cooked long-grain white rice
thinly sliced scallions
shiitake bacon (see page 40)

In a large pot or dutch oven, heat the vegetable oil over medium heat. When hot, add the flour and whisk until deeply browned and aromatic, about 7 to 10 minutes. Add the onion, celery, and red and green bell peppers, and sauté until the vegetables soften, 7 to 10 minutes. Add the garlic and cook for 1 minute. Add all the remaining ingredients, stir well, cover, and bring to a boil. Lower heat to a simmer and cook, stirring occasionally, for 2 hours. Serve hot, with a scoop of rice in each bowl, topped with scallions and shiitake bacon. Enjoy!

Notes

- For the okra, either fresh or frozen will work fine. If using frozen, there is no need to defrost before adding it to the pot.

- Cajun filé powder is available in the spice section of many grocery stores.

Chickpea Cacciatore

Serves 4 to 6

My all-time favorite meal before I became vegetarian was my grandma's chicken cacciatore. She prepared it so tenderly in that classic tangy red sauce that it would literally melt in your mouth. When I told my mom that we were including a meatless version in our cookbook, she mentioned that she saved my grandma's original handwritten recipe after she passed away. In this treasured entrée, we use that same recipe for the sauce and simply replace the chicken with chickpeas. Combined with cannellini beans, Parmesan cheese, bread crumbs, onions, celery, and spices, it nearly brought a tear to my eye after tasting it for the first time.

—*Adam*

FOR THE CHICKPEA PATTIES
- 1 15-ounce (425 g) can chickpeas, drained and rinsed
- 1 15-ounce (425 g) can cannellini beans, drained and rinsed
- 2 large eggs
- ½ cup (57 g) fine bread crumbs
- ½ ounce (2 tablespoons / 14 g) Parmesan cheese, grated
- 1 teaspoon salt
- ½ teaspoon freshly ground black pepper
- ½ teaspoon chili powder
- ½ teaspoon garlic powder
- ¼ teaspoon onion powder
- ½ teaspoon smoked paprika
- 1 tablespoon nutritional yeast flakes
- ½ teaspoon poultry seasoning blend
- 1 teaspoon red miso
- 1 tablespoon finely minced onion
- 1 tablespoon finely minced celery

FOR THE SAUCE
- 2 tablespoons extra-virgin olive oil, plus more if needed
- 1 cup (130 g) finely chopped onion
- ½ cup (65 g) thinly sliced green bell pepper
- 2 large garlic cloves (10 g), minced
- 1 28-ounce (794 g) can crushed or diced tomatoes
- ⅓ cup (85 g) tomato paste
- ¾ cup (177 ml) red wine
- 2 tablespoons (6 g) minced flat-leaf parsley
- 1½ teaspoons granulated sugar

- 1 teaspoon salt
- ½ teaspoon dried rosemary
- ½ teaspoon dried thyme
- ¼ teaspoon dried oregano

TO MAKE THE PATTIES

In a large bowl, mash together both types of beans until smooth and no lumps remain. Add all the remaining ingredients and stir to combine. Let rest for 10 minutes to allow the bread crumbs to absorb moisture. Form into 6 oval-shaped 4-inch patties.

TO MAKE THE SAUCE

Place a large, deep skillet over medium heat, and add the olive oil. When hot, arrange the patties in the skillet in a single layer and cook until the undersides are golden brown, 5 to 6 minutes. Flip and repeat with the second side. Remove the patties from the pan and transfer to a plate, but keep the stove on. There should still be oil remaining in the skillet, but if not, add a few tablespoons as needed. Then add the onion and bell pepper, and cook until softened, 7 to 9 minutes. Add the remaining ingredients, bring to a simmer, then cover and cook for 10 minutes. Use a spoon to make 6 indentations in the sauce, and place a patty in each one. Spoon the sauce over the patties, covering them evenly, then cover and cook for 8 minutes. Serve hot, and enjoy!

Moo Shu Vegetable Lettuce Wraps with Peanut Sauce

Serves 3 to 4   •   Gluten-Free Option, Vegan Option

When we decide where to eat out, we prefer to find a cozy family-run business or walk down the street to pick up a burrito from a local food truck, rather than order cookie-cutter dishes at chain restaurants where there are enough tables to seat customers by the hundreds. There is a Chinese place that some of our relatives enjoy, and every few years, we end up meeting there for a birthday or special occasion. We admit, the restaurant has a pretty mean lettuce wrap on the menu—which was the inspiration for this recipe—but we cannot tell a lie; ours runs circles around theirs. Gather your family because here, crisp iceberg lettuce cups are filled with marinated tofu and chopped vegetables sautéed in garlic and ginger, then topped with a peanut sauce that everyone will want to eat by the spoonful. These Asian wraps are so tasty, you just signed yourself up to be the host for all future family festivities.

FOR THE PEANUT SAUCE
1-inch piece of ginger, grated (about
    2 teaspoons / 12 g)
1 large garlic clove (5 g), minced or pressed
½ cup (127 g) creamy natural peanut butter
2 tablespoons tamari or soy sauce
2 tablespoons fresh lime juice
1 tablespoon honey
¼ teaspoon red pepper flakes

FOR THE MARINATED TOFU
2 tablespoons tamari or soy sauce
1 tablespoon rice vinegar
1 tablespoon sesame oil
1 teaspoon honey
1½ cups (214 g) extra-firm tofu, cut into small
    ¼-inch cubes

FOR THE LETTUCE WRAPS
4 tablespoons vegetable oil, divided
3 large eggs
1 teaspoon tamari or soy sauce
1 teaspoon sesame oil
1 cup (120 g) finely chopped onion
½ cup (65 g) finely chopped celery
2 cups (115 g) shredded green cabbage
2 cups (85 g) sliced mushrooms
1 tablespoon (16 g) grated ginger
2 large garlic cloves (10 g), minced
1 cup (60 g) sliced scallions (about 3 or
    4 scallions)
1 cup (80 g) mung bean sprouts
1 head iceberg lettuce, washed and pulled
    apart into individual leaves

TO MAKE THE PEANUT SAUCE
Combine all the ingredients in a small bowl, and
stir to blend. If the sauce is too thick, stir in water
a teaspoon at a time until the desired texture is
reached. Use immediately, or keep in a sealed
container in the fridge for up to a week.

TO PREPARE THE TOFU
In a shallow wide bowl, combine the tamari, rice
vinegar, sesame oil, and honey, and whisk to blend.
Add the tofu and toss to coat evenly. Let rest at room
temperature for 30 minutes, tossing occasionally.

TO MAKE THE WRAPS
In a wok or large heavy skillet, heat 2 tablespoons of
the vegetable oil over medium-high heat. While it is
heating, whisk together the eggs, tamari, and sesame
oil in a small bowl. Once the oil is hot, add the eggs
and stir gently until the eggs scramble and cook.
Remove the eggs from the pan and transfer to a plate,
breaking up the eggs into bite-size clumps.

Return the pan to heat, and add the remaining
2 tablespoons of vegetable oil. Add the onion
and celery, and cook until slightly softened, 3 to
5 minutes. Add the cabbage, mushrooms, ginger,
garlic, prepared tofu, and any remaining marinade,
and toss to combine. Cook until the cabbage and
mushrooms soften, 2 to 4 minutes. Add the scallions
and bean sprouts, and cook until wilted, about
4 minutes. Remove from heat, and stir in the eggs.

To serve, place lettuce leaf cups on a serving plate.
Top each one with a generous scoop of filling and
serve warm, drizzled with peanut sauce, with a bowl
of extra sauce at the table for dipping.

Notes

- To make this Gluten-Free: be sure to use
  gluten-free tamari instead of soy sauce.

- To make this Vegan: omit the eggs, and
  use maple syrup in place of honey.

Cuban Empanadas

Serves 8 to 10 • Vegan Option

My *abuelita* made empanadas like no one else. I can still picture her smiling as she removed them from the oven, standing in her kitchen with a pink 1960s refrigerator covered in colorful magnets and snapshots of her grandkids. Her method was unique because instead of folding individual hand pies, she always made one giant empanada—the size of an entire baking sheet. I would dance around impatiently, begging her to cut the warm pastry into squares, and she would laugh and say, "*Espérate*" (Be patient). Every time she prepared it, the filling was slightly different, depending on what she had available in the kitchen, but it was always perfect. This vegetarian version has all the same flavors I loved as a kid, just without the meat. With tender spiced lentils, caramelized onions, sautéed bell peppers, and minced garlic, the savory filling also has plump raisins and sliced green olives—traditional ingredients often found in Cuban empanadas. Wrapped in a flaky golden crust, these portable pies will have you salsa dancing in the kitchen in no time.

—*Ryan*

FOR THE CRUST
- 4½ cups (540 g) all-purpose flour
- 1 tablespoon salt
- 1 cup plus 2 tablespoons (254 g) unsalted butter, cubed
- 1 cup plus 2 tablespoons (267 ml) cold water

FOR THE LENTILS
- 1 cup (193 g) uncooked brown lentils
- 2 cups (473 ml) water
- ¼ teaspoon red pepper flakes
- ½ teaspoon ground cumin
- ½ teaspoon ground coriander
- 1 teaspoon smoked paprika
- ⅛ teaspoon ground cayenne pepper
- ¼ teaspoon garlic powder
- ¼ teaspoon onion powder
- ½ teaspoon salt
- ½ teaspoon freshly ground black pepper
- 1 teaspoon chopped chipotle chilies in adobo sauce

FOR THE FILLING AND ASSEMBLY
- 2 tablespoons extra-virgin olive oil
- 1 large onion (420 g), thinly sliced
- 1 red bell pepper (175 g), finely chopped
- 2 large garlic cloves (10 g), minced
- 1 teaspoon ground cumin
- 1 teaspoon smoked paprika
- 1 tablespoon chili powder
- 1 teaspoon salt
- ½ cup (80 g) pimiento-stuffed green olives, sliced in half
- ½ cup (75 g) raisins, soaked for 10 minutes in a bowl of warm water, then drained
- 1 large egg, to brush the crust

TO MAKE THE CRUST

In a large bowl, whisk together the flour and salt. Add the butter, and use a pastry knife or your fingers to work the butter into the flour until the largest pieces are the size of peas. Add the water, and use a spoon to stir until the dough comes together. Knead briefly, just enough for the dough to form one smooth ball. Divide the dough into 2 equal portions, and form each portion into a rough rectangle shape about 6 inches wide. Wrap in plastic, and let rest in the fridge for at least 30 minutes, up to one day.

TO MAKE THE LENTILS

First, spread the lentils on a baking sheet and sort through them, discarding any pebbles that you may find. Rinse them in a fine-mesh strainer and let drain briefly. Transfer the rinsed lentils to a medium saucepan, then add the water, red pepper flakes, cumin, coriander, paprika, cayenne pepper, garlic powder, and onion powder, and stir well to combine. Cover, bring to a boil over high heat, then lower to a simmer and cook until the lentils are tender, 30 to 40 minutes. If the water level dips below the surface of the lentils, add water as necessary to cover. When the lentils are tender, drain any remaining water, then return the lentils to the pan. Add the salt, pepper, and chipotle chilies, and stir well to combine. Use immediately, or keep in a sealed container in the fridge for up to a week.

TO MAKE THE FILLING

In a large, deep skillet or dutch oven, heat the oil over medium heat. Add the sliced onion and cook until lightly caramelized, 10 to 15 minutes. Add the lentils and cook for 2 minutes. Stir in the bell pepper, garlic, cumin, paprika, chili powder, and salt, and cook until the peppers soften, 3 to 4 minutes. Add the olives and raisins, and remove from heat. Use immediately, or

transfer to a sealed container in the fridge for up to a week.

TO ASSEMBLE THE EMPANADAS

Prepare a floured work surface, and place a rimmed 18×13-inch baking sheet nearby. Unwrap one of the dough rectangles, and roll out with a rolling pin until it is slightly larger than the baking sheet. Carefully transfer the dough to the baking sheet: roll the dough over the rolling pin, then unroll it over the baking sheet so the dough hangs over the edges by about 1 inch. Press the dough into the bottom and sides of the sheet, then spread the lentil filling into the crust, making an even layer. Roll out the second piece of dough in the same manner, laying it on top of the filling. Cut off any extra overhanging dough, then fold the edges over to seal them. Use a fork to press the edges closed and make a ridged design along the outside. Poke holes over the top of the crust using a fork, creating vents through which steam can escape. In a small bowl, whisk the egg until blended, then brush the entire surface of the crust with the beaten egg. Bake for 45 minutes, until the crust is golden brown and glossy. Cut into squares, and serve warm, room temperature, or chilled, and enjoy!

Notes

- To make this Vegan: use vegan butter in the crust, and omit the egg wash.

Lentil-Stuffed Cabbage

Serves 5 to 6　•　Gluten-Free, Vegan Option

The best part of visiting my grandma Gertrude was her homemade cooking. She lived nearby, so frequent weekends with game nights and sleepovers were like mini vacations for my brother and me. Whenever we visited, she prepared special meals for us, and our faces lit up every time she brought her famous stuffed cabbage to the table. This vegetarian version is adapted from her classic recipe—our only changes are the ingredients in the filling. She used ground meat to stuff the cabbage, but we found that brown lentils and a few spices give it a similar texture to the original with just as much flavor. Baked in a zesty tomato sauce, this satisfying dish is just like Grandma used to make.　　*—Adam*

FOR THE SAUCE
- 2 tablespoons extra-virgin olive oil
- 1 large onion (400 g), finely chopped
- 1 28-ounce (794 g) can crushed tomatoes
- ½ teaspoon salt
- ½ teaspoon freshly ground black pepper
- ¼ cup (53 g) brown sugar
- ¼ cup (59 ml) apple cider vinegar

FOR THE FILLING AND ASSEMBLY
- 1 cup (193 g) uncooked brown lentils
- 2 cups (473 ml) water
- 1 large egg
- ½ teaspoon dried oregano
- ½ teaspoon salt
- ½ teaspoon freshly ground black pepper
- ½ teaspoon dried thyme
- ¼ cup (33 g) finely chopped onions
- 1 large garlic clove (5 g), minced
- 1 ounce (about ¼ cup / 28 g) grated Parmesan cheese
- ⅓ cup (65 g) uncooked long-grain white rice
- 1 large head savoy cabbage

TO MAKE THE SAUCE
Pour the oil in a medium saucepan, and set over medium heat. Add the onion and cook until softened, 7 to 9 minutes. Add the remaining ingredients and simmer uncovered for 15 minutes.

Use immediately, or transfer to a sealed container in the fridge for up to a week.

TO MAKE THE FILLING
First, spread the lentils on a baking sheet and remove any pebbles. Transfer the lentils to a fine-mesh strainer, rinse well, and let drain briefly. Place the lentils in a medium saucepan, and add 2 cups water. Bring to a boil over high heat, then cover, lower heat, and simmer until the lentils are tender, 30 to 40 minutes, adding more water as needed if the water level dips below the top of the lentils. When tender, drain and return to the pot.

In a large bowl, mix together the egg, oregano, salt, pepper, thyme, onions, garlic, and Parmesan. Add the rice and cooked lentils and stir to combine. Add 1 cup of the sauce, and stir until blended. Use immediately, or transfer to a sealed container in the fridge for up to a week.

TO ASSEMBLE
Preheat oven to 350°F/177°C, and spread 1 cup of sauce in a large oven-safe skillet or a 2- to 3-quart baking dish. Bring a large pot of water to a boil.

Use a sharp paring knife to carefully cut out the hard center core from the head of cabbage. Place the

cabbage in the pot of boiling water to soften, using tongs to gradually peel away and remove each leaf as it separates from the head, transferring them to a cutting board to cool. You will need about 12 to 15 leaves.

To make the rolls, take one cabbage leaf and fill it with about ⅓ cup of lentil mixture. Roll up the leaf tightly like a mini burrito, and place it seam-side-down in the baking dish. Once all the filling is used and the baking dish is tightly packed with stuffed

cabbages, pour the remaining sauce over the top. Cover tightly with a lid or aluminum foil, and bake for 1 hour. Serve hot and enjoy!

Notes

- To make this Vegan: omit the Parmesan cheese, and replace the egg with a flax egg (page 8).

Notes

- Different brands of black beans vary widely in salt content, so when cooking the recipe, start with less salt and add more as needed.

Cuban Black Beans and Rice

Serves 3 to 4 • Gluten-Free, Vegan

Husbands That Cook was meant to be. Years before launching our website, we kept a travel blog—only for our close friends and family—sharing stories from our adventures and, most importantly, detailed descriptions of every meal we ate along the way. We even produced a few how-to cooking videos and posted them online, including one for black beans and rice, the simple dish that is the foundation of Cuban cuisine. While it's not exactly Emmy-winning material, even back then we loved sharing recipes, and ten years later, that same passion inspired us to start the blog together. In this classic dish, adapted from my *abuelita*'s original recipe, black beans are simmered until tender with sautéed onions and green peppers, minced garlic, and spices, and finished with a splash of vinegar. Served with a generous scoop of soft rice, this Cuban family recipe may be considered peasant food, but the flavor is fit for a king.

—Ryan

FOR THE BLACK BEANS
- 2 tablespoons extra-virgin olive oil
- 1 small onion (about 200 g), finely chopped
- 1 green bell pepper (about 200 g), finely chopped
- 4 large garlic cloves (20 g), minced
- ¾ to 1½ teaspoons salt (see note)
- ½ teaspoon freshly ground black pepper
- ½ teaspoon dried oregano
- ½ teaspoon ground cumin
- 1 bay leaf
- 2 15-ounce (425 g each) cans black beans
- 1 teaspoon red miso
- ¼ teaspoon liquid smoke
- ½ cup (118 ml) water
- 1 tablespoon white vinegar

FOR THE RICE
- 2 cups (473 ml) water
- pinch of salt
- 1 cup (200 g) uncooked long-grain white rice

TO MAKE THE BEANS
Pour the olive oil into a medium saucepan and place over medium heat. When hot, add the chopped onion and bell pepper, and sauté until golden, 15 to 20 minutes. Add the garlic, ¾ teaspoon salt, pepper, oregano, cumin, and bay leaf, then stir to combine and cook for 1 minute. Add the beans (including the liquid in the cans), miso, liquid smoke, and water. Bring to a boil, stirring occasionally, then lower heat and simmer uncovered for 15 to 20 minutes.

WHILE THE BEANS ARE SIMMERING, MAKE THE RICE
Pour the water and salt into a small saucepan, cover, and bring to a boil over high heat. Add the rice, stir to combine, bring back to a simmer, then lower the heat as low as possible, cover the pan, and cook without opening until the water is absorbed and the rice is fluffy, 18 to 20 minutes. Keep covered until ready to serve.

TO SERVE
When the beans and rice are both ready, add the vinegar to the beans, stir to combine, and remove from heat. Taste for salt, and adjust as needed. Serve the beans with a scoop of rice and enjoy!

Pad See Ew with Crispy Tofu

Serves 2 to 3

If you were to count the times we have enjoyed this classic Thai noodle dish, it would surely be in the hundreds. Between all the restaurants around Los Angeles and the numerous times we've ordered it for delivery on nights when we were too busy to cook, it is safe to say the two of us are passionate pad see ew enthusiasts. When soft, wide rice noodles are tossed with minced garlic, chinese broccoli, and ultra-crispy tofu in a sweet and savory sauce, you too will soon be craving this seductive Thai delicacy. And since it is cheaper than dining out and quicker than delivery, your pad see ew intake will soon be reaching the hundreds too.

FOR THE CRISPY TOFU

- 1 12- to 14-ounce (340 g to 397 g) package extra-firm tofu
- ¾ cup (88 g) cornstarch
- 1 teaspoon garlic powder
- 1 teaspoon salt
- ½ teaspoon freshly ground black pepper
- vegetable oil, for sautéing

FOR THE NOODLES

- 3 tablespoons vegetable oil
- 3 large garlic cloves (15 g), minced
- 4 cups (250 g) chinese broccoli, stems cut into 1-inch pieces, leaves left whole (see note)
- 1 pound (454 g) fresh wide rice noodles (see note), gently separated
- 3 tablespoons soy sauce
- 2 tablespoons kecap manis (see note)
- 4 teaspoons granulated sugar

FOR THE EGGS

- 2 large eggs
- ½ teaspoon soy sauce
- ½ teaspoon kecap manis

TO MAKE THE TOFU

Dice the tofu into ½-inch cubes. In a small, shallow bowl, whisk together the cornstarch, garlic powder, salt, and pepper with a fork. Lay a sheet of parchment or wax paper on a baking sheet, and set it next to the bowl. Dredge and toss the tofu cubes one at a time in the cornstarch mixture, evenly coating all sides, then place them on the prepared baking sheet to dry briefly.

Place a nonstick skillet over medium heat, and add approximately ⅛ inch of oil to cover the bottom of the pan. When hot, arrange the tofu cubes in a single layer in the oil without touching each other. (If there is not enough room in the skillet for all of the tofu, cook them in two rounds rather than crowding the pan.) Cook the tofu without stirring until the bottom is deeply browned, 4 to 6 minutes. Using tongs, flip each tofu piece over and repeat on the opposite side, 4 to 6 minutes. Then toss the cubes in the skillet and continue to cook the remaining sides for an additional 2 to 3 minutes. Line a plate with a layer of paper towels, and transfer the tofu to the plate to cool briefly.

TO MAKE THE NOODLES

Heat the vegetable oil in a wok or large, deep skillet (preferably nonstick) over medium heat. When hot, add the garlic and cook until sizzling, about 30 seconds, then add the chinese broccoli, rice noodles, soy sauce, kecap manis, and sugar. Toss gently with tongs and cook for 2 minutes until the noodles are coated in sauce, the broccoli stems are al dente, and the broccoli leaves are wilted. If the pan seems too dry, add vegetable oil as needed.

TO MAKE THE EGGS

While the noodles are cooking, crack the eggs into a small bowl. Add the soy sauce and kecap manis and whisk to blend. Set aside.

TO SERVE

Make a clear space in the center of the noodles. Pour the egg mixture in the middle, and scramble the eggs, stirring occasionally, about one minute.

Use tongs to toss and fold the eggs into the noodles, then transfer to individual bowls, top each with a handful of tofu (you will probably have tofu left over), and serve while hot. Enjoy!

Notes

- Leafy chinese broccoli is also sold as *gai lan* in Chinese markets or *kailan* in Thai markets. If you can't find it, substitute broccoli or bok choy.

- Wide rice noodles are sold fresh at some Asian markets, under the name *chow fun* at Chinese stores and *sen yai* at Thai stores. They can also be purchased dried online. If using dried noodles, they need to be soaked according to package directions before use.

- Kecap manis is a sweet, thick soy sauce used in Thai and Indonesian cooking. It is available at many grocery stores and online.

- Leftover tofu can be stored in an airtight container in the fridge for up to a week, but it loses its crispness quickly. Try it as a topping for our Kale Caesar Salad with Crispy Garlic Croutons (page 66) or in a bowl of Bibimbap (page 133), or toss it with vegetables in a skillet for a quick stir-fry.

Vegetarian Paella

Serves 5 to 6 • Gluten-Free, Vegan

Whenever my mom makes paella, it is an all-day project, endlessly stirring a giant bubbling cauldron filled with everything but the kitchen sink. It is an absolute showstopper and her go-to dish for entertaining. Thankfully, our vegetarian version takes a fraction of the time. Made with sautéed onions, three types of sweet peppers, asparagus, zucchini, capers, and artichoke hearts, this vibrant entrée comes together in under an hour. Filled with golden saffron rice and garnished with ruby-red peppers and green olives, this savory Spanish delicacy transforms any meal into a celebration.

—Ryan

FOR THE PAELLA
- 3 tablespoons extra-virgin olive oil
- 1 medium onion (350 g), finely chopped
- 3 jarred piquillo peppers (72 g), finely chopped
- ½ red bell pepper (120 g), finely chopped
- ½ green bell pepper (120 g), finely chopped
- 3 large garlic cloves (15 g), minced
- 2 tablespoons (26 g) capers, drained
- 8 ounces (227 g) asparagus, trimmed and sliced into 1½-inch pieces
- 1 medium zucchini (265 g), sliced into ½-inch rounds, halved if larger than bite-size
- 1½ cups (255 g) finely chopped tomatoes (about 1 large tomato)
- ¼ cup (59 ml) white wine
- 2½ teaspoons salt
- ½ teaspoon freshly ground black pepper
- pinch of ground cayenne pepper
- 1½ teaspoons smoked paprika
- 3 cups (710 ml) vegetable broth (page 46)
- 10 saffron threads (one small packet)
- 1½ cups (300 g) arborio rice or other short-grain rice, such as calrose
- 1 14-ounce (400 g) can artichoke hearts, drained and halved
- ½ cup (67 g) peas, frozen or fresh

FOR GARNISH
- 2 jarred piquillo peppers, sliced into thin ribbons
- 6 to 8 pimiento-stuffed green olives, halved
- flat-leaf parsley, finely chopped (optional)

Pour the olive oil into a large, deep pot or dutch oven, and place over medium heat. When hot, add the onion, piquillo peppers, and both bell peppers, then toss to combine and cook, stirring occasionally, until golden and beginning to caramelize, 12 to 15 minutes. Add the garlic, capers, asparagus, zucchini, tomatoes, white wine, salt, black pepper, cayenne pepper, and paprika, then stir to combine, cover the pan, and cook for 10 minutes.

While the vegetables are cooking, pour the vegetable broth into a small saucepan and add the saffron. Stir to combine, cover, bring to a simmer, then turn off heat.

Add the rice to the pot of vegetables, along with the broth, artichoke hearts, and peas. Stir to combine, cover, and gently simmer for 25 to 30 minutes, stirring occasionally until the rice is cooked. Transfer to a serving dish and decorate the top with strips of peppers and sliced olives. Serve hot and enjoy!

Notes

- The piquillo peppers are available in grocery stores, usually in the condiments section. You can also substitute jarred roasted red peppers.

Bibimbap

Serves 2 to 3 • Gluten-Free Option, Vegan Option

In high school, there was a new student sitting directly behind me in algebra class my sophomore year who had just moved to town from Seoul, South Korea. One day, I was drawing the logos of my favorite bands all over my notebook, not paying attention to the teacher as usual, when he tapped me on the shoulder and pointed to Pink Floyd with a glowing smile and an enthusiastic thumbs-up. At the time, he didn't speak a word of English, but we bonded over music and became instant friends. I always looked forward to dinner at his house, and his welcoming family introduced me to kimchi and other Korean delicacies for the very first time. It wasn't until years later, after becoming vegetarian, that I discovered bibimbap at a local restaurant when it was the only meatless item on the menu. In this recipe, a steaming bowl of rice is filled with sautéed vegetables and capped with a crispy fried egg. Accompanied by a spicy *gochujang* hot pepper sauce and served in a blazing-hot bowl known as a *dolsot,* the rice on the bottom sizzles, giving this popular dish a fiery kick and a pleasant crunch. My friend moved away and we lost touch years ago, but he would be thrilled to know that I still love Korean food—and I still listen to Pink Floyd.

—Adam

FOR THE RICE
1 cup (198 g) short-grain rice, such as calrose or sushi rice
2 cups (473 ml) water

FOR THE BLANCHED VEGETABLES
4 ounces (113 g) raw spinach
1 teaspoon minced scallion, divided
1 teaspoon minced garlic, divided
¼ plus ⅛ teaspoon salt, divided
1 teaspoon sesame seeds, divided
3¼ teaspoons toasted sesame oil, divided
4 ounces (113 g) mung bean sprouts
3 ounces (85 g) daikon radish, cut into ¼-inch matchsticks
¼ teaspoon granulated sugar

FOR THE SAUTÉED VEGETABLES
3 ounces (85 g) cucumbers, thinly sliced
½ plus ⅛ teaspoon salt, divided
4 tablespoons vegetable oil, divided
4 to 6 shiitake mushroom caps (75 g), thinly sliced
1 small zucchini (120 g), thinly sliced
2 small carrots (60 g), cut into matchsticks
½ teaspoon sesame seeds
¾ teaspoon toasted sesame oil

FOR THE SAUCE
2 tablespoons *gochujang* paste
1 tablespoon toasted sesame oil
¼ teaspoon granulated sugar
¼ teaspoon rice vinegar
1 large garlic clove (5 g), minced
¼ teaspoon water

FOR GARNISH
1 egg per serving
1 tablespoon vegetable oil, to cook the egg
nori seaweed, cut into thin 2-inch strips

TO COOK THE RICE

Place the rice in a fine-mesh strainer and rinse until the water runs clear, then let drain. Pour 2 cups water in a medium saucepan, cover, and bring to a boil over high heat. When boiling, add the rice and stir to combine. Return to a simmer, then cover the pan and turn the heat as low as possible. Cook without opening the lid for 18 to 20 minutes or until water is absorbed.

TO PREPARE THE BLANCHED VEGETABLES

While the rice is cooking, bring a medium pot of water (3 to 4 quarts) to a boil. When boiling, add the spinach and blanch until wilted, about 30 seconds. Remove with a spider strainer or slotted spoon and transfer to a colander, then rinse with cold water to stop the cooking process. Meanwhile, cover the pan and keep the water boiling. Squeeze the spinach tightly to remove excess water, then transfer to a cutting board and chop coarsely. Place in a bowl and toss with ½ teaspoon chopped scallion, ¼ teaspoon minced garlic, ⅛ teaspoon salt, ½ teaspoon sesame seeds, and 1½ teaspoons toasted sesame oil. Set aside.

Uncover the boiling pan of water and add the sprouts. Blanch until crisp-tender, 1 to 2 minutes. Remove with a spider strainer or slotted spoon and transfer to a colander, then rinse with cold water and drain. Place in a bowl and toss with ½ teaspoon chopped scallion, ¼ teaspoon minced garlic, ⅛ teaspoon salt, ½ teaspoon sesame seeds, and 1½ teaspoons toasted sesame oil. Set aside.

Uncover the pan one more time, and add the daikon. Cook until al dente, 4 to 5 minutes. Drain into a colander and rinse with cold water. Transfer to a bowl and toss with ⅛ teaspoon salt, ¼ teaspoon sugar, ½ teaspoon minced garlic, and ¼ teaspoon sesame oil. Set aside.

TO PREPARE THE SAUTÉED VEGETABLES

Place the sliced cucumbers in a small bowl, add ¼ teaspoon salt, and toss to combine. Let the cucumbers rest at room temperature for 15 to 20 minutes.

While the cucumbers are resting, set a large nonstick skillet over medium heat. Add 1 tablespoon of vegetable oil and, when hot, add the sliced

Notes

- To serve this dish as *dolsot* (hot bowl) bibimbap, preheat the oven to 425°F/218°C while cooking the rice, and place oven-safe ceramic serving bowls inside to heat up. When ready to serve, carefully remove the hot bowls from the oven and lightly brush the inside with a drizzle of toasted sesame oil. Add the rice, and press it down gently before adding the toppings. This creates a crispy rice crust on the bottom!

- All the vegetables and the sauce can be prepared up to a week ahead of time and kept in individual sealed containers in the fridge, allowing you to have bibimbap at a moment's notice.

- To make this Gluten-Free: make sure that the *gochujang* paste is labeled as gluten-free.

- To make this Vegan: omit the egg.

mushrooms and ⅛ teaspoon salt. Cook, stirring occasionally, until tender, 7 to 9 minutes, then transfer to a small bowl and return the skillet to heat.

Add another tablespoon of vegetable oil, the zucchini, and another ⅛ teaspoon salt, then cook until tender, 7 to 9 minutes. Transfer the zucchini to a separate bowl and return the skillet to heat.

Add another tablespoon of vegetable oil, followed by the carrots and the remaining ⅛ teaspoon salt. Cook until tender, 4 to 6 minutes, then transfer to a bowl and return the skillet to heat.

Once the cucumbers are done resting, gently squeeze them to remove excess water. Heat the final tablespoon of oil in the skillet, then add the cucumbers and sauté for 30 seconds. Add ½ teaspoon sesame seeds and ¾ teaspoon sesame oil, and continue cooking for another 30 seconds. Transfer the cucumbers to a small bowl and set aside.

TO MAKE THE SAUCE

Combine all ingredients in a small bowl and stir until smooth and blended.

TO ASSEMBLE THE BOWLS

Place a skillet over medium heat, and add one tablespoon of vegetable oil. For each serving, crack 1 egg into the skillet and cook until the whites are firm but the yolk is runny, 2 to 3 minutes.

While the egg is cooking, divide the rice between the serving bowls. Place the sizzling egg in the middle of the rice bowl and arrange about ¼ cup (or desired amount) of each topping around the egg: spinach, sprouts, daikon, mushrooms, zucchini, carrots, and sliced seaweed. Serve hot with a dollop of gochujang sauce to taste, and enjoy!

Six Root Vegetable Tagine with Roasted Garlic Couscous

Serves 6 to 8 • Gluten-Free Option, Vegan Option

We will never forget the night we were introduced to our first tagine. A friend invited us over for dinner, and from the moment we walked through the door, the sounds of traditional music transported us to Marrakech. We were treated to an elaborate vegetarian feast, where the highlight of the meal was a spicy carrot tagine, and for dessert, we enjoyed a unique Moroccan delicacy—cool cubes of melon sweetened with honey, mint, and rose water. In this fragrant tagine, not one, not two, but six root vegetables are slowly simmered with onions, garlic, and aromatic spices. Served with roasted garlic couscous, a spoonful of greek yogurt, fresh lemon wedges, and a crusty slice of *khobz* bread (page 85), it is a wonderful welcome to the world of North African cooking.

FOR THE ROASTED GARLIC COUSCOUS
1 head garlic, unpeeled
1 cup (237 ml) water
1 cup (195 g) dry couscous
2 tablespoons extra-virgin olive oil
⅛ teaspoon salt

FOR THE TAGINE
3 tablespoons extra-virgin olive oil
1 medium onion (300 g), finely chopped
2 large garlic cloves (10 g), minced
1 small sweet potato (325 g), peeled and diced into ¾-inch pieces
2 small carrots (100 g), diced into ¾-inch pieces
1 medium parsnip (85 g), peeled, tough core removed if needed, and diced into ¾-inch pieces
2 small golden beets (225 g), peeled and diced into ¾-inch pieces
1 small Yukon Gold potato (180 g), diced into ¾-inch pieces
4 to 6 small radishes (100 g), halved if tiny, quartered if medium-size
2 teaspoons ground turmeric

2 teaspoons cumin seeds
1 teaspoon ground cinnamon
⅛ to ¼ teaspoon ground cayenne pepper, to taste
½ teaspoon freshly ground black pepper
1 teaspoon salt
1 tablespoon honey
2 cups (473 ml) water
¼ cup (12 g) coarsely chopped cilantro

TO SERVE
lemon wedges
greek yogurt

First, roast the garlic. Preheat the oven to 400°F/ 204°C. Using a sharp knife, cut the top ¼-inch off the top of the garlic head, exposing the cut tops of the cloves. Place the garlic cut-side-up on a square of aluminum foil. Drizzle a small amount of olive oil on top, then gather the foil up to twist and seal the garlic tightly inside the foil packet. Place seam-side-up directly on the oven rack in the middle, and bake for 40 minutes. Remove and let cool for several minutes before opening the foil, as the steam inside can be very hot.

While the garlic is roasting, start the tagine. Heat the oil in a large, deep saucepan or dutch oven (or an actual tagine if you have one), and, when hot, add the onion. Cook until softened, 7 to 10 minutes. Add the garlic and cook for 30 to 60 seconds, then add the sweet potato, carrots, parsnip, golden beets, potato, radishes, turmeric, cumin seeds, cinnamon, cayenne pepper, black pepper, salt, and honey. Add the water and stir to combine. Cover and cook, stirring occasionally, until the vegetables are tender when pierced with a fork, 15 to 20 minutes.

While the tagine is cooking, prepare the couscous. Pour the water into a small saucepan, and bring to a boil over high heat. Add the couscous and return to a boil. Then cover the pan and turn off the heat, letting the couscous rest without opening the lid for 7 to 10 minutes. While the couscous is sitting, remove the soft garlic from the paper and place all the cloves in a small bowl. Use a fork to mash the garlic well, and set aside. When the couscous is ready and the water is absorbed, add the olive oil, salt, and mashed garlic. Stir to combine, then keep covered until ready to serve.

When the tagine is finished and the vegetables are tender, add the cilantro, stir to combine, and remove from heat. Serve with couscous, lemon wedges, and a dollop of greek yogurt, if desired, and enjoy!

Notes

- To make this Gluten-Free: use a gluten-free couscous.

- To make this Vegan: use maple or agave syrup instead of honey, and replace the greek yogurt with vegan sour cream.

Vegan Banh Mi Sandwich with Crispy Tofu

Serves 4 • Gluten-Free Option, Vegan

Traditionally, this Vietnamese and French fusion sandwich contains pork, but when you replace it with irresistibly crispy tofu marinated in a fiery chili sauce and top it with homemade pickled vegetables, vegan mayo, spicy sriracha, fresh cilantro, and sliced jalapeño peppers nestled beautifully in a crusty golden baguette, even the most committed carnivore won't miss the meat after trying this triumphant and tantalizingly tasty combo. Plus, this sandwich travels like a dream—easy to pack for a long hike, a convenient lunch that will elevate any workday, and perfect for a picnic with friends at the beach.

FOR THE PICKLED CARROTS AND DAIKON
½ cup (118 ml) white vinegar
¼ teaspoon salt
½ cup (100 g) granulated sugar
2 cups (200 g) carrots cut into matchsticks (about 3 medium carrots)
2 cups (200 g) daikon radish, peeled and cut into matchsticks (about 1 medium daikon)

FOR THE PICKLED CUCUMBER
2 small persian cucumbers (150 g)
1½ teaspoons sugar
¾ teaspoon salt
2¼ teaspoons rice vinegar

FOR THE CRISPY TOFU
1 12- to 14-ounce (340 g to 397 g) block of extra-firm tofu, drained
¼ cup (59 ml) tamari or soy sauce
¼ cup (17 g) nutritional yeast flakes
2 teaspoons sriracha hot sauce
1 teaspoon rice vinegar
2 teaspoons garlic powder, divided
¼ teaspoon smoked paprika
⅛ teaspoon ground cayenne pepper
½ teaspoon chili oil
½ teaspoon sesame oil
¾ teaspoon freshly ground black pepper, divided
¾ cup (88 g) cornstarch
1 teaspoon salt
vegetable oil, for frying

FOR ASSEMBLY
1 to 2 baguettes, cut into four 6-inch pieces
vegan mayonnaise
sriracha hot sauce
chopped cilantro
sliced fresh jalapeño peppers

TO MAKE THE PICKLED CARROTS AND DAIKON
In a medium bowl, mix together the white vinegar, salt, and sugar, and stir to dissolve. Add the sliced vegetables and toss to coat evenly. Cover and chill in the fridge for at least 2 hours or up to a week.

TO MAKE THE PICKLED CUCUMBER
Slice the cucumbers ⅛-inch thick, and place in a small bowl. Add the salt and sugar and toss to coat the cucumber slices evenly. Let sit for 20 minutes at room temperature, covered. Transfer to a strainer, then rinse with cold water and let drain. Place in a clean bowl, add the vinegar, and toss to combine. Use immediately or keep in a sealed container in the fridge for up to a week.

TO MAKE THE CRISPY TOFU
Cut the block of tofu into quarters, making one vertical cut and one horizontal cut to make 4 steaks, each about 3×4 inches in size.

In a shallow baking dish wide enough to fit the tofu in a single layer, whisk together the tamari, nutritional yeast flakes, sriracha, rice vinegar, 1 teaspoon of garlic powder, paprika, cayenne pepper, chili oil, sesame oil, and ¼ teaspoon black pepper. When smooth and evenly combined, lay the tofu steaks in the sauce, cover, and chill for 30 minutes. Then flip the tofu over, cover, and chill for another 30 minutes.

In a wide, shallow bowl, combine the cornstarch, 1 teaspoon garlic powder, ½ teaspoon black pepper, and salt, and whisk to combine. Place a plate near the bowl, and cover it with a sheet of parchment or wax paper. Remove a tofu steak from the marinade and dip it in the cornstarch, tossing until evenly coated on all sides. Transfer to the prepared plate and repeat with the remaining pieces of tofu.

Place a nonstick skillet over medium heat. Pour enough vegetable oil in the skillet to cover the bottom by ⅛ inch, and when hot, lay the tofu steaks in a single layer without touching. Cook without stirring until deeply golden on the bottom, 4 to 6 minutes. Flip and cook the second side without stirring until golden, 4 to 6 minutes. While the tofu is cooking, remove the parchment paper from the plate, and replace it with a layer of paper towels. When the tofu is done, transfer the steaks to the paper-lined plate to drain briefly.

TO ASSEMBLE THE SANDWICHES

Slice the baguette lengthwise to create two sandwich halves. Spread a light layer of vegan mayonnaise on both sides, then place a tofu steak on the bottom half of the bread. Drizzle the top with sriracha to taste, followed by a small handful of pickled carrots and daikon. Place a few slices of pickled cucumber on top, and finish with chopped cilantro and jalapeño slices. Place the other half of the bread on top, and repeat with the remaining sandwiches. Serve hot, and enjoy!

Notes

- When selecting a baguette, look for one about 4 inches wide. Skinny baguettes will be too small to fit all the toppings.

- To make this Gluten-Free: use tamari instead of soy sauce, and serve on gluten-free bread.

Sides

You'll be earning plenty of bonus miles in this chapter. With tasty stops in Spain, Japan, India, and Cuba, here are eleven colorful sides to inspire your appetite and decorate your plate. From the simplest six-ingredient Roasted Broccolini Limone (page 162) to a rich, Creamy Vegan Mac and Cheese (page 148) satisfying enough to be a main course, there is a dish for every occasion. Looking for a quick appetizer for a relaxing meal at home? Want to try something other than popcorn for your next movie night? Searching for something portable to bring to your next potluck party? Let the Husbands be your guides, and let us welcome you to the sides.

Samosas with Mango Chutney

Makes about 32 2-inch samosas   •   Vegan

Special Tools: Thermometer

You can taste the love in Indian cooking. Thoughtful combinations of exotic flavors and fragrant spices create an intimate experience with every bite, offering more vegetarian options than almost any other type of cuisine. Many meals begin with a warm, freshly made samosa—a savory pastry filled with creamy potatoes, vegetables, and spices. In our homemade version, we add fresh ginger and garlic to the filling, along with a serrano pepper for a hint of heat, wrapping it snugly in a crispy crust. Served with a sweet and spicy mango chutney alongside our Indian Curry with Chickpeas and Cauliflower (page 109), let the alluring aromas in your kitchen be a friendly distraction as they whisk you away to a fantasy of flavor.

FOR THE MANGO CHUTNEY
2 large ripe mangoes (about 435 g each), peeled and coarsely chopped
½ cup (62 g) finely chopped onion
1 tablespoon (12 g) finely minced ginger
¼ cup plus 2 tablespoons (75 g) granulated sugar
¼ cup (59 ml) apple cider vinegar
⅛ teaspoon red pepper flakes
⅛ teaspoon curry powder

FOR THE DOUGH
2⅓ cups (280 g) all-purpose flour
½ teaspoon cumin seeds
½ teaspoon salt
2 tablespoons vegetable oil, plus 1½ quarts (about 1½ L) for frying
¾ cup (177 ml) warm water

FOR THE FILLING
1½ pounds (680 g) russet potatoes, peeled and diced into ½-inch cubes
½ cup (75 g) finely chopped carrots
½ cup (66 g) peas, frozen or fresh
2 tablespoons vegetable oil
1 medium onion (290 g), finely chopped
1 large garlic clove (5 g), minced
1 teaspoon grated ginger

1 serrano pepper, seeded and finely chopped
¾ teaspoon garam masala
¼ teaspoon ground turmeric
1½ teaspoons salt
¼ teaspoon ground cumin
¼ teaspoon curry powder
2 tablespoons (6 g) finely chopped cilantro

TO MAKE THE MANGO CHUTNEY
Combine all the ingredients in a medium saucepan, stir to combine, cover, and place over medium-high heat. Bring to a boil, then lower heat to a simmer and cook covered for 45 minutes, stirring occasionally, until the mangoes and onion are soft and the mixture has the consistency of fruit preserves. Let cool, then use immediately or transfer to a sealed container and refrigerate for up to 2 weeks.

TO MAKE THE DOUGH
In a medium bowl, whisk together the flour, cumin seeds, and salt. Add the oil and water, and stir until the dough comes together. Transfer to a floured work surface, and knead until smooth and elastic, 5 to 10 minutes, adding more flour as needed if the dough

is too sticky. Form the dough into a disc, wrap in plastic to prevent it from drying out, and let rest at room temperature for 30 minutes, or in the fridge for up to two days.

TO MAKE THE FILLING

Place a large pot of unsalted water over high heat, and bring to a boil. When boiling, add the potatoes and set a timer for 10 minutes. Lower heat to a simmer, and when 5 minutes remain on the timer, add the carrots. When 3 minutes remain, add the peas. Drain, then transfer the cooked vegetables to a large heatproof mixing bowl. Use a spoon or rubber spatula to stir and slightly mash the potatoes, then set aside.

Place a skillet over medium heat and add the vegetable oil. When hot, add the onions and cook until very tender and beginning to caramelize, about 9 minutes. Add the garlic, ginger, serrano pepper, garam masala, turmeric, salt, cumin, and curry powder, and cook for 2 to 3 minutes. Add the chopped cilantro, stir to combine, and remove from heat. Pour the contents of the skillet into the bowl with the potatoes, and stir to combine. Use immediately, or refrigerate for up to 2 days.

TO ASSEMBLE THE SAMOSAS

Once the potato mixture has cooled enough to handle comfortably, scoop up about a tablespoon of the mixture, and use your palms to roll it into a 1-inch ball. Repeat until you have 32 balls. There may be filling left over, which can be saved for another use (see note), or simply enjoyed as is.

Unwrap the dough, and place on a floured work surface. Pour a few tablespoons of water into a small bowl and set aside. Use a knife or bench scraper to divide the dough into 16 equal slices. Place one in the palm of your hand, and form it into a ball. Roll the

ball out to a thin 6-inch circle, then cut the circle in half. Take one of the halves, and place it with the flat edge facing you. Dip a fingertip in the bowl of water, and moisten the flat edge of the half circle. Fold the dough in half from left to right, sealing and pressing the moistened edge together and forming a triangle shape. Pick up the dough triangle, and open it gently to form a cone. Place one of the balls of filling inside, then fold the edges over to seal the packet. Use a fork to crimp and seal the edges. Transfer to a parchment-lined baking sheet or platter, and repeat with the remaining dough and filling.

Pour about 1½ quarts of vegetable oil into a wide saucepan or skillet, and attach a candy thermometer to the pan with the probe submerged in the oil without touching the bottom. Place over medium-high heat until the temperature reaches 350°F/177°C. Set a wire rack on a baking sheet, and place it next to the pan. When the oil is hot, add as many samosas as will fit without crowding—about 5 or 6 at a time—and cook until golden brown, approximately 3 minutes, turning occasionally and adjusting the heat as needed to maintain the temperature. Use a spider strainer or tongs to lift the samosas out of the oil and onto the wire rack to drain. Repeat with the remaining samosas. Serve immediately with the mango chutney, and enjoy!

Notes

- Leftover filling can be used to make samosa veggie burgers: Place the filling in a medium bowl, then add an egg and stir to combine. Form into patties and sauté over medium heat until golden on both sides. Serve with the mango chutney or on a hamburger bun with condiments of your choice.

Onigiri Four Ways

Makes about 8 • Gluten-Free, Vegan

Finding vegetarian meals in Japan is sometimes difficult, so we always carried *onigiri*—seaweed-wrapped rice balls with an assortment of tasty fillings—in our backpacks to keep us from getting hangry while exploring the beautiful countryside. They are easy to find in Japan, but the tricky part is locating vegetarian *onigiri* among the many meat-filled varieties, since these tasty treats all look alike from the outside and have nearly identical labels, and neither of us can read Japanese. They were our snack savior during the vacation, and we've been obsessively making them at home ever since. Whether you choose the tart *umeboshi* plum, creamy avocado, spicy kimchi, or pickled cucumber, these triangular treats are perfect to serve at a party, a cute side to accompany your dinner, and a healthy snack to enjoy any time of day.

FOR THE PICKLED CUCUMBER
2 small persian cucumbers (150 g)
1½ teaspoons sugar
¾ teaspoon salt
2¼ teaspoons rice vinegar

FOR THE *ONIGIRI*
2¼ cups (460 g) uncooked short-grain rice
(3 "rice cooker cups")
2 tablespoons rice vinegar
1½ teaspoons granulated sugar
1 teaspoon salt
1 teaspoon mirin rice wine (see note)
2 sheets of nori seaweed, cut into strips
about 6×2 inches

FILLINGS
umeboshi pickled plums, seeds removed
avocado slices topped with sesame seeds
and sea salt
prepared kimchi
pickled cucumber

TO MAKE THE PICKLED CUCUMBER
Slice the cucumbers ⅛-inch thick, and place in a small bowl. Add the salt and sugar and toss to coat the cucumber slices evenly. Let sit for 20 minutes at room temperature, covered. Transfer to a colander, then rinse with cold water and let drain. Place in a clean bowl, add the vinegar, and toss to combine. Use immediately or keep in a sealed container in the fridge for up to a week.

TO MAKE THE *ONIGIRI*
Place the rice in a fine-mesh strainer and rinse until the water runs clear.

If cooking the rice on the stove, start by pouring 4½ cups of water in a medium saucepan, cover, and bring to a boil over high heat. Add the rice, return to a simmer, then cover the pan and set heat as low as possible. Cook without opening the lid for 20 minutes.

If using a rice cooker, prepare the rice according to the manufacturer's directions.

While the rice is cooking, mix together the vinegar, sugar, salt, and mirin in a measuring cup or small bowl, and stir to dissolve. Set aside.

As soon as the rice is done, transfer it to a large bowl, pour over the vinegar mixture, and use a rice paddle or rubber spatula to fold and toss the rice—coating it and cooling it without breaking or mashing the rice grains.

When the rice is cool enough to handle, line a small teacup with plastic wrap, leaving a few inches hanging over the sides. Fill the cup about ⅔ full of rice, using the back of a spoon to press the rice down into the cup. Place your desired topping in the middle of the cup—half an *umeboshi* plum, a few thin slices of avocado, a spoonful of kimchi, or a few slices of pickled cucumber. Top with another scoop of rice, sealing the filling inside. Gather the plastic wrap and twist the ends to squeeze and compress the rice into a tight ball. Gently form the rice ball into a triangle shape, then discard the plastic and wrap it with a strip of seaweed. Serve immediately, and enjoy!

Notes

- If making *onigiri* in advance, leave the triangles in plastic at room temperature, then just before serving, remove the plastic and wrap the *onigiri* in seaweed.

- Mirin is a type of rice wine used for cooking. Look for true mirin, which contains about 14 percent alcohol, rather than imitation mirin, which has no alcohol plus added sugar and salt. It is sold in the Asian section of many grocery stores and adds a delicious flavor, but if you cannot find it, feel free to leave it out.

Creamy Vegan Mac and Cheese

Serves 4 • Gluten-Free Option, Vegan

We interrupt this chapter to bring an important message to every mac-and-cheese lover out there. If you are just as obsessed with that classic dish as we are, please do not to be alarmed by the *V* word that appears after the word *creamy* in the recipe title. Let us assure you that this wonderful non-dairy version is exceptionally creamy, remarkably cheesy, and able-to-leap-tall-buildings-in-a-single-bound delicious. If you haven't tried cashew cream before, this is your golden ticket to the world of this miraculous alternative. The irresistible blend is made from tender potatoes, carrots, onions, and cashews, seasoned with garlic, nutritional yeast flakes, savory red miso, and fresh lemon. Garnished with chopped chives, your lactose-intolerant friends will be indebted to you forever, and even cheese snobs will be asking for seconds.

10 ounces (284 g) dried macaroni pasta
1½ cups (200 g) russet potato, peeled and chopped into ½-inch pieces
½ cup (67 g) raw cashews
¼ cup (37 g) carrots, peeled and chopped into ½-inch pieces
½ cup (67 g) finely chopped onion
1 small garlic clove (2 g), minced or pressed
¼ cup (20 g) nutritional yeast flakes
1 teaspoon smoked paprika
2 tablespoons extra-virgin olive oil
1 tablespoon red miso paste
1 to 2 tablespoons freshly squeezed lemon juice
½ teaspoon salt
¼ teaspoon freshly ground black pepper
¼ teaspoon ground turmeric
chives, for garnish (optional)

Notes

- To make this Gluten-Free: use gluten-free pasta.

Place a large covered pot of salted water over high heat, using 1 teaspoon of salt for every quart of water. When boiling, add the macaroni, and cook according to package directions until al dente. Reserve about 1 cup of the pasta cooking water, then drain the macaroni and return it to the pan.

Meanwhile, place the potato, cashews, carrots, and onion in a medium saucepan. Add enough water to cover the vegetables by an inch or two. Cover the pan and set over medium-high heat. When boiling, lower heat to a simmer and cook for 10 minutes. Reserve some of the cooking water, then drain the vegetables.

Transfer the drained vegetables to a blender or food processor, and add the garlic, nutritional yeast flakes, paprika, olive oil, miso paste, lemon juice, salt, pepper, and turmeric. Blend until smooth, adding a few tablespoons of the vegetable cooking water as needed to thin the mixture to a creamy consistency. Pour into the pan with the cooked macaroni, and toss to coat the pasta evenly, adding some of the pasta water to create a creamy sauce. Note that the sauce will dry somewhat as it cools, so add plenty of water as you stir to keep it silky. Taste for lemon and adjust as needed. Serve immediately, and enjoy!

Barbecue Baked Beans

Serves 6 to 8 • Gluten-Free, Vegan

A barbecue without baked beans is like a wedding without champagne. They are a crucial part of the Barbecue Essentials Starter Kit according to rule number 3.1 in the respected *Outdoor Barbecue Society of America Official Guidebook*. Arm in arm, they pair musically with grilled veggie burgers, fresh corn on the cob, and our no-mayo Tangy Potato Salad with Lemon and Capers (page 77). These smoky homemade baked beans are summer-perfect, and your pool party plate would feel incomplete without them.

2 15-ounce (425 g each) cans navy beans, great northern beans, or cannellini beans
2 tablespoons extra-virgin olive oil
1 small onion (240 g), finely chopped
2 large garlic cloves (10 g), minced
¼ cup (60 ml) Smoky Tamarind Barbecue Sauce (page 286) or your favorite store-bought barbecue sauce
¼ cup (52 g) brown sugar
4 teaspoons prepared yellow mustard
2 teaspoons apple cider vinegar
½ teaspoon liquid smoke
½ teaspoon salt
½ teaspoon freshly ground black pepper

Preheat oven to 325°F/163°C. Open the cans of beans, and pour all the contents, including the liquid, into a small dutch oven, covered casserole dish, or oven-safe saucepan.

Pour the oil in a medium skillet and place over medium heat. When hot, add the onion and cook until golden and quite soft, 12 to 15 minutes. Add the garlic and cook for 1 minute. Remove from heat and pour the contents of the skillet into the pan with the beans. Add the remaining ingredients and stir gently to combine. Cover and bake for 45 minutes. Serve hot, and enjoy!

Life-Changing Corn Bread

Makes 1 8×8-inch square or 9-inch circle, about 9 pieces

This is a story about corn bread and the power of saying *yes*. In late December 2013, I found a hand-written note in the mailbox, dropped off by the couple who used to live in our house. They wanted to meet the new owners, so they left a festive card inviting us to their New Year's Eve party. Ryan was out of town, but I decided to step out of my comfort zone and show up by myself. As soon as I walked in, I was introduced to a woman named Kacy who happened to live just a few blocks from us, and we instantly bonded over our love of gardening and animals. We stayed in touch, and a few weeks later, she invited us to her house for an evening of snacks and live music in her backyard. The two musicians that performed were a young neighborhood couple from a band called Fire Chief Charlie, singing an acoustic set of original folk songs around a small fire pit under the stars. After that night, Jonah and Jamie became some of our closest friends, and I ended up producing their debut record, released just two years later. This momentous side dish is adapted from a secret recipe that Jonah's family has been making his entire life. Not only is this corn bread truly life-changing—somewhere between a moist cake and bread pudding—but its name is also appropriate because of the life-changing events that led up to this historic day.

—Adam

½ cup (69 g) yellow cornmeal
¾ cup plus 2 tablespoons (105 g) all-purpose flour
⅓ cup (66 g) granulated sugar
2¾ teaspoons baking powder
1 tablespoon cornstarch
2 large eggs
1 15-ounce (425 g) can creamed corn
1 cup (227 g) sour cream
½ cup (113 g) unsalted butter, melted, plus 1 tablespoon for greasing the pan

Preheat oven to 350°F/177°C, and grease an 8-inch square or 9-inch round baking pan with 1 tablespoon unsalted butter.

In a small bowl, whisk together the cornmeal, flour, sugar, baking powder, and cornstarch.

In a large bowl, whisk together the eggs, creamed corn, and sour cream. Add the melted butter, and whisk until smooth. Add the flour mixture, and whisk just until blended. Pour into the prepared pan and bake until a toothpick inserted into the center comes out clean, about 60 minutes.

Toasted Orzo with Brussels Sprouts and Wilted Greens

Serves 4 as a side, 2 as a main course

Roll out the red carpet for this easy one-pan appetizer. If you have never toasted pasta before, you are in for a treat; it completely transforms the flavor, adding a deep golden-brown color and a fragrant nutty aroma. Complemented with fresh swiss chard and brussels sprouts, and seasoned with sharp pecorino cheese, minced garlic, and basil, you'll feel like a celebrity as this deeply satisfying dish comes together in under thirty minutes with a round of applause. Whether you serve it as a light dinner or a healthy side, your family—and the paparazzi—will love every bite.

2 tablespoons (28 g) unsalted butter
6 ounces (170 g) uncooked orzo pasta
4 large garlic cloves (20 g), minced
1 cup (237 ml) vegetable broth (page 46)
1 cup (237 ml) water
6 to 8 brussels sprouts (165 g), trimmed and halved
3 ounces (85 g) coarsely chopped chard or kale leaves, stem removed (about 2 large leaves)
2 ounces (57 g) pecorino romano cheese, finely grated
10 basil leaves (about 6 g), thinly sliced
¼ to ½ teaspoon salt
¼ teaspoon freshly ground black pepper
pinch of ground cayenne pepper

Place a skillet over medium heat. Add the butter and, when melted, add the orzo and cook uncovered, stirring often, until the pasta is deeply toasted and fragrant, about 7 minutes. Add the garlic and cook for about 30 seconds. Add the broth, water, and brussels sprouts, then stir to combine, and cover the pan. Lower the heat to a simmer and set a timer for 15 minutes. When 4 minutes remain, lift the lid and scatter the chopped chard leaves over the orzo, then replace the lid. When the timer rings, remove from heat, add the cheese, basil, salt, black pepper, and cayenne pepper, and stir to combine. Serve immediately, and enjoy!

Spanish Tortilla

Makes 1 9-inch tortilla • Gluten-Free

I had never heard of Spanish tortilla before meeting Ryan. It is entirely different from the floppy white tortillas used in Mexican cuisine. Similar to a frittata, this simple egg dish is cooked in a skillet with thinly sliced potatoes and sautéed onions. Ryan's *abuelita* knew how much I loved it, so every time we were in Portland for a visit, she would make two tortillas—one for the rest of the family to share, and a personal one just for me. She was one of the kindest and most welcoming people I have ever known, and she treated me like family from the first day we met, with warm hugs and contagious laughter. Spanish tortilla was one of her specialties—served hot or cold, day or night, it is an expression of love, and we are honored to share this family recipe in our first cookbook.   —*Adam*

1¼ pounds (567 g) russet potatoes (about 2)
1 small onion (about 300 g)
1 cup (237 ml) extra-virgin olive oil
2½ teaspoons salt, divided
7 large eggs

Peel the potatoes, and use a sharp knife or mandoline to slice them into ⅛-inch-thick rounds. Cut the rounds into quarters. Repeat the process with the onion: peel, slice ⅛-inch thick, and cut into quarters.

Place a 10-inch skillet with sloping sides—preferably nonstick—over medium heat and add the oil. When hot, add the potatoes, onion, and 1¼ teaspoons of salt. Toss to evenly distribute in the skillet and cook until tender, about 15 minutes, tossing occasionally. Remove from heat and pour the contents of the skillet into a heatproof strainer set over a heatproof bowl or large measuring cup. Let the vegetables drain for 5 minutes, reserving the oil.

In a large bowl, whisk together the eggs and the remaining 1¼ teaspoons salt. Add the drained vegetables and toss gently to combine without breaking up the potatoes. Let the mixture rest for 10 minutes.

Place the skillet over medium-low heat, and add 2 tablespoons of the drained oil. When hot, pour in the egg mixture and use a spatula to even out the top. Cook without stirring until the edges are set but the middle is still runny, and the bottom is golden brown in patches, 3 to 4 minutes. Find a 10-inch plate—preferably with gently sloping sides—the same size as the skillet. Place the plate facedown on top of the skillet. Put one hand on the plate, and hold the skillet handle with the other. Take a deep breath (you can do this!), and quickly flip the skillet over, inverting the tortilla onto the plate. Now slide the tortilla back into the skillet, browned-side-up, and cook for another 2 to 4 minutes, then transfer to a clean plate. Cut into wedges and serve warm, at room temperature, or chilled, and enjoy! Tortilla will keep fresh for up to a week in the fridge.

Yuca con Mojo

Serves 6 to 8 as a side • Gluten-Free, Vegan

No, that is not a typo—there really are 20 cloves of garlic in this traditional Cuban delicacy. My *abuelita* cooked with this potent herb in almost every recipe, but here it proudly takes center stage as the star ingredient in a tangy liquid-gold mojo sauce, accompanied by tender cubes of yuca—a starchy Caribbean root similar to a potato. Over the years, I watched her prepare this aromatic side dish from memory, observing and taking detailed notes so that her perfected *yuca con mojo* would remain a family tradition for years to come. The recipe below has not been changed or modernized in any way—it comes directly from the loving kitchen of Teresa Alvarez, and I am so proud to share my *abuelita*'s creation.

—*Ryan*

FOR THE YUCA
- 3 pounds (1.36 kg) yuca (also sold as cassava)
- 4 teaspoons salt
- 2 tablespoons lemon juice

FOR THE *MOJO* SAUCE
- 20 large garlic cloves (100 g)
- 1 teaspoon salt, divided
- ⅔ cup (158 ml) extra-virgin olive oil
- ½ cup (118 ml) white vinegar
- ¼ teaspoon freshly ground black pepper

First, prep the yuca. They are usually sold with a coating of wax and do not need to be washed. Slice into 2-inch rounds. Lay one piece flat-side-down, and use a sharp knife to trim off the brown skin and the thin cream-colored layer just underneath the skin. Cut into quarters, and remove the tough fiber in the center. Repeat for the remaining yuca rounds. Cut the pieces approximately the same size, about 1×2 inches, so they cook evenly. Once they are all prepped, place the pieces in a strainer and rinse them with cold water.

Place the yuca pieces in a large pot, and add enough water to cover them by about an inch. Add the salt and lemon juice, and stir. Cover pot, place over high heat, and bring to a boil. When boiling, lower heat to a simmer and cook, stirring a few times, until the yuca is quite tender when pierced with a fork, 30 to 45 minutes (the time will depend on the size of the yuca pieces). The best way to tell if they are done is to simply taste a piece: it should have a soft, tender texture.

While the yuca is cooking, make the *mojo* sauce. In a mortar and pestle, mash the garlic well. Add ½ teaspoon of salt to the mortar, and continue to mash until it resembles a thick, chunky paste. Transfer the garlic to a medium bowl, then add the remaining ½ teaspoon salt, olive oil, vinegar, and pepper. Stir well to combine.

When the yuca is done, drain, then return it to the pot. Pour the *mojo* sauce over the yuca, and toss well to combine. Serve hot, and enjoy!

Notes

- Yuca is known as *cassava* in English and is available at many grocery stores, especially those that carry Latin American food. It is pronounced *yoo-kah* and is unrelated to the spiky ornamental plant called yucca (pronounced *yuck-ah*).

- Yuca con Mojo is just as good—if not better—the next day, as the flavors marinate overnight in the fridge. We often make this dish the day before a dinner party, to save time.

Chili-Lime Garlic Fries

Serves 4 • Gluten-Free, Vegan

While we don't really follow baseball, we love going to the occasional Dodger game. Honestly, we mostly look forward to the concessions, even though buying a single beer is equivalent to putting a down payment on a house. There's a magical feeling inside that historic ballpark, especially on a warm summer night, with a bag of peanuts in your lap alongside a veggie Dodger Dog and, of course, an order of their famously addictive garlic fries. No game is complete without them, and our spicy version of that sporty side was inspired by those crispy potatoes smothered in sautéed garlic found at almost every food stand in the stadium. They are the perfect pairing for a Meatless Western Bacon Cheeseburger (page 106) and a grand slam snack for your next movie night.

FOR THE POTATOES
1½ pounds (680 g) Yukon Gold potatoes
1½ quarts (1.4 L) neutral vegetable oil, such as canola or peanut (use more or less as needed)
½ to ¾ teaspoon salt

FOR THE GARLIC
3 tablespoons extra-virgin olive oil
5 large garlic cloves (25 g), finely chopped
1 serrano pepper, finely chopped (seeds removed for mild, or left in for spicy)
4 tablespoons (12 g) finely chopped italian parsley
2 tablespoons freshly squeezed lime juice, plus more to taste
lime wedges, for serving

TO MAKE THE POTATOES
Wash and dry the potatoes, then slice into ¼-inch sticks. Transfer them to a wide and deep saucepan, and add enough oil to cover them completely. Turn heat to high and bring to a boil, about 5 minutes. Cook for 15 minutes without stirring, and at the 20-minute mark, stir slightly, gently scraping any that have stuck to the bottom. Cook for 8 to 10 minutes more, stirring only if needed, until the desired level of color and crispness is reached. Place a baking sheet next to the pan, and line it with paper towels. Remove the fries with a spider strainer and place them on the prepared sheet. Let drain for a few seconds, then remove the paper towels, leaving the fries on the baking sheet, and immediately sprinkle with salt, tossing gently to combine. Taste for salt and add more if needed.

TO MAKE THE GARLIC AND SERVE
Place the olive oil, garlic, and chopped pepper in a small skillet, toss to combine, and place over medium heat. As soon as the garlic begins to sizzle, turn off the heat and add the parsley and lime juice, stirring to combine. Pour over the hot fries and toss to coat them evenly. Serve immediately with lime wedges and enjoy!

Roasted Broccolini Limone

Serves 2 to 4 • Gluten-Free, Vegan

This is the perfect example of how a dish with very few ingredients can be so vibrant and flavorful. One of the simplest recipes in our book, this light broccolini can accompany almost any entrée and comes together in just fifteen minutes, leaving you more time to sort out that all-important dinner playlist. This lemony-garlicky side is high in vitamin C, oh so pleasant to see, and known for its green excellency.

1 bunch (about 325 g) broccolini, sliced into long-stemmed florets
4 tablespoons extra-virgin olive oil, divided
½ teaspoon plus ⅛ teaspoon salt, divided
½ teaspoon freshly ground black pepper
3 large garlic cloves (15 g), finely chopped
¼ cup (60 ml) freshly squeezed lemon juice

Preheat oven to 375°F/191°C, and line a baking sheet with parchment paper. Place the broccolini on the sheet in a single layer, and drizzle over 2 tablespoons of the olive oil. Sprinkle ½ teaspoon of salt and the pepper over the top, toss to coat evenly, and bake in the oven until crisp-tender, 10 to 15 minutes.

While the broccolini is cooking, place the remaining 2 tablespoons of olive oil and the garlic in a small, unheated skillet, then set over medium heat. As soon as the garlic begins to sizzle, remove the pan from heat and pour the contents into a small bowl to stop the cooking process. Add the lemon juice and ⅛ teaspoon salt, and stir to combine.

When the broccolini is cooked to your liking, remove it from the oven and pour over the garlic mixture. Toss to combine, and serve hot.

Cheesy Spinach and Artichoke Pull-Apart Bread

Fills 1 Bundt pan or 3-quart dutch oven • Serves 6 to 8

The best part of being nominated for the Saveur Blog Awards was becoming friends with the other finalists. One of those friends, Alexandra Stafford—nominated for Most Inspired Weeknight Dinners—wrote a revolutionary cookbook called *Bread Toast Crumbs,* released the following year. The centerpiece of this innovative book was her mom's famous peasant bread, which she claims is "the easiest bread you will ever make." With an inconceivable no-knead, no-thermometer, five-minute prep, the results are astounding and will fundamentally change the way you bake. In this recipe, we use her genius techniques for the foundation of a savory pull-apart bread, resulting in a pillow-soft interior that is chewy, buttery, and delicious. Mix in handfuls of sautéed spinach, melted Parmesan and gruyère cheese, tangy artichoke hearts, and mounds of garlic, and the results are simply staggering. Serve this magnetic bread with dinner or bring it to a party, and watch how quickly it attracts everyone in the room.

FOR THE DOUGH

- 4½ cups (512 g) all-purpose flour, plus more for flouring the counter
- 1¾ teaspoons salt
- 2 teaspoons granulated sugar
- 2¼ teaspoons instant yeast
- 2 cups (473 ml) warm water (see note)

FOR THE FILLING

- ½ cup (113 g) unsalted butter, plus more at room temperature to grease the pan
- 12 ounces (340 g) spinach, coarsely chopped
- 6 large garlic cloves (30 g), minced
- ½ cup (24 g) italian parsley, finely chopped
- ½ teaspoon salt
- 2 14-ounce (397 g each) cans artichoke hearts, drained and quartered
- 6 ounces (170 g) Parmesan cheese, grated
- 6 ounces (170 g) gruyère cheese, grated

In a large mixing bowl, whisk together the flour, salt, sugar, and yeast. Add the warm water and stir with a rubber spatula to combine. Place the bowl in a cold oven, cover loosely with a kitchen towel, shut the door, and set the temperature to 400°F/204°C for 60 seconds, then shut the oven off (this creates the perfect warm, draft-free place for the dough to rise). Let rise for 90 minutes, until doubled in volume.

Meanwhile, make the filling. Melt the butter in a medium saucepan over medium heat. When hot, add the spinach, garlic, parsley, and salt, and stir to combine. Sauté until the spinach is wilted, 1 to 2 minutes, then add the artichoke hearts, stir to combine, and remove from heat. Transfer the mixture to a bowl to stop the cooking process.

In a small bowl, mix together the two grated cheeses.

After 90 minutes, remove the bowl from the oven, and preheat the oven to 350°F/177°C. Generously grease a Bundt pan or 3-quart dutch oven with a few tablespoons of unsalted butter.

Spread ¼ cup of flour on a clean, dry work surface. Deflate the dough by using two forks to pull the wet dough away from the sides, toward the center of the bowl. Use the two forks to divide the dough in half, then lift one half onto the floured counter. Using as much flour as needed to prevent sticking, and handling it as little as possible, gently gather the loose dough into one mound, then use a knife or bench scraper to divide it into 12 equal pieces. Repeat with the remaining dough.

Sprinkle a few spoonfuls of the spinach mixture into the bottom of the greased Bundt pan, and add a small handful of the grated cheese blend. Place 3 or 4 dough pieces around the pan, then cover the dough with more spinach and cheese. Continue adding dough pieces, spinach mix, and cheese, layering as you go to ensure that every piece is surrounded by filling. When all the dough pieces have been added, top them with any remaining spinach mixture and cheese. Let rise uncovered at room temperature for 20 to 25 minutes. Set the pan on a rimmed baking sheet to catch any spills, and place in the oven. Bake until the crust is golden brown and sounds hollow when tapped with the back of a spoon, 35 to 40 minutes. Let cool in the pan for 5 minutes, then invert onto a serving platter. Serve immediately while hot, and enjoy!

Notes

- To make 2 cups of warm water, simply mix 1½ cups (355 ml) of cold water with ½ cup (118 ml) of boiling water in a heatproof measuring cup and stir to combine. It should feel warm to the touch, perfect for proofing.

- Instant yeast—also labeled as bread machine yeast—does not need to be proofed before use, and is mixed directly with the dry ingredients when making bread. Do not substitute Active Dry yeast, as it will not rise properly, and will result in a flat, dense loaf.

Desserts

No matter what anyone says, dessert is the most important meal of the day. In this decadent chapter, we offer twenty-one enticing ways to bring some happiness into the world. Your kids will be cheering when you surprise them with Gooey Butterscotch Blondies (page 215) on a rainy day. Your loved one's eyes will light up when you set down a Molten Peanut Butter Chocolate Cake (page 210) after a romantic dinner. And be prepared for a standing ovation when you exit the kitchen carrying a gorgeous Trifle with Kiwi and Fresh Strawberries (page 183). Desserts spread joy and love, helping make any meal—and the world—a little bit sweeter. In the following pages, you will be tempted by rich and decadent chocolate cakes, flaky pastries and cookies, and delicious vegan options like our smooth Salted Caramel Nice Cream with a Candied Pecan Crumble (page 204). We will be visiting Spain, Thailand, Cuba, and the Middle East, so pack your belongings and get ready for the trip of a lifetime.

Communication Breakdown Carrot Cake with Whipped Goat Cheese Frosting

Makes 1 2-layer, 8-inch cake • Serves 12 to 16

Special Tools: Electric Mixer

Kitchen disasters can happen to anyone—even on your birthday. Every August, Ryan bakes me a cake (best husband ever), and one year, I requested a carrot cake with cream cheese frosting. While he was busy baking, I stepped into the kitchen and it was like walking into a Jackson Pollock painting. There were masses of grated carrots covering the walls, bits scattered over the floor, and even a few dangling from the ceiling. Since we didn't have a food processor at the time, he had been strenuously grating carrots for the last half hour, and the first words out of my mouth were, "What did you do in here?!" Tensions rose and words not worth repeating were exchanged, but the story gets worse. While Ryan continued mixing the batter, I thought it would be helpful to clean the kitchen, so I gathered up peels from every inch of the room, then stuffed them all down the disposal, which began producing terrifying murky sounds while water backed up and started filling the sink. Then, suddenly, the pipe under the cabinet exploded, sending a torrent of filthy water and carrot peels pouring onto the floor. We laugh about it now, and thankfully, the cake—and our relationship—survived the Great Carrot Flood of 2005. This recipe is appropriately named after that chaotic day. We kissed and made up, and we learned two valuable lessons: don't ever put carrot peels down the garbage disposal, and be nice to your significant other, especially when they are making you a birthday cake.

—*Adam*

FOR THE CAKE
1 tablespoon unsalted butter, for greasing the pans
2 cups (240 g) all-purpose flour
2 teaspoons baking soda
1 teaspoon ground cinnamon
½ teaspoon salt
2 cups (396 g) granulated sugar
1½ cups (355 ml) toasted walnut oil (see note)
4 large eggs
3 cups (300 g) grated carrots (about 5 medium carrots)

FOR FROSTING AND ASSEMBLY
6 ounces (170 g) goat cheese, at room temperature
3 tablespoons (42 g) unsalted butter, at room temperature
1½ teaspoons vanilla extract
3 cups (340 g) powdered sugar
⅓ cup (45 g) finely chopped pecans, for garnish

TO MAKE THE CAKE

Preheat oven to 350°F/177°C. Grease two 8-inch cake pans with butter, line the bottoms with circles of parchment, and grease the parchment.

In a medium bowl, sift together the flour, baking soda, cinnamon, and salt. Whisk to combine, and set aside.

In a large bowl, combine the sugar and walnut oil, and whisk until smooth and blended. Add the eggs, and whisk until combined. Gradually add the flour mixture, stirring until just combined. Then fold in the carrots until blended. Divide the batter evenly between the two cake pans, and bake until a toothpick inserted in the center comes out clean, about 40 to 45 minutes. Let the cakes cool for a few minutes in the pans, then invert the cakes onto wire racks, remove the parchment paper, and cool completely. Use immediately, or wrap tightly in plastic and refrigerate for up to 3 days.

TO MAKE THE FROSTING

Place the goat cheese and butter in a large mixing bowl. Beat with an electric mixer on medium until smooth and evenly combined, stopping to scrape down the sides of the bowl as needed. Add the vanilla and continue beating until smooth. Gradually sift the powdered sugar into the mixing bowl in several additions, stopping to mix between each one. Continue to beat until light and fluffy.

TO ASSEMBLE THE CAKE

Place one cake layer on a serving plate. Spread half the frosting over the layer, all the way to the edge. Place the second cake layer on top of the first, then spread the remaining frosting over the top. Sprinkle the nuts over the frosting. Kiss and make up, serve, and enjoy!

Notes

- Toasted walnut oil adds a delicious nutty flavor and can be found in many supermarkets and online. If you can't find it, any neutral vegetable oil can be used instead.

- Don't ever throw carrot peels down the garbage disposal (see cautionary tale above).

- To make a 6-inch, 2-layer cake that serves 6 to 8 people, cut the cake recipe and frosting recipe in half. The layers will be slightly taller, so be sure the cake pans have sides at least 2 inches high.

Vegan Chocolate Puddle Cake

Makes 1 single-layer, 8- or 9-inch cake   •   Serves 8 to 10   •   Vegan

When I was five years old, I took my first cooking class. While other kids wanted to play soccer or baseball, I did everything in my power to avoid them—including once when I picked up a soccer ball in the middle of a game, handed it to the referee, and walked off the field. Thankfully, my parents quickly realized I had no interest in sports and signed me up for a "Mini Gourmet" children's class at the local recreation center. It was a dream come true; we spent every session cooking a variety of treats, and from the very first day, I was in heaven. I still have all the recipes, complete with *Ryan A.* scribbled across the front in my wobbly five-year-old handwriting, and there is one dessert I still continue to make. It has different names depending where you live—puddle cake, wacky cake, depression cake—but they all refer to the same thing: a one-layer cake that is rich, moist, and intensely chocolaty, yet contains no butter, eggs, or milk. Made with common ingredients that are probably in your kitchen right now, everything gets mixed in one bowl, and this foolproof recipe turns out flawlessly every time. When swirled with a silky chocolate frosting and showered with rainbow sprinkles, it is an elegant dessert—yet so simple a five-year-old can make it.

—Ryan

FOR THE CAKE
1 tablespoon vegan butter, to grease the pan
1½ cups (180 g) all-purpose flour
1 cup (198 g) granulated sugar
5 tablespoons (27 g) unsweetened cocoa
   powder
1 teaspoon baking soda
½ teaspoon salt
6 tablespoons vegetable oil
2 tablespoons white vinegar
1 teaspoon vanilla extract
1 cup (237 ml) water

FOR THE FROSTING
5 tablespoons (27 g) unsweetened cocoa
   powder
1¼ cups (142 g) powdered sugar
½ cup (113 g) vegan butter, at room
   temperature
1½ teaspoons vanilla extract
1 to 2 tablespoons milk of your choice,
   if needed to thin
vegan rainbow sprinkles, for garnish,
   if desired

TO MAKE THE CAKE

Preheat the oven to 350°F/177°C. Grease an 8- or 9-inch round cake pan with vegan butter. Line the bottom of the pan with a circle of parchment, and set aside.

In a large bowl, sift together the flour, sugar, cocoa, baking soda, and salt, and whisk until evenly mixed. Add the oil, vinegar, vanilla, and water, and stir just until blended to avoid overmixing. Pour the batter into the prepared cake pan and bake until a toothpick inserted into the center comes out clean with a few crumbs sticking to it, 25 to 30 minutes. Let the cake cool in the pan for 5 minutes, then invert onto a wire rack, peel off the parchment paper, and let cool completely.

TO MAKE THE FROSTING

In a medium bowl, sift together the cocoa and powdered sugar to remove any lumps. In a large mixing bowl, blend the vegan butter on medium-high speed until light and fluffy. Add the cocoa mixture to the bowl with the butter, then add the vanilla, and blend on medium-high speed until creamy. If the frosting seems too thick, add milk 1 to 2 teaspoons at a time and blend until smooth and spreadable.

TO SERVE

Once the cake has cooled completely, place it on a serving plate. Frost the top (and sides, if desired) evenly with the frosting, and garnish with rainbow sprinkles. Enjoy!

Notes

- The cake will stay fresh in a covered container at room temperature for a day or up to 3 days in the fridge. If refrigerating, allow the cake to warm to room temperature before serving.

- The cake can be baked in either an 8- or 9-inch cake pan. An 8-inch cake will be slightly taller and will take up to 5 minutes longer to bake than a 9-inch cake.

- To make a 6-inch cake that serves 6 to 8, simply halve the recipe for both the cake and frosting.

Toasted Hazelnut Fudge

Makes 1 8-inch square pan, about 25 pieces   •   Gluten-Free

The holidays would not be complete without my mom's homemade chocolate fudge. Every year, we travel to Portland, Oregon to celebrate with my family, and on Christmas Eve, we all bundle up for a wintry nighttime walk to deliver it to lucky friends in the neighborhood as the streets glow from twinkling lights on every rooftop. My mom's version is rich and chocolaty, silky smooth, and studded with chopped walnuts. We put a spin on her recipe, adding deeply roasted hazelnuts and generous dollops of Nutella for a toasty fudge that makes a great gift, if you can bear to part with it.

—Ryan

½ cup (76 g) raw hazelnuts
7 ounces (198 g) Marshmallow Fluff or other marshmallow spread
¾ cup (149 g) granulated sugar
⅔ cup (158 ml) evaporated milk
2 tablespoons unsalted butter, plus 1 tablespoon for greasing the pan
¼ teaspoon salt
9 ounces (255 g) semisweet chocolate chips
1 cup (295 g) Nutella or other chocolate hazelnut spread
1 teaspoon vanilla extract

Grease the bottom and sides of an 8-inch square baking pan, then set aside.

Scatter the hazelnuts in a dry skillet and place over medium heat. Cook until the nuts are toasted and fragrant, 7 to 9 minutes, shaking the pan occasionally to roll them around. Transfer the nuts to a plate and place in the freezer until cool enough to handle comfortably, about 5 to 10 minutes. Remove any loose skins, and transfer the nuts to a cutting board. Chop coarsely, then set aside in a small bowl.

In a medium saucepan, combine the Marshmallow Fluff, sugar, evaporated milk, butter, and salt. Place on the stove but do not turn on the heat yet. Prepare the remaining ingredients by measuring the chips and placing them in a bowl, having the Nutella measured and ready, and setting the bottle

of vanilla with a measuring spoon nearby—this is because when the mixture is finished cooking, all the remaining ingredients need to be added at once.

Set the stove to medium heat, and bring the mixture to a boil, stirring constantly and making sure to scrape along the sides and bottom of the pan to prevent scorching (when the mixture is fully boiling, it will have vigorous bubbles over the entire surface, not just around the edges). Once it reaches a full boil, set a timer for 5 minutes and continue stirring constantly. If the mixture is boiling too rapidly and sputtering hot liquid, lower the heat to a simmer. Once the timer rings, turn off the heat and stir in the chocolate chips, Nutella, vanilla, and chopped hazelnuts. Stir vigorously until smooth and blended. Pour into the prepared baking pan, and shake the pan gently to spread the mixture into an even layer. Let cool at room temperature for 1 to 2 hours, then slice into 25 individual squares and enjoy!

Notes

- The fudge will stay fresh for up to a week at room temperature in a sealed container.

Dark Chocolate Florentine Cookies

Makes about 36 cookies

Our local bakery makes the best florentine cookies. We wanted our recipe to be just as delicate and delicious, so in the interest of science, we bought a dozen freshly baked florentines and brought them back to our house to run some important side-by-side cookie taste tests. We invited a few friends to partake in the confectionery experiment, and everyone agreed that ours was the winner. Crisp and chewy, with toasted almonds, a hint of honey, and drizzled with dark chocolate, these lace cookies are dangerously addicting and scientifically proven to bring a smile to your face.

2 cups (235 g) slivered almonds
3 tablespoons (25 g) all-purpose flour
¼ teaspoon salt
¾ cup (149 g) granulated sugar
3 tablespoons heavy cream
2 tablespoons honey
6 tablespoons (85 g) unsalted butter
½ teaspoon vanilla
4 ounces (113 g) dark chocolate, coarsely chopped

Scatter the almonds in a dry skillet, and place over medium heat. Stirring occasionally, cook until toasted, fragrant, and golden brown, about 5 to 7 minutes. Transfer to a plate and place in the fridge or freezer for 5 to 10 minutes until cool.

Place the cooled almonds in a food processor, and pulse until coarsely ground. Add the flour and salt, and pulse to combine, then transfer to a small bowl and set aside.

In a medium saucepan, combine the sugar, cream, honey, and butter, and set over medium heat. Stirring often, bring to a boil, then cook for 1 minute until the sugar dissolves completely. Remove from heat and add the vanilla and the almond mixture, stirring to combine. Let cool 15 to 20 minutes. While the mixture is cooling, preheat the oven to 350°F/177°C, and line a baking sheet with parchment paper.

Once cool, scoop a heaping teaspoon of the almond mixture, and place it on the prepared baking sheet, flattening the ball slightly. Repeat until the sheet is full, leaving about 3 inches of space between each ball of dough. Bake 10 to 12 minutes, until the edges are deeply golden. The cookies may look soft, but they will harden as they cool. Let cool on the sheet for about 4 minutes, then transfer to a wire rack to cool completely. Repeat with the remaining dough.

Melt the chocolate using either the stove or a microwave. If using the stove, set a small heatproof bowl over a pan of simmering water, add the chopped chocolate, and stir until melted. If using the microwave, heat the chocolate in 20- to 30-second bursts, stirring between each one, until smooth and creamy. Using a spoon, drizzle the melted chocolate over the cooled cookies, let cool, and enjoy!

Notes

- The cookies will stay crispy in a sealed container at room temperature for up to 3 days.

Pillow-Soft Glazed Doughnuts

Makes 12 to 14

Special Tools: Thermometer

There are three types of doughnuts in the world: the cold, packaged ones found in grocery stores, filled with artificial flavors and preservatives; the sad, stale doughnut-shop variety prepared in the early morning and sitting lonely on a shelf all day; and the fresh, homemade kind that melts in your mouth, hot off the stove. If you have never had the pleasure of experiencing a warm glazed doughnut, allow these light pillow-soft delicacies to be your first, and dough-nut be fooled by any others again.

FOR THE DOUGHNUTS
2 tablespoons water
¾ cup (177 ml) milk of your choice
¼ cup (50 g) granulated sugar
2¼ teaspoons (1 packet) active dry or instant yeast
1 large egg
3 tablespoons unsalted butter, melted
½ teaspoon salt
3 to 3½ cups (360 g to 420 g) all-purpose flour
1½ quarts (1½ L) vegetable oil for frying

FOR THE VANILLA GLAZE
1 cup (113 g) powdered sugar
1½ tablespoons milk of your choice
1 teaspoon vanilla extract

FOR THE CHOCOLATE GLAZE
¾ cup (85 g) powdered sugar
2 tablespoons (13 g) unsweetened cocoa powder
1½ tablespoons milk of your choice
1 teaspoon vanilla extract

In a glass measuring cup, combine the water, milk, and sugar. Microwave in 20-second bursts until the mixture reaches 115°F/46°C. Pour into a large mixing bowl, add the yeast, and stir briefly to combine. Let the mixture rest at room temperature until the yeast forms a foamy layer on top, about 7 to 10 minutes. Add the egg, melted butter, and salt, and stir to combine. Add the flour ½ cup at a time as you stir until a dough forms that holds together and pulls away from the sides of the bowl. Transfer to a floured work surface and knead for 5 minutes, adding more flour 1 tablespoon at a time if the dough is too sticky. Return the dough to the mixing bowl, cover with a kitchen towel, and let rise at room temperature until doubled in size, 45 to 60 minutes.

Transfer the dough to a floured work surface, and roll it out to ½-inch thick. Use a doughnut cutter (or a 3½-inch circle cutter and a 1-inch circle cutter) to make doughnut-shaped rings and doughnut holes. Gather the scraps, roll them out again, and repeat with the remaining dough. Let the doughnuts rest at room temperature until puffy, about 30 to 45 minutes.

While the doughnuts are resting, make your glazes. Combine the vanilla glaze ingredients in a small, shallow bowl and whisk with a fork until smooth and blended. Repeat with the chocolate glaze in a second bowl.

Fill a wide, deep saucepan with 2 to 3 inches of vegetable oil, and attach a deep-fry or candy thermometer to the side of the pan with the tip submerged in oil but not touching the bottom. Place on the stove, set the heat to medium-high, and raise the temperature to 375°F/191°C. Once the temperature is reached, adjust the burner lower or higher as needed to maintain it. The oil is extremely hot, so carefully add several doughnuts to the pan, just enough to fill it without crowding. Cook until the underside is golden brown, 45 to 60 seconds, then use a spider strainer or tongs to flip them and repeat on the second side. Remove the doughnuts and transfer to a wire rack to drain for 1 minute. Use tongs to dip a doughnut in your desired glaze, coating the bottom evenly. Then place it back on the rack glaze-side-up so it drips down the sides. Repeat with the remaining doughnuts and doughnut holes. Serve warm, and enjoy!

Notes

- These doughnuts are best served warm and fresh the day they are made, as they lose their softness with time.

Schokoladen Cake

Makes 1 8-layer, 9-inch cake, serves 16 to 20

Special Tools: Electric Mixer

My mom had a slice of *schokoladen* cake just hours before I was born. I must have been sending her a message, because after dinner with friends, she felt a sudden yearning for something chocolaty. Searching in the fridge, she found a piece of cake from a local bakery, our cacao cravings were cured, and I was born just a few hours later. Clearly, I needed a slice of cake to celebrate my grand entrance into the world, and growing up, *schokoladen* continued to be my all-time favorite. Unfortunately, the bakery stopped making it more than twenty years ago, so we re-created it for our cookbook. Made with eight thin layers of vanilla buttermilk cake and surrounded by a smooth milk chocolate ganache, this towering torte is for all the chocolate lovers in your life—even if they haven't been born yet.

—Ryan

FOR THE YELLOW BUTTERMILK CAKE
1 cup (2 sticks / 226 g) unsalted butter at room temperature, plus more for greasing the pans
4 cups plus 2 tablespoons (495 g) cake flour
2 teaspoons baking powder
1½ teaspoons baking soda
1 teaspoon salt
2 cups (396 g) granulated sugar
2 teaspoons vanilla extract
4 large eggs, at room temperature
2 cups (473 ml) buttermilk

FOR THE MILK CHOCOLATE GANACHE FROSTING
32 ounces (907 g) milk chocolate, coarsely chopped
1⅓ cups (315 ml) heavy cream
2 cups (4 sticks / 452 g) unsalted butter at room temperature, cut into cubes

TO MAKE THE CAKE
Preheat oven to 350°F/177°C. Grease two 9-inch round cake pans, and line the bottoms with circles of parchment paper.

In a medium bowl, sift together the cake flour, baking powder, baking soda, and salt. Set aside.

In a large mixing bowl, beat the butter and sugar together on medium speed until fluffy. Add the vanilla, then the eggs one at a time, beating between each addition. Add the buttermilk and beat until blended. Add the flour in 3 equal additions, stopping to scrape down the sides and blending again between each addition. Divide the batter between the prepared cake pans, spreading each one into an even layer. To remove any bubbles in the batter, pick up the pans an inch or two off the counter and drop them gently a few times. Transfer to the middle oven rack and bake until a toothpick inserted into the center comes out dry with a few crumbs, 35 to 40 minutes. Cool in the pans for 10 minutes, then invert onto wire racks, remove the parchment, and cool completely.

TO MAKE THE GANACHE FROSTING

While the cakes are cooling, set a medium heatproof mixing bowl over a pan of simmering water, and place the chopped chocolate and cream in the bowl. Stir until melted and creamy, then remove from heat, add the butter, and whisk until smooth and blended. Refrigerate until cooled and spreadable, 30 to 60 minutes. If it becomes too thick to spread, let rest at room temperature until softened.

TO ASSEMBLE AND SERVE

Once the cakes are completely cool, cut each layer in half horizontally, creating 4 layers. Then carefully cut each of the 4 layers in half again, creating 8 thin layers. The two methods we use are a cake leveler or a serrated knife. The cake leveler quickly cuts the most even layers, but a knife can work just as well. If using a knife, you can simply eye it—although your layers may not be perfectly even—or use toothpicks as a guide by inserting them halfway up the sides of the cake all around, and use them to keep the blade level.

To assemble, place one layer on a serving plate. Dollop a spoonful of frosting in the middle, and use a thin spatula to spread it evenly all the way to the edge. The layer of frosting should be about ⅛-inch thick, so add more if needed. Place the second layer of cake on top, then repeat with another layer of frosting. Continue with the remaining layers in the same manner, then once all the layers have been stacked, use the remaining frosting to evenly cover the top and sides of the cake. If desired, use a decorating comb to create ridges on the sides and a piping bag fitted with a narrow circle tip to create dots around the bottom border, as pictured. Keep refrigerated and serve cold, since the ganache will soften too much at room temperature. Enjoy!

Notes

- The cake layers can be made up to 2 days ahead of time. Once they are baked and completely cooled, wrap tightly in plastic and refrigerate. Don't cut the cakes into layers until you are ready to assemble, as they will stay fresher when kept whole.

- The finished cake should be kept covered and will stay fresh in the refrigerator for up to 3 days.

- To make a 6-inch, 8-layer cake that serves 8 to 10 people, cut the cake recipe and ganache recipe in half.

Trifle with Kiwi and Fresh Strawberries

Serves 8 to 10

Special Tools: Electric Mixer

Trifles are the ultimate make-ahead recipe. When hosting a dinner or holiday gathering, you want to relax and enjoy yourself, so time-saving dishes are the key to a stress-free evening, and these British desserts are ideal, since they are assembled and chilled the day before. Served in a decorative glass bowl, layers of soft homemade pound cake, vanilla custard, and sliced kiwis and strawberries mingle together, creating a fluffy cloud-like dessert in a kaleidoscope of colors. Spread with a generous layer of whipped cream, set this showstopper on the table, and prepare to take a bow to a chorus of *oohs* and *aahs* from your astonished guests.

FOR THE POUND CAKE
- 1 cup (226 g) unsalted butter at room temperature, plus more for greasing the pan
- 1¾ cups (210 g) cake flour, plus more for dusting the pan
- ½ teaspoon baking soda
- ¼ teaspoon salt
- 1¼ cups (248 g) granulated sugar
- 4 large eggs
- 2 large egg yolks
- 1½ teaspoons vanilla extract
- ¼ cup (59 ml) buttermilk or kefir

FOR THE VANILLA CUSTARD
- 9 large egg yolks
- ¾ cup (149 g) granulated sugar
- 1½ cups (355 ml) whole milk
- 1½ cups (355 ml) heavy cream
- 1 tablespoon vanilla extract

FOR THE WHIPPED CREAM AND ASSEMBLY
- 4 large kiwis (about 335 g), peeled and thinly sliced, for assembly
- 12 ounces (340 g) fresh strawberries, stem removed, thinly sliced, for assembly
- ¾ cup (177 ml) heavy cream
- 2 teaspoons granulated sugar
- ½ teaspoon vanilla extract

TO MAKE THE POUND CAKE
Preheat oven to 350°F/177°C. Grease a 9×4-inch loaf pan, then add a spoonful of flour to the pan, tilting it to coat the bottom and sides evenly. Pour out the excess flour and set aside.

In a medium bowl, sift together the flour, baking soda, and salt.

In a large mixing bowl, combine the butter and sugar and beat on medium speed until fluffy. Add the eggs and egg yolks one at a time, beating between each addition, then add the vanilla. Add the buttermilk and beat until blended. Add the flour mixture in 3 additions, stopping to scrape down the sides and beating between each one. Pour the batter into the prepared loaf pan, and bake until golden brown on top and a toothpick inserted into the center comes out clean, 55 to 75 minutes. Let cool in the pan for 10 minutes, then remove and transfer to a wire rack to cool completely before assembling the trifle. Use immediately, or wrap in plastic once fully cooled, and keep refrigerated for up to 3 days.

TO MAKE THE VANILLA CUSTARD
In a medium heatproof bowl, whisk together the egg yolks and sugar and set aside.

In a medium saucepan, combine the milk and cream. Place over medium heat, and when bubbles just begin to appear around the edges, remove the pan from heat and slowly pour the hot milk into the bowl with the eggs in a slow, small stream as you whisk constantly. This tempers the eggs so they don't scramble when you add them to the pan in the next step. Pour the mixture back into the pan, then get a clean bowl—or wash and dry the one you just used—and set a fine-mesh strainer over the bowl. Return the pan to medium heat and stir constantly until the mixture just begins to thicken, then remove from heat and stir for 2 minutes. Pour the custard through the strainer into the bowl, using a rubber spatula to press it through. Add the vanilla extract, and stir to combine. Use immediately, or cover the bowl with plastic, pressing it directly onto the surface of the custard to prevent a skin from forming, and refrigerate for up to 3 days.

TO MAKE THE WHIPPED CREAM
AND ASSEMBLE THE TRIFLE
Cut the pound cake into ½-inch slices, and arrange a layer in the bottom of a glass serving bowl. Trim the slices as needed to fit together in a single layer without overlapping. Arrange a layer of kiwi and strawberry slices on top of the cake, with the slices on the side pressed against the glass so they are visible. Pour about half the custard over the fruit, spreading if needed to create an even layer. Arrange another layer of pound cake slices on top, cutting the slices into smaller pieces as needed to fill the space evenly. Cover with another layer of fruit, with the slices on the sides pressed up against the glass as before. Pour the remaining custard over the top and spread evenly. Cover the bowl with plastic, pressing the plastic directly onto the custard to prevent a skin from forming. Refrigerate for at least 8 hours, or overnight.

When almost ready to serve, place a clean, dry mixing bowl and beaters in the freezer for about 10 minutes to chill. When cold, remove from the freezer and pour the heavy cream into the bowl. Add the sugar and vanilla, and beat on high speed until soft peaks form when you lift the beaters. Uncover the trifle, and scoop the whipped cream on top, spreading into an even layer. Decorate with additional fruit slices or whole strawberries, then serve and enjoy!

Notes

- Trifles are delicious with a variety of fruit, so try other combinations and get creative!

Cinnamon Crumb Coffee Cake

Makes 1 ring cake, serves 8 to 10

Special Tools: Electric Mixer

In June 1964, my grandmother won a whopping five dollars for her coffee cake that was featured in the *Los Angeles Times.* There was a cooking column called My Best Recipe, and each week, they featured a lucky reader who had mailed in their favorite recipe, hoping to be published. The original title—Sour Cream Coffee Cake—and the story about my grandma inheriting it from her Austrian friend caught the attention of the columnist, and they selected hers to be printed in the newspaper. I heard my grandma proudly tell the story at gatherings and parties over the years, and she served it after every meal when I was growing up. Ryan and I left the cake recipe the same, but I always felt it needed more of the best part—the cinnamon crumb topping—so we decided to double it! Introducing Grandma Gertrude's prizewinning coffee cake . . . now with even more topping!   —*Adam*

FOR THE COFFEE CAKE

- ½ cup (113 g) unsalted butter, at room temperature, plus more for greasing the pan
- 2 cups (240 g) all-purpose flour
- 1 teaspoon baking powder
- 1 teaspoon baking soda
- ½ teaspoon salt
- 1 cup (198 g) granulated sugar
- 2 large eggs
- 1 teaspoon vanilla extract
- 1 cup (227 g) sour cream

FOR THE CRUMB TOPPING

- ½ cup (99 g) granulated sugar
- ½ cup (107 g) brown sugar
- ½ cup (57 g) finely chopped walnuts
- 4 teaspoons ground cinnamon

Preheat oven to 350°F/177°C. Grease a tube pan, preferably with a removable bottom, and set aside.

In a medium bowl, sift together the flour, baking powder, baking soda, and salt.

In a large mixing bowl, combine the butter and sugar, and beat on medium speed until fluffy. Add the eggs one at a time, beating after each addition, then the vanilla. Add the flour mixture in three additions, alternating with two additions of the sour cream, stopping to scrape down the sides and beating between each one. Spread half the batter in the prepared tube pan in an even layer.

In a small bowl, make the crumb topping by mixing together the granulated and brown sugars, chopped walnuts, and cinnamon. Sprinkle half the crumb topping over the cake batter, then spread the remaining cake batter over the crumbs. Top with the remaining crumb mixture, then place on the center oven rack and bake for 45 minutes, or until a toothpick inserted into the center comes out clean.

Let the pan cool for 10 minutes on a wire rack, then remove the cake from the pan and transfer to a large plate if serving warm, or leave on the wire rack to cool completely. The cake can be served warm or at room temperature and will stay fresh in a covered container for up to 4 days. Enjoy!

Part V—THURS., JUNE 4, 1964   Los Angeles Times

MY BEST RECIPE

Sour Cream Coffee Cake From Austria

"I fell heir to this exceptional recipe many years ago when an Austrian friend gave it to me in repayment for a kindness," writes Mrs. Gertrude Blender. "It has remained our favorite coffee cake over the years."

SOUR CREAM COFFEE CAKE

1/2 cup butter or margarine
1 cup sugar
2 eggs
1 tsp. vanilla
2 cups sifted flour
1 tsp. baking powder
1 tsp. soda
1/2 tsp. salt
1 cup dairy sour cream

Cream butter and sugar thoroughly. Beat in eggs, one at a time. Add vanilla. Sift flour with baking powder, soda and salt. Add to c r e a m e d mixture alternately with sour cream.

Pour half of batter in greased 12x8x2-in. pan. Sprinkle with half of topping mixture. Add remaining batter, and sprinkle with remaining topping. Bake at 350 deg., 45 min., or until cake tests done.

Topping: Mix together 1/4 cup granulated sugar, 1/4 cup brown sugar (packed), 1/4 cup chopped walnuts and 2 tsp. cinnamon.

MRS. GERTRUDE BLENDER,
6459 Lubao Ave.,
Woodland Hills.

The Times pays $5 for Southern California readers' recipes published in this exchange column. Send recipes you consider your best and that are unusual and not widely publicized. Explain interesting features and how you found the recipe. Sign or print your complete name and address on each one. Address entries, "My Best Recipe," c/o Anita Bennett, Los Angeles Times, Times Mirror Square, Los Angeles 90053. All recipes become the property of The Times, and none will be returned.

Churros con Chocolate

Makes about 15 to 20 small churros

Special Tools: Thermometer

The most common variety of churro in the US is Mexican-style—almost a foot long and generously rolled in cinnamon sugar. In Central America, they are often prepared as giant spirals two feet across, and in other places, they are filled with rich *dulce de leche* or vanilla custard. The churros that hold a special place in my heart are from Spain—thinner and less sweet, often made without any sugar. With an exceedingly crispy outside and a chewy interior, this Spanish specialty is served warm and fresh with a thick hot-chocolate dip that coats the churro's ridges. Make our Vegetarian Paella (page 130) for dinner, pop open a bottle of wine, and serve these crispy treats for a grand chocolate finale and an authentic taste of Spain. —*Ryan*

FOR THE HOT CHOCOLATE
2 cups (473 ml) milk of your choice
1 tablespoon cornstarch
¼ cup (50 g) granulated sugar
7 ounces (200 g) dark chocolate (70 percent cacao), coarsely chopped

FOR THE CHURROS
1 cup (120 g) all-purpose flour
¼ teaspoon salt
1 cup (237 ml) water
½ cup (113 g) unsalted butter
3 large eggs
1½ to 2 quarts (about 1½ to 2 L) vegetable oil for frying

TO MAKE THE HOT CHOCOLATE
Pour half the milk into a small saucepan, leaving half in the measuring cup. Add the cornstarch to the milk in the measuring cup and stir well to combine. Add the sugar and dark chocolate to the pan, and place over medium heat, stirring often. When the chocolate melts, add the cornstarch mixture and continue stirring. Once the mixture comes to a boil, lower heat to a simmer and stir for 1 to 2 minutes until thickened. Remove from heat, and keep warm until ready to serve.

TO MAKE THE CHURROS
In a small bowl, sift together the flour and salt and set aside. In a medium saucepan, combine the water and butter, and place over medium-high heat.

When boiling, add the flour mixture all at once and immediately begin stirring rapidly until a ball of dough forms. Remove from heat and transfer the hot dough to a mixing bowl. Beat with an electric mixer on medium speed for a few minutes until warm, but no longer hot. With the mixer running, add the eggs one at a time, then continue beating for 2 to 3 more minutes. Let the dough rest for 10 to 15 minutes at room temperature, then transfer to a piping bag fitted with a wide star tip, and set aside.

Pour the vegetable oil into a wide saucepan or deep skillet. Attach a candy thermometer to the side so the tip is submerged in the oil but not touching the bottom of the pan. Turn the heat to medium-high, until the oil reaches 360–375°F/182–191°C, then lower and raise the heat as needed to keep the oil in that temperature range. Twist and seal the top of the piping bag, then squeeze 4 to 6 inches of dough onto the hot oil, cutting it off with a pair of scissors. Repeat 3 or 4 times without crowding the pan with too many churros at once. Cook until golden brown on the bottom, about 2½ minutes, then flip and repeat on the second side. Remove with a spider strainer or tongs, and transfer to a wire rack or paper-towel-lined plate to drain. Serve immediately with a small cup of hot chocolate for dipping and enjoy!

Sweet and Salty Cake

Makes 1 2-layer, 9-inch cake, serves 16 to 20

Special Tools: Electric Mixer

What is better than chocolate cake, you ask? After some deep chocolate-reflecting, we concluded that the answer is simply this: multiple layers of chocolate cake, each one drizzled in rich salted caramel, layered with crunchy potato chips, swirled in a lush chocolate buttercream frosting, and garnished with a potato chip bouquet. Any questions?

FOR THE CHOCOLATE CAKE
1 tablespoon unsalted butter, for greasing
   the pans
2½ cups (300 g) all-purpose flour
1 cup (85 g) unsweetened cocoa powder
1¼ teaspoons baking powder
2 teaspoons baking soda
1 teaspoon salt
½ cup plus 2 tablespoons (148 ml) vegetable oil
2 cups (396 g) granulated sugar
2 large eggs
1 large egg yolk
2 teaspoons vanilla extract
1½ cups (355 ml) buttermilk
3 ounces (85 g) bittersweet chocolate, coarsely
   chopped (about 70 percent cacao)
1 cup (237 ml) hot strong coffee

FOR THE SALTED CARAMEL FILLING
1 cup (198 g) granulated sugar
2 tablespoons light corn syrup
2½ tablespoons water
½ cup (118 ml) heavy cream
2 tablespoons unsalted butter
1 teaspoon flaky sea salt
1 teaspoon vanilla extract

FOR THE CHOCOLATE FROSTING AND ASSEMBLY
1 cup (226 g) unsalted butter at room
   temperature
2½ cups (284 g) powdered sugar
⅔ cup (57 g) unsweetened cocoa powder
2 teaspoons vanilla extract
¼ teaspoon salt
1 medium bag of plain salted potato chips,
   for assembly
½ teaspoon flaky sea salt, divided,
   for assembly

TO MAKE THE CAKE
Preheat the oven to 350°F/177°C. Grease two 9-inch round cake pans with butter, line the bottoms with circles of parchment paper, and set aside.

In a medium bowl, sift together the flour, cocoa powder, baking powder, baking soda, and salt to eliminate any lumps.

In a large mixing bowl, combine the oil, sugar, eggs, egg yolk, and vanilla, and beat until smooth. Add the flour mixture in three additions, alternating with two additions of the buttermilk, stopping to scrape down the sides and beat between each one.

Place the chopped chocolate in a small heatproof bowl. Pour the hot coffee over the chocolate, and whisk until it melts and the mixture is smooth. Pour the coffee mixture into the cake batter, and beat until just combined. Divide the batter equally between the two prepared cake pans, then place on the center oven rack and bake 30 to 35 minutes, until a toothpick inserted in the center comes out clean. Let cool in the pans on wire racks for 10 to 15 minutes, then invert onto the racks, remove the parchment, and let cool completely. Once cool, the cakes can be used immediately or wrapped tightly in plastic and stored in the fridge for up to 3 days.

TO MAKE THE SALTED CARAMEL FILLING
In a small saucepan, combine the sugar, corn syrup, and water. Set over medium heat and cook, stirring often, until amber-colored, 8 to 10 minutes. Remove from heat and add the cream, butter, salt, and vanilla. Stir until smooth and blended, then transfer to a sealed container in the fridge to cool. The caramel will stay fresh for up to a week in the fridge, but needs to be heated to a spreadable consistency in the microwave or on the stove before use.

TO MAKE THE FROSTING AND ASSEMBLE
Place the butter in a large mixing bowl, and beat until fluffy. Sift the powdered sugar and cocoa into the bowl, then add the vanilla and salt. Beat on low speed at first, scrape down the sides as needed, then beat on medium-high until light and creamy.

Open the bag of chips and select the best-looking 6 to 8 chips to set aside. Those will be the chip bouquet garnish (yes!) in the center of the cake. Close the bag, and use your hands to crush the remaining chips into tiny pieces. Transfer the crushed chip pieces to a bowl, and set aside.

Place one cake layer on a serving plate. Pour ¼ cup of caramel over the cake, spreading it into an even layer and leaving about ½ inch of space around the edges, then sprinkle evenly with a generous pinch of flaky sea salt (about ¼ teaspoon). Scoop ¾ cup of frosting and place it over the caramel. Spread into an even layer, going all the way to the edge of the cake, then top with ¼ cup of crushed potato chips. Place the second cake on top, and add another ¼ cup of caramel in an even layer. Add another ¼ teaspoon of sea salt, then use the remaining frosting to cover the top and sides of the cake. Sprinkle crushed potato chips around the top edge of the cake, and press them into the lower sides of the cake so they adhere to the frosting—note that you will likely have some extra crushed chips left over. Arrange the good-looking chips decoratively in the middle of the cake in a bouquet or other design. Serve and enjoy!

Notes

- The finished cake will stay fresh for up to 4 days in the fridge, but the crunchy texture of the chips is best on the day the cake is assembled.

- To make a 6-inch, 2-layer cake that serves 6 to 8 people, cut the caramel, frosting, and cake recipes in half.

Strawberry Apricot Rugelach

Makes 18 to 20 • Vegan Option

Special Tools: Electric Mixer; Food Processor or Blender

Rugelach are light and flaky Jewish pastries rolled with an assortment of fillings. When I was growing up, my mom would buy the chocolate kind from the store, and I would enjoy one—or three—in the morning with my bowl of cereal before school. These versatile, mini-cookie-like treats can be a simple dessert after a heavy meal and a sublime midday snack to calm a hectic afternoon at the office. Filled with strawberry jam, dried apricots, walnuts, brown sugar, and cinnamon, our version of these bite-size pastries are cozy companions for your morning cup of coffee, so feel free to enjoy one—or three—and start your day with something sweet.

—Adam

FOR THE DOUGH
- 4 ounces (113 g) cream cheese, at room temperature
- ½ cup (113 g) unsalted butter, at room temperature
- 1 cup (120 g) all-purpose flour
- ¼ teaspoon salt

FOR THE FILLING AND ASSEMBLY
- ⅔ cup (250 g) strawberry jam
- 2 tablespoons brown sugar
- ¾ teaspoon ground cinnamon
- ¼ cup (28 g) walnuts, finely chopped
- ¼ cup (50 g) dried apricots, finely chopped
- 1 large egg
- 1 teaspoon water
- coarse decorating sugar, for garnish

TO MAKE THE DOUGH
In a large mixing bowl, beat the cream cheese and butter until light and fluffy, about 2 minutes. Add the flour and salt, and beat until just blended. Gather the dough together, then divide in half. Roll each half into a ball, then flatten slightly to make a disc shape. Wrap tightly in plastic and refrigerate for at least 1 hour, or up to 24 hours.

TO MAKE THE STRAWBERRY SPREAD
Place the strawberry jam in a food processor or blender, and purée until smooth and pourable. Set aside.

TO MAKE THE CINNAMON-SUGAR FILLING
In a small bowl, combine the brown sugar and cinnamon, and stir to break up any lumps. Add the walnuts and apricots, and stir to combine.

TO ASSEMBLE
Line a baking sheet with parchment paper, and set aside.

Unwrap one of the discs of dough, and place it on a lightly floured work surface. Roll out the dough to a 9-inch circle about ⅛-inch thick. Spread half the jam over the circle, leaving a ½-inch border around the sides. Use a pizza cutter or sharp knife to cut the circle into 8 to 10 triangular slices. Top with half the filling mixture, spreading it evenly over the jam, and use your hands to gently press the filling into the dough so it sticks. Separate one of the slices and roll it up, starting at the wide end and tucking the point of the slice underneath so it doesn't unroll as it bakes. Some of the filling will ooze out as you roll, but that is expected and nothing to worry about. Transfer to the prepared baking sheet, and repeat with the remaining rugelach slices and the remaining dough.

In a small cup, mix together the egg and 1 teaspoon water, whisking with a fork until smooth. Brush the tops of the rugelach with egg wash, then sprinkle each one with a pinch of decorating sugar. Set the baking sheet in the fridge to chill for 30 minutes and preheat the oven to 350°F/177°C. Once the sheet has chilled for 30 minutes, transfer it to the middle rack of the oven and bake until the rugelach are golden brown, 15 to 25 minutes.

Notes

- To make this Vegan: use a nondairy cream cheese and vegan butter, and omit the egg wash.

No-Bake Cherry Cheesecake Parfaits

Makes 4 to 6 • Vegan Option

Special Tools: Electric Mixer; Food Processor

Please proceed with caution. These parfaits are known to be habit-forming and ridiculously easy to make. You didn't misread the title—this miracle dessert does not need an oven, and parfait paradise is just a few ingredients and a few minutes away. Sporting a toasted almond graham cracker crust swirled between smooth layers of silky cheesecake and tangy cherry purée, this is heaven in a cup. Generously topped with fresh cherries and a mint leaf garnish, a dessert this extraordinary needs to include a warning.

FOR THE TOASTED ALMOND CRUST

½ cup (57 g) slivered almonds
4 ounces (113 g) graham crackers (about 8 crackers)
4 tablespoons melted butter or coconut oil

FOR THE VANILLA CHEESECAKE LAYER

1 pound (454 g) cream cheese at room temperature
1 tablespoon vanilla extract
pinch of salt
2 cups (226 g) powdered sugar

FOR ASSEMBLY

1 pound (454 g) fresh or frozen cherries (pitted)
mint leaves, for garnish (optional)

TO MAKE THE CRUST

Scatter the almonds in a dry skillet, and place over medium heat. Cook until deeply toasted and golden, 5 to 7 minutes. Transfer to a plate and place in the fridge or freezer for 5 to 10 minutes until cool.

Place the graham crackers in a food processor, breaking them up slightly with your hands. Add the cooled almonds and pulse until finely ground. Transfer the sandy mixture to a small bowl, add the melted butter, and stir to combine. Use immediately, or transfer to a sealed container in the fridge for up to a week.

TO MAKE THE CHEESECAKE

Place the cream cheese in a large mixing bowl. Beat it on medium speed until light and fluffy. Add the vanilla and salt, then place a fine-mesh strainer over the bowl. Pour the powdered sugar into the strainer, and sift it directly into the mixing bowl. Beat on low speed for a few seconds to incorporate the sugar, then raise speed to medium-high and beat until light and fluffy, 1 to 2 minutes. Use immediately, or transfer to a sealed container in the fridge for up to 3 days.

TO ASSEMBLE

Place half the cherries in a food processor and blend until puréed. Cut the remaining cherries into quarters, setting aside a few whole ones for garnishing the glasses, if desired.

In a dessert glass or small glass cup, place a few spoonfuls of the crust mixture. Use the back of a spoon to gently press it into the bottom of the glass, creating a crust. Pour a few spoonfuls of cheesecake filling over the crust, spreading it evenly. Add a layer of chopped cherries, then top them with another layer of cheesecake. Pour a layer of the cherry purée on top, followed by a final dollop of cheesecake. Top with a sprinkle of the crust mixture, and repeat with the remaining parfaits. Serve immediately, garnished with a whole cherry and a mint leaf, if desired, or keep refrigerated for up to one day.

Notes

- To make this Vegan: use a nondairy cream cheese in the filling and coconut oil in the crust.

Thai Iced Tea Popsicles

Makes about 10 • Gluten-Free

When Ryan and I first started dating, we spent hours on the phone every night. One evening, I noticed something was different—he seemed extra chatty and energetic, speaking so fast I could barely keep up with his rapid-fire sentences. Apparently, he had just finished eating Thai takeout with his college roommates and had polished off an entire super-size Thai iced tea in a matter of minutes, not realizing it contained caffeine. Since he was not a regular coffee drinker, it lit him up like a fireworks display on the Fourth of July, and after a sleepless night bouncing off the walls, he vowed to never drink tea before bedtime again. In this peppy dessert, we take traditional Thai iced tea and turn it into cool, creamy popsicles. Blended with fragrant spices like cinnamon, vanilla, cloves, and star anise, then swirled with sweet condensed milk and cream, these chilly ice pops are light and refreshing and will surely put a spring in your step.

—Adam

2½ cups (591 ml) water
3 black tea bags
1 whole star anise
2 whole cloves
⅛ teaspoon ground cinnamon
3 tablespoons (37 g) granulated sugar
¾ teaspoon vanilla extract
¼ cup (95 g) condensed milk
¼ cup (59 ml) heavy cream
popsicle sticks, if needed

Pour the water in a small saucepan, and bring to a boil. Turn off the heat and add the tea bags, anise, cloves, and cinnamon. Cover pan and steep for 10 minutes. Remove the tea bags and whole spices with a slotted spoon, then pour the tea into a pitcher or large measuring cup and add the sugar, vanilla, condensed milk, and cream. Stir until the mixture is evenly blended and the sugar dissolves.

Pour the tea mixture into popsicle molds, add sticks in the center of each one, and place in the freezer until frozen solid, at least 4 hours. When ready to remove the popsicles, run each mold under warm water for a few seconds, and the popsicles should slide right out. Enjoy!

Margarita Caramels

Makes about 64 bite-size caramels • Gluten-Free

Special Tools: Thermometer

OK, so maybe we did come up with this idea at 2:00 a.m. after a few margaritas. How else would we get inspired to transform one of our favorite drinks into a candy? In this experiment gone right, we took all the flavors of a classic margarita and condensed them into one chewy caramel. Made with freshly squeezed citrus, tequila, brown sugar, and vanilla, it is impossible to have just one of these festive cocktail confections. Start your evening with Easy Homemade Tortilla Chips with Roasted Tomatillo Salsa (page 258), followed by Enchiladas with Chipotle-Marinated Tofu (page 114), then serve these bite-size candies for a Taco Tuesday you will never forget.

½ cup (118 ml) lime juice
½ cup (118 ml) tequila
1 cup (237 ml) orange juice
½ cup (113 g) unsalted butter at room temperature, cut into cubes
1 cup (198 g) granulated sugar
½ cup (107 g) brown sugar
⅓ cup (79 ml) heavy cream
2 teaspoons flaky sea salt, plus more for sprinkling, if desired
1 teaspoon vanilla extract

Line the bottom and sides of an 8-inch square baking pan with two overlapping strips of parchment paper, forming a sling to lift out the caramels later.

Pour the lime juice, tequila, and orange juice through a fine-mesh strainer into a medium saucepan to remove any pulp. Place the pan over medium-high heat, bring to a boil, and simmer, stirring occasionally, until the mixture reduces down to just ½ cup of thick, syrupy liquid, about 30 to 45 minutes.

Remove the pan from heat, then add the butter, granulated sugar, brown sugar, and cream. Stir until blended, then attach a candy or deep-fry thermometer to the side of the pan, with the tip of the probe submerged in the caramel but not touching the bottom. Return the pan to medium heat, bring to a boil, and continue to stir until the temperature reaches 252°F/122°C on the thermometer, about 10 to 12 minutes. Remove from heat, remove the thermometer, then add the salt and vanilla and stir to combine. Pour into the prepared baking pan, jiggling the pan slightly to spread the mixture into an even layer. Transfer to the fridge and cool completely, 3 to 4 hours.

When cool, use the parchment to lift the square of caramel out of the pan. Use a large sharp knife to cut the caramel into squares, sized according to your preference. If desired, top each caramel with flaky sea salt. Wrap the caramels in individual squares of wax paper, and store in the fridge in a sealed container for up to a week. Enjoy!

Abuelita's Flan

Serves 6 to 8 • Gluten-Free

My mom makes the best flan in the world, using a recipe that has been in our family for genera-tions. She learned everything from her mother-in-law, my *abuelita,* whose secret was all in her tech-nique. While most recipes use the oven—often resulting in a spongy dessert closer to a wet cake than custard—she cooked hers on the stove, steaming it gently using a double boiler, resulting in the creamiest flan I have ever tasted. With only four ingredients—five if you count water—it is one of the simplest desserts in this chapter. Ultrasmooth and drizzled in caramel sauce, this silky Cuban custard will change the way you cook flan forever.

—Ryan

1 14-ounce (414 ml) can condensed milk
3 large eggs
⅔ cup (158 ml) water
1 teaspoon vanilla extract
¾ cup (149 g) sugar

In a medium bowl, combine the condensed milk, eggs, water, and vanilla, and blend with an electric mixer or blender until completely smooth and creamy. Set aside.

Place a medium saucepan filled with a few inches of water on the stove. Set a double boiler or a heatproof bowl on top, with the bottom of the bowl resting 3 to 4 inches down inside the pan, just above the water (see note). Set the stove to medium heat, and bring to a simmer.

While the water is heating, place a small saucepan on the stove and add the sugar. Set the heat to medium, and cook until the sugar melts into a light amber liquid, stirring continuously. Once all the sugar has melted, carefully pour the hot caramel into the heated double boiler bowl. Using oven mitts,

carefully turn and rotate the hot bowl to evenly coat the entire inside with a thin layer of caramel. Once coated, set the bowl back onto the pan of simmering water, and pour in the egg mixture. Cover the bowl tightly with foil, and cook until the edges are golden and until a butter knife inserted in the center and moved slightly creates a hole that does not fill with liquid, 30 to 45 minutes. Begin checking the flan with a knife at the 30-minute mark, even if it appears wobbly when the pan is jiggled. Periodically check the water level in the pan to ensure that it does not go dry, adding boiling water from a kettle as needed to keep it at least half an inch deep at all times. Once the flan is finished, remove the bowl from the pan using oven mitts and let cool for 15 minutes, still covered with foil. Transfer to the fridge until fully chilled, at least 4 hours or up to overnight. When ready to serve, uncover the bowl and place the serving plate facedown on top. Invert quickly, and the flan should slip right out onto the plate. Cut into slices, drizzle with any liquid caramel remaining in the bowl, and enjoy!

Notes

- When selecting a bowl to use as a double boiler, it is important that the bowl sits several inches down into the pan (rather than sitting on top), so the steam can heat around the sides of the bowl, not just the bottom.

- After unmolding the flan, there will be a layer of rock-solid caramel at the bottom of the bowl. To clean it out, simply soak the bowl in hot, soapy water and the sugar will dissolve.

Salted Caramel Nice Cream with a Candied Pecan Crumble

Serves 4 • Gluten-Free, Vegan

Special Tools: Food Processor or Blender

Nice cream is one of the greatest inventions in history. Smoother than gelato, as healthy as a plate of steamed broccoli, and just as tasty as any soft serve, this refreshing dairy-free dessert is made by simply blending frozen bananas until creamy—and that's it. In this vegan recipe, we add a splash of almond milk and vanilla, then top it with a salted caramel you will want to eat by the spoonful. Completed with a candied pecan crumble, you can now have an indulgent ice cream sundae without a trace of dairy . . . and none of the guilt!

FOR THE CANDIED PECAN CRUMBLE

1 tablespoon vegan butter
1 cup (100 g) coarsely chopped pecans
¼ cup (53 g) brown sugar
¼ teaspoon ground cinnamon
¼ teaspoon salt

FOR THE CARAMEL

10 medjool dates (175 g), pits removed
¼ cup (59 ml) milk of your choice
1 tablespoon almond butter
½ teaspoon vanilla extract
⅛ teaspoon salt

FOR THE NICE CREAM

12 ounces (340 g) frozen sliced bananas
   (about 3 or 4 medium bananas; see note)
4 to 5 tablespoons milk of your choice
1 teaspoon vanilla extract

TO MAKE THE CANDIED PECAN CRUMBLE

Line a baking sheet with parchment paper and set aside. In a small skillet, melt the butter over medium heat. Add the chopped pecans, brown sugar, cinnamon, and salt, and toss to combine. Cook, stirring occasionally, until the sugar is melted and bubbly, 5 to 8 minutes. Transfer to the prepared parchment paper and spread into an even layer. Let cool completely, 30 to 45 minutes, then break into pieces by hand. Use immediately, or store at room temperature in a sealed container for up to 3 days.

TO MAKE THE SALTED CARAMEL

In a food processor or blender, combine the pitted dates, milk, almond butter, vanilla, and salt. Blend until smooth and creamy, stopping to scrape down the sides as needed. Use immediately, or transfer to a sealed container and keep refrigerated for up to a week.

TO MAKE THE NICE CREAM

Place the frozen banana slices in a food processor or blender, and process until smooth, adding milk a few tablespoons at a time and scraping down the sides as needed. This will likely take a few rounds of mixing, since the bananas tend to clump at first, so gently break them up, stir to loosen, and continue blending. Once the bananas are smooth, fluffy, and creamy like gelato, add the vanilla and 4 tablespoons of the caramel, and blend. Transfer to serving bowls, and top each one with extra caramel to taste and a generous handful of candied pecan crumble.

Notes

- The easiest way to prepare the bananas is to peel them when ripe, then slice into 1-inch rounds. Place them in a plastic ziplock bag in a single layer, then lay the bag flat in the freezer. Once frozen, they will stay fresh for weeks or even months, so they're easy to keep around for any last-minute ice cream cravings.

Chocolate Whoopie Pies with Peppermint Cream Filling

Makes 8 large whoopie pies

Special Tools: Electric Mixer

Look! Up in the sky! Is it a cookie? Is it a cake? No, it's a whoopie pie! This superhero of a dessert is here to save the day. When a cool and creamy peppermint filling is sandwiched between two soft and ultramoist mini chocolate cakes, their powers combine to create a stellar after-dinner treat that will have you and your guests shouting, "Whoopie!" with every bite.

FOR THE CAKES

2 cups (240 g) all-purpose flour

½ cup (42 g) unsweetened cocoa powder

½ teaspoon baking powder

1¼ teaspoons baking soda

½ teaspoon salt

½ cup (113 g) unsalted butter at room temperature

1 cup (213 g) brown sugar

1 large egg

1 teaspoon vanilla extract

1 cup (237 ml) buttermilk

FOR THE FILLING

1 cup (226 g) unsalted butter at room temperature

1 cup (113 g) powdered sugar

7 ounces (198 g) Marshmallow Fluff or other marshmallow spread

2 teaspoons peppermint extract

¼ cup (57 g) crushed peppermint candies or candy canes

TO MAKE THE CAKES

Preheat the oven to 350°F/177°C, and line 2 baking sheets with parchment paper.

In a medium bowl, sift together the flour, cocoa, baking powder, baking soda, and salt. Whisk to combine and set aside.

In a large mixing bowl, beat the butter until light and fluffy. Add the brown sugar and continue beating until smooth. Add the egg and vanilla, and beat until creamy. Add the flour mixture in three additions, alternating with the buttermilk, beating between each addition and stopping as needed to scrape down the sides of the bowl. The batter will be smooth and slightly thicker than regular cake batter.

Scoop about 3 tablespoons of batter onto one of the prepared baking sheets in a small mound, then repeat with the remaining batter, leaving a few inches of space between each scoop of batter. You should end up with about 16. Bake on the two center racks in the oven, swapping positions halfway through, until the edges are dry and the centers of the cakes are set but still appear wet, 10 to 15 minutes (If you have only one oven rack, the pans can be baked one at a time; the batter will be unaffected). Let the cakes cool on the pans for 5 minutes, then transfer to a wire rack to cool completely, 45 to 60 minutes.

TO MAKE THE FILLING

In a large mixing bowl, beat the butter until fluffy. Sift the powdered sugar into the bowl, then continue beating until smooth and creamy. Add the Marshmallow Fluff and peppermint extract, and continue beating until silky. Stir in the crushed candies by hand.

TO ASSEMBLE

Place one of the cooled cakes flat-side-up on a piece of parchment. Scoop or pipe several tablespoons of filling on the cake in an even layer about ½-inch thick. Top with a second cake flat-side-down to make a sandwich. Serve immediately, or keep in a covered container at room temperature for up to 3 days. Enjoy!

Notes

- The cupcakes will stay fresh for up to 4 days in a sealed container in the fridge or at room temperature.

Pumpkin Cupcakes with Chai Frosting

Makes 18

Special Tools: Electric Mixer

News flash! You don't have to wait until October to eat pumpkin. Just because every grocery store turns into a pumpkin parade on the first day of fall doesn't mean you can't enjoy this sweet, orange squash throughout the year—especially when it is presented in the form of a soft, moist cupcake with a velvety chai frosting. Winter, spring, summer, or fall, these warmly spiced cakes are suitable for every season.

FOR THE CUPCAKES
- 2 cups (240 g) all-purpose flour
- 1½ teaspoons ground cinnamon
- ½ teaspoon ground nutmeg
- ½ teaspoon ground cloves
- 1 teaspoon baking powder
- 1 teaspoon baking soda
- ½ teaspoon salt
- 4 tablespoons (57 g) unsalted butter, at room temperature
- ½ cup (106 g) brown sugar
- ½ cup (99 g) granulated sugar
- ⅓ cup (79 ml) vegetable oil
- 2 large eggs
- 10 ounces (284 g) pumpkin purée
- ⅓ cup (79 ml) milk of your choice

FOR THE FROSTING
- 1 cup (226 g) unsalted butter at room temperature
- 3 cups (340 g) powdered sugar
- ½ teaspoon ground ginger
- 1 teaspoon ground cinnamon, plus more for garnish
- ½ teaspoon ground cardamom
- ½ teaspoon ground allspice
- ¼ teaspoon ground cloves
- ½ teaspoon freshly ground black pepper
- ⅛ teaspoon salt
- 2 teaspoons vanilla extract

TO MAKE THE CUPCAKES

Preheat the oven to 350°F/177°C, and line 18 muffin cups with paper liners. Set aside.

In a medium bowl, sift together the flour, cinnamon, nutmeg, cloves, baking powder, baking soda, and salt, and whisk to combine.

In a large mixing bowl, beat the butter, brown sugar, and white sugar until fluffy and creamy. With the machine running, add the oil in a slow stream. Once blended, add the eggs one at a time, mixing after each addition, then the pumpkin purée, and continue beating until smooth. Add half the flour mixture, beat to combine, then add the milk and beat again. Add the remaining flour mixture and beat until just combined. Divide the batter among the prepared muffin cups, filling each one about ¾ full. Bake until a toothpick inserted in the center of a cupcake comes out clean, 15 to 25 minutes. Let cool in the pans for 5 minutes, then remove the cupcakes and transfer to a wire rack to cool completely.

TO MAKE THE FROSTING AND ASSEMBLE

In a large mixing bowl, beat the butter until light and fluffy. Sift the powdered sugar directly into the bowl, then add all the spices and the vanilla, and beat until smooth and creamy.

Once the cupcakes are completely cool, pipe or spread a generous layer of frosting on top of each one and sprinkle with a pinch of cinnamon. Serve and enjoy!

Molten Peanut Butter Chocolate Cakes

Makes 5

Special Tools: Electric Mixer

Attention all chocolate peanut butter lovers out there! This dessert is for you. These luxurious cakes use three kinds of chocolate and reveal a creamy molten peanut butter center when you slice into them. Whether you present these rich and chocolaty personal-size cakes to your significant other on Valentine's Day or wow your dinner guests at the end of a special meal, these freshly baked warm chocolate peanut butter treats are pure decadence on a plate.

FOR THE PEANUT BUTTER FILLING
½ cup (135 g) creamy no-stir peanut butter (see note)
4 tablespoons powdered sugar
¼ teaspoon salt

FOR THE CHOCOLATE CAKES
½ cup (113 g) unsalted butter, cubed, plus more for greasing the ramekins
1 to 2 teaspoons unsweetened cocoa powder, for dusting
3 ounces (85 g) semisweet chocolate (50–60 percent cacao), coarsely chopped
3 ounces (85 g) bittersweet chocolate (70–80 percent cacao), coarsely chopped
¼ cup (30 g) all-purpose flour
½ cup (57 g) powdered sugar
⅛ teaspoon salt
2 large eggs
2 large egg yolks
1 teaspoon vanilla
vanilla ice cream (optional, but necessary in our opinion)

TO MAKE THE PEANUT BUTTER FILLING
In a small bowl, mix together the peanut butter, powdered sugar, and salt. Set aside.

TO MAKE THE CAKES
Preheat oven to 425°F/218°C.

Grease five 4-ounce ramekins with butter, then place a spoonful of cocoa in one of the greased ramekins and tilt it around until the sides and bottom are evenly coated in a layer of cocoa. Pour any excess cocoa into the next ramekin, and repeat until all of them have been dusted.

Make a double boiler by placing a heatproof mixing bowl over a pan of simmering water over medium heat, making sure the bottom of the bowl does not touch the water. Add the butter and both kinds of chopped chocolate, and stir until the mixture is melted and completely smooth with no lumps remaining, about 3 to 5 minutes. Remove the bowl from the pan of water, and place on a rack to cool.

In a small bowl, whisk together the flour, powdered sugar, and salt, then set aside.

In a medium mixing bowl, combine the eggs and egg yolks. Beat on high speed until thick, foamy, and the mixture forms ribbons when the beaters are lifted, about 4 to 6 minutes. Add the flour mixture, vanilla, and warm chocolate, then beat until smooth.

Fill each prepared ramekin about ⅓ full. Scoop a dollop of peanut butter filling in the middle of each one, dividing it evenly between the ramekins (you should not have any filling left over). Pour the remaining batter over the peanut butter, filling the ramekins. There should be about ¼-inch of space at the top of each one, so do not overfill. Arrange the ramekins on a rimmed baking sheet, and bake on the middle oven rack for 13 to 16 minutes, until the edges appear set and dry, and the centers still look soft. Cool on the baking sheet for 1 minute, then carefully invert each ramekin onto a serving plate, and lift to release it onto the plate. Dust with cocoa, if desired, and serve immediately while hot, with vanilla ice cream, if desired.

Notes

- For the peanut butter, using a no-stir variety like Jif will give better results. Natural peanut butters can be oily and don't work well here.

I'm Dreaming of a White Christmas Cake

Makes 1 4-layer, 8-inch cake • serves 16 to 20

Special Tools: Electric Mixer

Sleigh bells will surely be jingling this Christmas when this cheerful beauty makes its grand entrance. In this wintry recipe, four layers of soft vanilla cake are hidden beneath a silky-smooth white coconut frosting. With a smooth and tart key lime filling, and garnished with fresh rosemary sprigs and sparkling sugar-coated cranberries, that white Christmas you have always dreamed of is now a sweet reality. And when it is no longer the holiday season, skip the red and green decorations and enjoy this white wonderland all year long.

FOR THE KEY LIME FILLING
(MAKES ABOUT 2 CUPS)
    finely grated zest from one lime
    ½ cup (118 ml) freshly squeezed lime juice
        (about 3 to 4 large limes)
    1 14-ounce (414 ml) can condensed milk
    2 large egg yolks
    1 tablespoon cornstarch

FOR THE WHITE CAKE
    1 cup (226 g) unsalted butter, at room
        temperature, plus more for greasing
        the pans
    2¼ cups (270 g) cake flour
    1 tablespoon baking powder
    ¾ teaspoon salt
    1½ cups (297 g) granulated sugar
    6 large egg whites, at room temperature
    1½ teaspoons vanilla extract
    1 cup (237 ml) milk of your choice, at room
        temperature

FOR THE SUGARED CRANBERRIES
    1¼ cups (248 g) granulated sugar, divided
    ½ cup (118 ml) water
    1 cup (105 g) cranberries

FOR THE COCONUT FROSTING
    1¼ cups (283 g) unsalted butter, at room
        temperature
    4 cups (400 g) powdered sugar
    ⅛ teaspoon salt
    1 teaspoon coconut extract

FOR GARNISH
    fresh rosemary sprigs

TO MAKE THE KEY LIME FILLING
In a small saucepan, combine the lime zest, lime juice, condensed milk, egg yolks, and cornstarch. Whisk to combine, then set over medium heat. Cook until the mixture thickens, about 5 to 7 minutes, then pour into a heatproof bowl and cover with plastic, pressing the plastic wrap directly onto the surface of the custard to prevent a skin from forming. Refrigerate until completely chilled, at least 4 hours or up to 5 days.

TO MAKE THE WHITE CAKE
Preheat oven to 350°F/177°C. Grease two 8-inch round cake pans, and line the bottoms with circles of parchment. Set aside.

In a medium bowl, sift together the cake flour, baking powder, and salt. Set aside.

In a large mixing bowl, beat the butter and sugar on medium speed until light and fluffy. Add the egg whites and vanilla, and beat until smooth. Add the flour mixture in three additions, alternating with the milk, stopping to scrape down the sides and beating between each addition. Once all the flour is added, beat just until no dry streaks remain, being careful not to overmix. Divide the batter evenly between the two prepared pans, then bake on the center rack until a toothpick inserted into the center comes out clean, 25 to 35 minutes. Transfer the pans to a wire rack to cool for 10 minutes, then invert the cakes onto the racks, remove the parchment paper, and cool completely. Once completely cool, the cakes can be used immediately, or wrapped tightly in plastic and refrigerated for up to 3 days.

TO MAKE THE SUGARED CRANBERRIES
In a small saucepan, combine ½ cup sugar and the water. Set over medium heat and stir until the sugar

dissolves. Remove from heat, add the cranberries, and steep for 10 minutes. While the berries are steeping, line a plate or baking sheet with parchment paper. When the 10 minutes are up, remove the berries with a slotted spoon and spread them on the parchment paper without letting them touch each other. Let dry for 1 hour.

Pour the remaining ¾ cup sugar in a small, wide bowl. Using tongs, drop one cranberry in the sugar and roll it around until evenly coated. Place on a clean dry plate, and repeat with the remaining cranberries. Use immediately, or cover loosely and keep at room temperature for up to 2 days.

TO MAKE THE COCONUT FROSTING

Place the butter in a large mixing bowl and beat until fluffy. Sift in half the powdered sugar, and beat until smooth. Sift in the remaining powdered sugar, then add the salt and coconut extract and beat until creamy, stopping to scrape down the sides as needed.

TO ASSEMBLE

Use a long, serrated knife to cut the cake layers in half horizontally, creating 4 thin layers.

Scoop about 1 cup of coconut frosting into a piping bag or a ziplock plastic bag with a corner cut off. Set aside.

Place one of the cake layers on a serving plate. Pipe a ½-inch-thick band of frosting around the top edge of the cake, which creates a "dam" to hold the filling in place so it doesn't leak out. Scoop a third of the lime filling (about ⅔ cup) onto the center of the cake, and use an offset spatula to spread it into an even layer about ¼-inch thick, spreading it all the way to the ring of frosting. Top with the second layer of cake, repeating the ring of frosting and another third of the filling. Repeat with the third cake layer, making a final ring of frosting and using the remaining filling. Top with the final cake layer. Use the remaining frosting to cover the top and sides of the cake, smoothing it out evenly.

Garnish the top of the cake with the sugared cranberries and arrange sprigs of rosemary around the bottom like a wreath. Serve and enjoy!

Notes

- Almost every component of this recipe can be prepared ahead of time to make things easy. The lime filling will stay fresh in the fridge for up to 5 days. The cake layers can be baked, fully cooled, then wrapped in plastic and refrigerated for up to 3 days before assembly. The sugared cranberries will stay fresh for up to 3 days if stored loosely covered at room temperature. The coconut frosting is best when freshly made, but can be stored covered in the fridge for up to 3 days—but before use, let it return to room temperature and beat again until fluffy.

- Once the cake is assembled and frosted, it can be kept in a covered container in the refrigerator for up to 3 days at peak freshness. If making ahead, do not decorate with the cranberries until just before serving, as the moisture from the frosting will melt the sparkly sugar.

- Bring the cake to room temperature before serving, since cold cake has a more muted flavor.

- To make a 6-inch, 2-layer cake that serves 8 to 10 people, cut the filling, frosting, and cake recipes in half. The layers will be slightly taller, so be sure the cake pans have sides at least 2 inches high.

Gooey Butterscotch Blondies

Makes 9 large or 16 small bars • Vegan

The next time you are craving a brownie, allow us to tempt you with a rich and chewy butterscotch blondie instead. Ooier and gooier than your average chocolate brownie, these one-bowl caramel-y squares are easy to prepare, and when you add a few secret ingredients to the mix, the outcome is pure blondie bliss. With a hint of coffee and a few scoops of almond butter, these celestial treats just so happen to be vegan, ensuring dessert nirvana for all parties involved.

1 tablespoon vegan butter, for greasing the pan
½ cup (160 g) almond butter
1 tablespoon refined coconut oil
1 cup (213 g) brown sugar
1 tablespoon vanilla extract
½ teaspoon salt
¼ teaspoon instant coffee crystals
¼ cup (59 ml) water
1⅓ cups (160 g) all-purpose flour
½ teaspoon baking powder
⅔ cup (120 g) butterscotch chips (see note)

Notes

- To keep the recipe vegan, be sure to buy nondairy butterscotch chips.

Preheat oven to 350°F/177°C, and grease an 8-inch square baking pan with vegan butter. Line the bottom and sides of the pan with two overlapping strips of parchment paper, forming a sling to lift out the blondies later. Set aside.

In a large bowl, combine the almond butter, coconut oil, brown sugar, vanilla, salt, coffee crystals, and water, and whisk until smooth and blended. Add the flour and baking powder, using a spoon or rubber spatula to stir just until no streaks of dry flour remain. Add the butterscotch chips and stir until evenly distributed in the batter. Transfer to the prepared baking pan, and spread into an even layer. Bake 20 to 25 minutes, then set on a wire rack to cool. Use the parchment to lift the blondies out of the pan, and cut into 9 to 16 pieces, depending on your size preference.

The blondies can be served warm from the oven or, once cooled, can be covered and left overnight at room temperature since they are even gooier the next day. Enjoy!

Drinks

Drinks are a sacred part of the human experience. Whether you are enjoying an intimate moment alone or clinking glasses with a large group of friends at a party, we have a beverage for every occasion, from hot, soothing herbal teas to cool, frosty milkshakes and fresh green juices. In this chapter, there are batch cocktail and margarita ideas to make planning your next party a breeze, plus romantic potations to kick things up a notch on your next date night. We'd like to propose a toast to all of you for cooking along with us, so pour something refreshing, raise your glass, and have fun mixing! Cheers!

Pomegranate Moscow Mule

Serves 1 • Gluten-Free Option, Vegan

In this simple spin on a Moscow mule—a cocktail made with vodka, ginger beer, lime juice, and mint—we start with the same fresh ingredients, then add a splash of tart pomegranate juice. You can mix this drink for friends year-round, and it is especially festive during the holidays, with its cheerful ruby-red and mint-green colors served in a shiny copper mug. Pick up a case of your favorite ginger beer—the spicier the better—and let every day of the year be merry and bright.

2 ounces (60 ml) vodka
½ ounce (15 ml) freshly squeezed lime juice
1 ounce (30 ml) pomegranate juice
4 mint leaves
5 ounces (150 ml) ginger beer (see note)
ice, for serving
mint sprigs, for garnish

In a copper mug or similar-size glass, combine the vodka, lime juice, pomegranate juice, and mint leaves. Crush the mint leaves using a muddler or the back of a wooden spoon, then fill the glass ¾ full of ice, add the ginger beer, and stir. Garnish with a sprig of mint. Cheers!

Notes

- Ginger beer is more intensely flavored than ginger ale and is widely available in grocery stores and online. Our favorite is Reed's, which has a bold ginger flavor and a spicy kick.

- To make this Gluten-Free: be sure to use a gluten-free vodka.

Rise and Shine

Serves 6 to 8 • Gluten-Free, Vegan Option

Up and at 'em! The sun is rising, the birds are singing . . . and it's time for a cocktail. There is nothing more appropriate than starting bright and early with a glass of something bubbly at dawn. No need to get dressed or fix your hair—just put on some slippers, stroll leisurely to the kitchen, ignoring the pile of dishes from last night's festivities, and focus your attention on this sparkling glass. Simply made with Earl Grey tea, honey, lemon, and a splash of champagne, this invigorating drink is a distant cousin to a mimosa—with a gently caffeinated kick. Garnished with a slice of fresh citrus, this morning tonic will help make those daily chores just a little bit easier.

3 Earl Grey tea bags
3¼ cups (770 ml) boiling water
1 tablespoon honey
1 tablespoon freshly squeezed lemon juice
1 bottle (750 ml) sparkling wine, such as
    champagne or prosecco
citrus slices, for garnish, if desired

Notes

- To make this Vegan: substitute maple or agave syrup for the honey.

Place 3 Earl Grey tea bags in a heatproof pitcher or quart measuring cup, and add 3¼ cups boiling water. Steep for 2 to 3 minutes, then remove the tea bags. Add the honey and lemon, and stir to dissolve. Cover and refrigerate overnight or until chilled, 3 to 4 hours.

When ready to serve, fill each champagne flute halfway with tea, then the remainder with champagne. Garnish with a slice of lemon or orange, if desired. Cheers!

Strawberry Sangria Sparkler

Makes about 7 cups • Gluten-Free, Vegan

Batch cocktails are ideal for get-togethers. You mix all the ingredients before the guests arrive, taking care of the entire party in a matter of seconds. Plus, this pretty pink drink travels like a charm. Bring it to the beach, and while the kids are building sandcastles and sipping Strawberry Ginger Lemonade (page 240), the parents can enjoy the adult version made with white wine and a splash of sparkling club soda—just make sure to label the pitchers correctly!

FOR THE SANGRIA
1 bottle (750 ml) white wine, such as pinot grigio
3 cups (710 ml) Strawberry Ginger Lemonade (page 240)
1 kiwi, peeled and sliced
1 lemon, sliced
4 to 5 strawberries, sliced
¾ cup (177 ml) club soda

FOR GARNISH
strawberry slices
lemon slices
ice, if desired

In a large pitcher, combine the wine and lemonade, stirring until blended. Add the kiwi and lemon slices, cover, and refrigerate until chilled, about 2 hours. When ready to serve, add the strawberry slices and the club soda to the pitcher, and stir gently to combine. Fill each glass with a few ice cubes, top with more strawberry and lemon slices, then pour in the chilled sangria. Cheers!

Notes

- Strawberries will fade to a whitish-pink color when soaked in sangria, which is why they are added just before serving.

Cool as a Cucumber

Serves 1

Gluten-Free Option, Vegan

Special Tools: Cocktail Shaker

Southern California is famous for its glorious weather. Yes, on certain summer days, leaving the house is like stepping into a hot oven, and the breeze feels like a hair dryer blowing in your face, but other than occasional scorching triple-digit temperatures, we are happy to call this arid metropolis our home. When our city becomes a furnace, we must find preventative ways from overheating—enter this lifesaving drink. Made with freshly squeezed lime juice, your favorite gin, simple syrup, and sliced cucumbers, this light libation is cheaper than running your air conditioner and can make even the hottest of days feel as cool as a cucumber.

2 ounces (57 g) cucumber slices (about 2 inches in length)
1¾ ounces (52 ml) gin
¾ ounce (22 ml) lime juice
½ ounce (15 ml) simple syrup (see note)
thinly sliced cucumber ribbons, for garnish

Place the cucumber slices in a cocktail shaker, and use a muddler or the back of a wooden spoon to mash them. Add the gin, lime juice, and simple syrup, then fill the shaker about ¾ full of ice and shake for 15 seconds. Strain into a chilled cocktail glass garnished with a thin ribbon of cucumber. Cheers!

Notes

- Simple syrup (page 280) is made by combining equal parts water and granulated sugar in a pan on the stove and stirring over medium heat until the sugar dissolves. The syrup will stay fresh in a jar in the fridge for up to 2 weeks.

- To make thin ribbons of cucumber, use a vegetable peeler for the best results.

- To make this Gluten-Free: be sure to use a gluten-free gin.

Love Potion #10

Serves 1 • Gluten-Free Option, Vegan

Special Tools: Cocktail Shaker

Ryan and I met in a recording studio where I was the head engineer. He was a member of the USC jazz choir, which had booked several weeks at our studio to make an album. I noticed him immediately, so I would purposely spend extra time setting up the microphones in his section of the choir, hoping to strike up a conversation. One afternoon, Ryan arrived early with two girls from the group, and while I could tell the ladies were trying to flirt with me, I deflected their questions and directed my attention to the cute, skinny boy in glasses. After the singers left, the choir director and I worked long hours together mixing the songs and became instant friends. One evening, I admitted to him that I had a crush on one of the basses, and the very next day, without my knowledge, he told Ryan my secret after class. Within a few days, we met up for our first date (page 109) before Ryan went home for the summer. We chatted online every day, and when he returned in the fall, we were inseparable. Some people fall in love at first sight, while others take a bit longer to bloom—this light and refreshing cocktail is dedicated to both. Simply made with fresh pineapple juice, vodka, peach schnapps, and elderflower liqueur, this magic potion truly is love at first sip! —*Adam*

FOR THE COCKTAIL
1 ounce (30 ml) vodka
2 ounces (60 ml) St-Germain liqueur
1½ ounces (45 ml) pineapple juice
½ ounce (15 ml) peach schnapps

FOR GARNISH
strawberry cut-out hearts
dry ice chunks, if desired (see note)

Combine vodka, St-Germain liqueur, pineapple juice, and peach schnapps in a cocktail shaker. Fill the shaker about ¾ full of ice and shake for 15 seconds. Strain into a cocktail glass and serve immediately. Garnish with a strawberry heart and drop a chunk of dry ice in the drink to make it bubble and steam, if desired. Cheers!

Notes

- Important: Do not ingest dry ice cubes. Dry ice is safe to use in cocktails, but should never be consumed. Be sure to wait for the ice to dissolve before drinking.

- To make this Gluten-Free: be sure to use a gluten-free vodka.

Tropical Rum Punch

Serves 10 to 12 • Gluten-Free, Vegan

Treat your friends to an island getaway. Light the tiki torches, dust off those string lights, and let's throw a party! This drink couldn't be easier to make; you mix everything in a large punch bowl, then wait for your guests to arrive—and that's it. Garnished with rainbow umbrellas and colorful slices of citrus, the simple prep leaves you more time to make Chili-Lime Garlic Fries (page 161) and hang up tropical tiki decorations—just don't forget to invite us!

12 ounces (355 ml) light rum
12 ounces (355 ml) coconut rum
12 ounces (355 ml) orange juice
12 ounces (355 ml) pineapple juice
6 ounces (177 ml) lime juice
3 ounces (90 ml) grenadine
12 dashes Angostura bitters
18 ounces (532 ml) club soda
ice, for serving
citrus slices, for garnish

In a large serving bowl, stir together the light rum, coconut rum, orange juice, pineapple juice, lime juice, grenadine, and bitters. Keep refrigerated until ready to serve. Just before serving, add the club soda and several cups of ice. Garnish the bowl and serving glasses with citrus slices, and serve with a ladle. Cheers!

The Bee's Knees

Serves 1 • Gluten-Free, Vegan Option

Special Tools: Cocktail Shaker

A few years ago, we became interested in urban beekeeping. We enthusiastically bought a few books on the subject and made a list of supplies to get started, but our research came to a sudden halt after learning that getting stung is a routine part of the hobby. Since there are already several beekeepers in the neighborhood and a healthy population of bees on our property, we decided to find a friendlier pastime that didn't involve so much pain. Thankfully, no one was stung making this citrusy bourbon-based cocktail. Mixed with golden honey, freshly squeezed grapefruit juice, sparkling club soda, and a dash of Angostura bitters, your friends will be buzzing over the Bee's Knees.

1½ ounces (45 ml) bourbon
3 ounces (90 ml) freshly squeezed pink
    grapefruit juice
½ ounce (15 ml) honey
dash of Angostura bitters
1½ ounces (45 ml) club soda
grapefruit slice, for garnish

In a cocktail shaker, combine the bourbon, grapefruit juice, honey, and bitters. Fill the shaker about ¾ full of ice and shake vigorously for 15 seconds. Strain into a cocktail glass and top with club soda. Garnish with a slice of grapefruit. Cheers!

Notes

- To make this Vegan: use maple or agave syrup instead of honey.

Mango Margarita with a Chili-Lime Rim

Serves 4 • Gluten-Free, Vegan

Special Tools: Blender

Transform your next taco night with these delicious margaritas. Blended with frozen mango, lime juice, triple sec, and tequila, this smooth cocktail is crowned by a Tajín rim—a zesty Mexican seasoning made from red chili peppers, lime, and salt. Whether you are observing Margarita Monday or Tequila Tuesday, bust out the blender, invite your friends, and turn any night of the week into a celebration.

---

1 cup (237 ml) silver or gold tequila
½ cup (118 ml) triple sec
¼ cup (59 ml) lime juice
¼ cup (59 ml) simple syrup (see note)
20 ounces (567 g) frozen mango chunks
2 cups ice cubes
Tajín spice, to rim the glasses (see note)
4 lime slices, for garnish

In a blender, combine the tequila, triple sec, lime juice, simple syrup, mango chunks, and ice. Blend just until smooth and no chunks of ice remain, usually less than 30 seconds.

Pour a few tablespoons of Tajín spice onto a small rimmed plate. Wet the rim of a glass by rubbing it with a cut wedge of lime, then dip the rim in the Tajín, coating it evenly. Repeat with the remaining glasses, and garnish each one with a slice of lime. Pour the blended margaritas into the prepared glasses and serve. Cheers!

Notes

- Simple syrup (page 280) is made by combining equal parts water and granulated sugar in a pan on the stove, and stirring over medium heat until the sugar dissolves. The syrup will stay fresh in a jar in the fridge for up to 2 weeks.

- Tajín is a spice blend made with chilies, lime, and salt. Look for it in the produce section of your local grocery store.

Peach on the Beach

Serves 1 • Gluten-Free Option, Vegan

Special Tools: Food Processor or Blender; Cocktail Shaker

Do you hear that? Those are the sounds of summer—sweet grilled corn sizzling on the barbecue, logs crackling in the fire pit, and clinking glasses as you celebrate with friends under the stars. An intimate August evening like this requires a refreshing cocktail, and we have just the solution. Mixed with fresh seasonal peaches, vodka, peach schnapps, a splash of pomegranate juice, lime, and a dash of bitters, then shaken till cool and frosty, this summer sipper will be glowing in the moonlight around your next campfire.

2 ounces (60 ml) vodka
1 ounce (30 ml) peach schnapps
2 ounces (60 ml) unsweetened pomegranate juice
2 ounces (60 ml) peach purée (see note)
1 ounce (30 ml) lime juice
dash of Angostura bitters

In a cocktail shaker, combine all the ingredients. Fill with ice and shake vigorously for 15 seconds. Strain into a cocktail glass. Cheers!

Notes

- To make peach purée, cut a few unpeeled peaches into wedges, discarding the pits. Place them in a food processor or blender, and blend until liquefied, stopping to scrape down the sides as needed. Each peach makes enough purée for 2 to 3 drinks, depending on the size of the peach.

- To make this Gluten-Free: be sure to use a gluten-free vodka.

The Cat's Eye

Serves 1 • Gluten-Free Option, Vegan

Special Tools: Cocktail Shaker

We adopted our cat, Sylvia, from the local humane society in 2010. She was the most social and engaging kitten there, reaching her paws through the cage as we walked by, trying to capture our attention. She is sweet and playful, and she loves to keep us company while we cook—just don't be offended if she hisses at you and hides under the couch, as she is extremely shy around new people. This herbal potion is called the Cat's Eye, in honor of our funny and ferocious ball of fluff. Made with gin, green chartreuse, St-Germain, lime juice, and rosemary simple syrup, this purr-fect drink will have you feline fine in no time.

---

2 ounces (60 ml) gin
½ ounce (15 ml) chartreuse liqueur (see note)
1 ounce (30 ml) rosemary simple syrup
 (page 281)
½ ounce (15 ml) lime juice
½ ounce (15 ml) St-Germain liqueur (see note)
dash of Angostura bitters
rosemary sprig, for garnish

In a cocktail shaker, combine the gin, chartreuse liqueur, rosemary simple syrup, lime juice, St-Germain liqueur, and bitters. Fill with ice and shake vigorously for 15 seconds, then strain into a cocktail glass, and garnish with a sprig of rosemary. Cheers!

Notes

- Chartreuse, a bittersweet herbal liqueur, and St-Germain, a sweet elderflower liqueur, are available in many liquor stores.

- To make this Gluten-Free: be sure to use a gluten-free gin.

The First Kiss

Serves 1 • Gluten-Free

Special Tools: Cocktail Shaker

Our first kiss was on September 23, 2001, at my Los Feliz apartment while watching the entertaining—and apparently romantic—Ken Burns *Jazz* documentary. Neither of us had ever had a boyfriend before, and we were both feeling nervous, as earlier that day, Ryan had proposed a question over Instant Messenger inquiring about where we stood in our relationship. We were anxiously staring at the television screen, our minds racing, wondering if tonight would finally be the night, after four months of chatting online and several dates without a kiss. The space on the couch between us seemed to be growing smaller, as if something were gradually pulling us closer together. Electricity filled the air, then it happened—our lips met for the first time, we completely forgot about the movie, and five years later were married in front of all our friends and family. This velvety after-dinner drink is inspired by that romantic autumn evening that we now recognize as our first anniversary. Mixed with brandy, Kahlúa, chocolate liqueur, vanilla, and cream, you are guaranteed to get a sweet kiss with this drink—since it is garnished with a chocolate kiss on the rim of the glass.   **—Adam**

chocolate kiss, for garnish
1½ ounces (45 ml) brandy
1½ ounces (45 ml) half-and-half
1 ounce (30 ml) chocolate liqueur
½ ounce (15 ml) simple syrup (see note)
½ teaspoon Kahlúa
¼ teaspoon vanilla extract
unsweetened cocoa, for garnish

Notes

- Simple syrup (page 280) is made by combining equal parts water and granulated sugar in a pan on the stove and stirring over medium heat until the sugar dissolves. The syrup will stay fresh in a jar in the fridge for up to 2 weeks.

Garnish the glass with a chocolate kiss before mixing the cocktail: Hold the tip of the kiss between your fingers, and using a match or a lighter, hold the base of the kiss near the flame to soften it—this only takes a few seconds. Gently press the softened part of the kiss onto the rim of a coupe or martini glass, balancing it and holding it in place for a few seconds as the chocolate cools and hardens.

In a cocktail shaker, combine the brandy, half-and-half, chocolate liqueur, simple syrup, Kahlúa, and vanilla. Fill the shaker with ice, then shake vigorously for 15 seconds. Strain into the prepared glass and dust the cocktail with cocoa, if desired. Cheers!

Soothing Ginger-Honey Tea

Serves 2 • Gluten-Free, Vegan Option

When you're feeling under the weather, or just want to get cozy, let a cup of this soothing, hot ginger-honey tea work its wonders. A relaxing way to start the morning, a quiet moment in the afternoon, or a late-night herbal tonic to wind down before bed, this aromatic remedy is a miracle tea. Simmered gently on the stove with sliced ginger, cinnamon, mint, star anise, honey, and fresh lemon juice, this calming blend will warm you up on a cold day and soothe your spirit when it needs a little TLC.

3 cups (710 ml) water
1 ounce (28 g) ginger, thinly sliced (about one 2-inch piece)
1 cinnamon stick
6 mint leaves
1 star anise pod
3 tablespoons honey, divided
1 tablespoon freshly squeezed lemon juice, divided

Notes

- To make this Vegan: use maple or agave syrup instead of honey.

Pour the water into a small saucepan. Add the ginger slices, cinnamon stick, mint leaves, and star anise pod, then place over medium-high heat, cover, and bring to a boil. Lower the heat to a bare simmer, and keep covered for 10 minutes.

While the tea is simmering, prepare the two glasses by pouring 1½ tablespoons of honey and ½ tablespoon lemon juice in each one.

When the tea is done simmering, remove the pan from heat. Remove the herbs and spices using a slotted spoon, or pour the tea through a fine-mesh strainer into a large measuring cup, kettle, or pitcher. Divide the tea evenly between the two prepared glasses, stir well, then serve hot and enjoy!

Strawberry Ginger Lemonade

Makes 6 cups • Gluten-Free, Vegan

We are the proud uncles of two lovely nieces, Stella and Lucia. They live in Portland and have both flown to Los Angeles to stay with us for action-packed weekend visits—cooking their favorite dishes, gardening, and riding every roller coaster at Disneyland until the park closed. During Lucia's trip, she guest-starred on our weekly live Instagram cooking show, making vegan chocolate chip cookies in front of our global audience. When Stella was here, she had the creative idea to add sliced ginger and strawberries as we made lemonade using fruit we picked from our tree. Inspired by those flavors, this three-ingredient thirst-quencher combines our tangy strawberry-ginger simple syrup (page 281) and freshly squeezed lemon juice, making a pretty pink potion that is prepared in just seconds. Served over ice and garnished with slices of lemon, this recipe is dedicated to two of the coolest girls we know.

—*Ryan*

4 cups (945 ml) water
¾ cup (177 ml) freshly squeezed lemon juice (from about 6 large lemons)
1¼ cups (296 ml) strawberry-ginger simple syrup (page 281)
lemon slices, for garnish
ice, for serving

In a large pitcher, combine the water, lemon juice, and simple syrup. Stir to blend, adding a few lemon slices, if desired, then cover and refrigerate until chilled. Serve over ice with lemon slices for garnish. Cheers!

Post-Hike Pick-Me-Up

Serves 2 • Gluten-Free, Vegan

Special Equipment: Electric Juicer or Blender

Just twenty minutes from our house is the breathtaking Angeles National Forest, with hundreds of scenic trails, roaring waterfalls, and landscapes so lush they feel like Hawaii. Considering the number of residents in Los Angeles, we are always shocked at how few people we see on the trails, each time feeling like we have the mountains to ourselves. After a day of hiking, it feels rewarding to return home and rejuvenate with fresh homemade juice, chock-full of vitamins and minerals. Blended with green apples, spinach, ginger, lime, celery, cucumber, and parsley, this emerald-green pick-me-up will help nourish your body and revive you after a long workout on the trails.

2 small handfuls (70 g) spinach
4 green apples (about 150 g each)
juice from 1 lime
2 inch piece of ginger (about 28 g)
2 large celery stalks (about 50 g each)
1 small handful of parsley (about 5 g)
1 large cucumber (about 280 g)

Use an electric juicer to juice all the ingredients into a large measuring cup. Stir to combine, pour into two glasses, serve, and enjoy!

Notes

- No juicer? No problem! Dice all ingredients into chunks, then use a high-powered blender to purée them before straining the mixture through a nut milk bag or a few layers of cheesecloth set over a fine-mesh strainer. Squeeze the pulp to remove as much juice as possible.

Affogato Milkshake with Toasted Marshmallow

Serves 1 • Gluten-Free Option, Vegan Option

Special Tools: Blender

An *affogato* (meaning "drowned" in Italian) is a scoop of vanilla ice cream drowned in a shot of hot espresso. We were feeling imaginative one sweltering summer day and transformed this simple European dessert into a cool, layered milkshake. With just six ingredients and ornamented with a toasted marshmallow the size of your head, you are about to make somebody very happy—especially if that somebody is you.

**FOR THE ESPRESSO SYRUP
(MAKES ENOUGH FOR ABOUT 4 MILKSHAKES)**
1 cup (237 ml) water
1 tablespoon instant espresso powder (see note)
1 tablespoon cornstarch

FOR EACH MILKSHAKE
1 large marshmallow
3 large scoops vanilla ice cream
¼ cup (59 ml) milk of your choice

Notes

- Instant espresso powder is available in the coffee aisle of many grocery stores and online. If you prefer, you can use an espresso maker to brew 8 ounces of espresso, then cool it to room temperature. Pour the cooled coffee into a small saucepan, add the cornstarch, bring to a simmer and cook for 2 minutes until thickened. Chill until ready to serve.

- To make this Gluten-Free: use marshmallows labeled as gluten-free.

- To make this Vegan: use vegan marshmallows, nondairy ice cream, and vegan milk of your choice.

TO MAKE THE ESPRESSO SYRUP
In a small saucepan, combine the water, espresso powder, and cornstarch, whisking to combine. Bring to a boil and simmer for 2 minutes, until slightly thickened. Remove from heat, transfer to a heatproof container, and keep refrigerated until ready to serve, up to a week.

TO ASSEMBLE
First, toast the marshmallows. If you have a gas stove, skewer a marshmallow on a long flameproof stick and hold it above the flame, rotating it slowly for about 30 to 60 seconds until the outside is golden brown—or burned, if you prefer.

If you do not have a gas stove, this can also be done in the oven under the broiler. Set the broiler to 500°F/260°C, and place an oven rack just under the heating element. Place the marshmallows on a baking sheet and set under the broiler until golden and toasted, about 1 to 2 minutes.

To make the milkshake, place the vanilla ice cream and milk in a blender and process until smooth and creamy. Pour into a large serving glass and garnish the rim with a toasted marshmallow. Pour 2 to 3 tablespoons of the espresso syrup over the milkshake, and enjoy!

Horchata with Almond Milk

Serves 4 to 6 • Gluten-Free, Vegan

Special Equipment: Blender; Nut Milk Bag or Cheesecloth

This traditional rice drink is prepared differently around the world. Living in Southern California, we are most familiar with the Mexican version found at every restaurant and taco stand in the city. When you're enjoying a spicy plate of enchiladas, *horchata* tames the tongue and dials down the heat. Lightly sweetened and flavored with cinnamon, vanilla, and a hint of almond, this refreshing dairy-free beverage is the original Kool-Aid.

1 cup (200 g) uncooked long-grain rice
5 cups (1.2 L) water
1 cup (237 ml) almond milk
¾ cup (149 g) granulated sugar
1¾ teaspoons ground cinnamon, plus more for garnish, if desired
1½ teaspoons vanilla extract
¼ teaspoon almond extract

To make rice milk, place the rice in a fine-mesh strainer and rinse until the water runs clear. Let the rice drain briefly, then transfer to a blender. Add 5 cups of water and blend on high speed for 1 minute. Without opening the blender, let the mixture rest at room temperature for 3 hours. Strain through a fine-mesh nut milk bag or several layers of cheesecloth, squeezing to extract all the liquid, then discard the solids. Rinse out the blender, then pour the rice milk back inside. Add the almond milk, sugar, cinnamon, vanilla, and almond extract, and blend until smooth. Transfer to a pitcher and chill until ready to serve. Stir well before pouring, as settling will occur. Serve chilled over ice and garnish with a pinch of cinnamon.

Hot Vanilla with Cinnamon Whipped Cream

Serves 2 to 3   •   Gluten-Free

Special Tools: Electric Mixer

This sweet and comforting recipe is for anyone who doesn't like chocolate. For a simple drink that is just as cozy, hot vanilla should be on every menu where hot chocolate is served. There are no tricks here—just milk and cream, powdered sugar, cinnamon, and vanilla—the only tricky part is not eating the all the cinnamon whipped cream while the hot vanilla is simmering on the stove!

FOR THE CINNAMON WHIPPED CREAM
¾ cup (177 ml) heavy cream
1 tablespoon powdered sugar
¼ teaspoon ground cinnamon, plus more for garnish

FOR THE HOT VANILLA
3 cups (710 ml) milk of your choice
2 tablespoons heavy cream
½ cup (56 g) powdered sugar
¼ teaspoon ground cinnamon
pinch of salt
2 teaspoons vanilla extract

TO MAKE THE CINNAMON WHIPPED CREAM
Place a mixing bowl and beaters in the freezer until chilled, 5 to 10 minutes. Remove the bowl from the freezer, pour in the cream, sugar, and cinnamon, and beat on high speed until soft peaks form, 1 to 2 minutes. Keep the bowl in the fridge while you prepare the hot vanilla.

TO MAKE THE HOT VANILLA
In a small saucepan, combine the milk, cream, sugar, cinnamon, and salt. Whisk to combine, and place over medium heat. Stirring often, heat the milk until it is steamy (not boiling), then remove from heat, whisk in the vanilla, and pour into serving mugs. Top with dollops of cinnamon whipped cream and serve immediately.

Entertaining

Every meal is a celebration. It's how we learn about other cultures, share in centuries-old family traditions, and connect with our friends. In this entertaining chapter, there are twelve crowd-pleasing recipes dressed to the nines and ready to party all night long. From the simplest Heirloom Tomato and Wild Mushroom Bruschetta (page 276) and Easy Homemade Tortilla Chips with Roasted Tomatillo Salsa (page 258) to the mesmerizing Ratafruitie (page 265)—hang up strings of twinkling lights, set a table filled with delicious snacks, and let us know what time you'd like us to arrive.

Tots Two Ways

Special Tools: Food Processor (Cajun Cauliflower Tots)

Tots in twos are better than one, so we had to include a few. Whether you choose the spicy Cajun made with cauliflower or the mashed potato tots filled with a whole head of roasted garlic, the decision is entirely up to you—although we all know that the correct answer is to make both. Surprise your friends with a tater tower at the next Super Bowl party, brighten someone's day by serving these golden puffs with dinner, or enjoy them as a savory snack while you're binge-watching *Stranger Things* for the third time.

Cajun Cauliflower Tots • Makes about 25

12 ounces (340 g) cauliflower florets (about 1 large head)
1 large egg
¼ cup (35 g) finely minced onion
⅔ cup (45 g) panko bread crumbs
⅔ cup (74 g) grated Parmesan cheese
1 teaspoon salt
½ teaspoon freshly ground black pepper

½ teaspoon garlic powder
½ teaspoon smoked paprika
½ teaspoon dried oregano
½ teaspoon dried thyme
½ teaspoon onion powder
⅛ teaspoon ground cayenne pepper
extra-virgin olive oil, for brushing

Garlic Mashed Potato Tots • Makes about 25

1 head garlic
1 teaspoon extra-virgin olive oil
12 ounces (340 g) russet potatoes, peeled and cubed (about 1 large potato)
½ cup (75 g) goat cheese, softened at room temperature
1 tablespoon unsalted butter, melted
1 tablespoon milk of your choice

1 large egg
¼ cup (35 g) finely minced onion
⅔ cup (45 g) panko bread crumbs
1 teaspoon salt
1 teaspoon minced chives
½ teaspoon freshly ground black pepper
extra-virgin olive oil, for brushing

Preheat oven to 400°F/204°C, and line a baking sheet with parchment paper or a silicone baking mat.

FOR THE CAJUN CAULIFLOWER TOTS

Bring a medium pot of water to a boil, then add the cauliflower florets, return to a simmer, and cook 1 minute until blanched. Drain and rinse with cold water to stop the cooking process. Leave in strainer to dry briefly, then transfer to a food processor and pulse until finely chopped. Transfer to a large mixing bowl, then add the egg, onion, bread crumbs, Parmesan, salt, black pepper, garlic powder, paprika, oregano, thyme, onion powder, and cayenne pepper, and stir until evenly blended.

FOR THE GARLIC MASHED POTATO TOTS

First, start with a whole head of unpeeled garlic, and cut off the top ¼-inch so the tops of the cloves are exposed. Place the head cut-side-up on an 8-inch square of foil, then drizzle the top with a teaspoon of olive oil and wrap tightly in the foil, creating a sealed packet. Place in the oven directly on the rack and roast for 45 minutes.

While the garlic is roasting, place the cubed potatoes in a medium saucepan and cover with several inches of cold water. Set over medium-high heat and bring to a boil. Lower heat and simmer until the potatoes are tender when pierced with a fork, 8 to 10 minutes. Drain the potatoes and transfer to a large mixing bowl. Once the garlic is roasted, carefully unwrap the foil packet, let cool for 5 to 10 minutes, then squeeze out the softened garlic cloves, discarding the papery skins. Add the garlic cloves to the potatoes and mash until smooth. Add the goat cheese, melted butter, and milk of your choice, mashing to combine. Stir in the egg, onion, bread crumbs, salt, chives, and pepper until evenly blended.

FOR BOTH TOTS

Use your hands to form the mixture into cylindrical tots, using about 1 tablespoon of the mixture for each one. Place the tots on the prepared baking sheet, leaving about ½ inch between each one, then brush them lightly with olive oil.

Bake on the center oven rack for 15 to 20 minutes, then flip the tots and bake for another 15 to 20 minutes, until browned on both sides. Serve hot, and enjoy!

Notes

- The unbaked tots can be frozen for up to 3 months. After forming the tots and placing them on a baking sheet, simply place the entire sheet in the freezer until the tots are frozen, about 3 hours. Transfer the frozen tots to a sealed container or ziplock bag. When ready to serve, place them on a baking sheet while still frozen, then bake until golden brown, which takes 5 to 10 minutes longer than fresh tots.

Avocado Egg Rolls with Tangy Tamarind Dipping Sauce

Makes 10 to 12 • Vegan Option

Special Tools: Blender or Food Processor; Thermometer

We eat an avocado almost every morning with breakfast and may just weep with joy the day our baby avocado tree starts producing fruit and we get to make our first bowl of homegrown guacamole. In this recipe, inspired by the famed appetizer at the Cheesecake Factory, we feature avocados in the form of a crispy, golden egg roll filled with sun-dried tomatoes, carrots, red onion, and fresh cilantro. Dipped in a mouthwatering tamarind sauce, make sure to have a box of tissues close by since you may just shed a tear too.

FOR THE DIPPING SAUCE
1 tablespoon white wine vinegar
1 teaspoon balsamic vinegar
½ teaspoon tamarind paste (see note)
¼ cup (59 ml) honey
⅔ cup (32 g) coarsely chopped cilantro
¼ cup (32 g) coarsely chopped cashews
2 scallions (30 g), coarsely chopped
1 large garlic clove (5 g), minced or pressed
1 tablespoon granulated sugar
1 teaspoon ground cumin
¾ teaspoon freshly ground black pepper
1 teaspoon freshly squeezed lime juice
¼ cup (59 ml) extra-virgin olive oil

FOR THE EGG ROLLS
3 medium avocados (about 225 g each), halved, peeled, pit removed
¼ cup (45 g) coarsely chopped sun-dried tomatoes
¼ cup (35 g) finely chopped red onion
½ medium carrot (25 g), cut into matchsticks
2 tablespoons (6 g) coarsely chopped cilantro
1½ tablespoons freshly squeezed lime juice
1¼ teaspoons salt
½ teaspoon freshly ground black pepper
1 large garlic clove (5 g), minced or pressed
12 to 15 egg roll wrappers
1 to 2 quarts (1 to 2 L) vegetable oil, for frying
lime wedges, for garnish

TO MAKE THE DIPPING SAUCE

In a small bowl, combine the white wine vinegar, balsamic vinegar, tamarind paste, and honey. Whisk with a fork to dissolve the paste. Pour into a food processor or blender, and add the cilantro, cashews, scallions, garlic, sugar, cumin, pepper, and lime juice. Blend until smooth, stopping to scrape down the sides as needed. Then, with the motor running, add the olive oil in a slow, steady stream, and continue to blend until smooth. If not using immediately, transfer to a sealed container in the fridge for up to 4 days.

TO MAKE THE EGG ROLLS

Place the avocado halves in a medium bowl and mash slightly. Add the sun-dried tomatoes, onion, carrot, cilantro, lime juice, salt, pepper, and garlic, and stir to combine evenly.

Prepare a clean work surface with the stack of egg roll wrappers and a small bowl of water nearby. Lay an egg roll wrapper on the counter with one corner facing you. Spoon about 2 tablespoons of the avocado mixture onto the wrapper, making a horizontal line of filling across the middle. Dip a finger in the bowl of water and lightly moisten the edges of the wrapper. Fold the bottom corner over the filling, then roll the egg roll about halfway up. Take the side corners and fold them toward the center over the filling. Then continue to roll it up from the bottom until it forms a tight cylinder, pressing the moistened edges closed to seal. Transfer the egg roll to a plate, and repeat with the remaining wrappers until all the filling is used.

Pour the vegetable oil into a large, wide saucepan until it is about 2 inches deep. Attach a candy thermometer to the side of the pan, with the tip of the probe submerged in oil but not touching the bottom. Place over medium-high heat and bring the oil to 375°F/191°C, adjusting the burner as needed to maintain a constant temperature. Carefully add a few egg rolls to the oil without crowding—usually about 3 to 4, depending on the size of the pan. Cook until evenly golden on all sides, about 3 to 4 minutes total. Remove the egg rolls from the hot oil using tongs or a spider strainer and transfer to a wire rack to drain briefly. Serve hot with tamarind dipping sauce, and enjoy!

Notes

- Tamarind paste—also used in our Smoky Tamarind Barbecue Sauce (page 286)—is sold in jars in some Asian grocery stores, or you can easily make it yourself. Peel a few tamarind pods, breaking up the fruit with your hands. Place the fruit in a small bowl, pour boiling water over the top to cover, and let sit for 30 minutes. Drain the fruit, remove the seeds, and press the pulp through a fine-mesh strainer to remove the fibers. You will be left with a smooth, tangy paste that is ready to use, and any leftovers can be refrigerated for up to 2 weeks.

- To make this Vegan: use maple or agave syrup instead of honey.

Kale Bites with Lemon Ranch Dressing

Makes about 45

In one of the first photos we took as a couple, the two of us are wearing pajamas, sitting on the floor of Ryan's tiny college bedroom with a plate of kale bites in front of us, about to watch a movie. Staying home and relaxing with games and snacks has always been our favorite way to spend an evening, and while the treats back then may have been frozen packages from the store, over the years we have stepped up our appetizer game. These mini bites are loaded with kale, seasoned with garlic and scallions, and filled with melty gruyère and pecorino romano cheese. Served with tangy lemon ranch dressing for dipping, these irresistible hors d'oeuvres were made for movie nights with friends, cozy on the couch.

FOR THE KALE BITES
- 16 ounces (454 g) coarsely chopped kale, thick stems removed and discarded
- 1½ cups (106 g) panko bread crumbs
- ½ cup (55 g) Italian-style bread crumbs
- 2 ounces (57 g) pecorino romano cheese, grated (about ½ cup)
- 2 ounces (57 g) gruyère cheese, grated (about ½ cup)
- ½ cup (104 g) coconut oil or unsalted butter, melted
- 4 scallions (about 40 g), thinly sliced
- 3 large eggs
- 1 teaspoon salt
- ½ teaspoon freshly ground black pepper
- ¾ teaspoon garlic powder
- ½ teaspoon onion powder

TO SERVE
Vegan Lemon Ranch Dressing (page 283)

Preheat oven to 375°F/191°C, and line a baking sheet with parchment or a silicone mat.

Bring a large pot of water to a boil. Add the chopped kale, using a spoon to press the kale down into the water. Cook for 3 minutes to blanch the kale, then drain and rinse with cold water to stop the cooking process. Dry the kale by the handful, squeezing it tightly to remove excess water, then transfer it to a large mixing bowl. Add the remaining ingredients and toss to combine evenly.

Form the mixture into walnut-size balls, and arrange them on the prepared baking sheet, leaving about ½-inch of space between each one. Bake until golden and crispy, 15 to 18 minutes. Serve warm with Vegan Lemon Ranch Dressing, and enjoy!

Easy Homemade Tortilla Chips
with Roasted Tomatillo Salsa

Serves 4 to 6 • Gluten-Free, Vegan

Special Tools: Blender

In 2012, we traveled to Puerto Vallarta for our cousin's wedding. It was our first time in Mexico together, and during the trip, we signed up for a bus tour that took us outside the city, deep into the jungles of Jalisco. The highlight was visiting a private home, owned by an elderly lady who prepared handmade tortillas over an open flame with simmering clay pots of beans, which we turned into tacos topped with fresh *pico de gallo*. We learned how simple it is to make corn tortillas and how easy it is to transform them into chips. Since you can't throw a party without them, and three ingredients is all you need—corn tortillas, vegetable oil, and salt—why not make them yourself? Still warm, crispy, and fresh from the oven, and served with a spicy green salsa made from roasted tomatillos, onion, jalapeños, garlic, and lime, you will never need to buy chips from the store again.

FOR THE SALSA
1 pound (454 g) tomatillos, paper husks removed
1 medium onion (about 300 g)
1 jalapeño pepper
1 large garlic clove (5 g)
¼ cup coarsely chopped cilantro (about 12 g)
4 teaspoons freshly squeezed lime juice
1¼ teaspoons salt
½ teaspoon freshly ground black pepper

FOR THE TORTILLA CHIPS
10 corn tortillas
1 to 2 tablespoons vegetable oil
several generous pinches of salt, to taste

TO MAKE THE SALSA
Preheat the broiler to 500°F/260°C, arrange an oven rack just under the broiler, and leave the door ajar.

Cut the tomatillos in half, and arrange them cut-side-down on a baking sheet. Cut the onion into quarters or eighths, and place it on the sheet as well. Slice the pepper in half vertically, and if desired,

remove the seeds and white ribs to reduce the heat level—for a mild salsa, remove all seeds and ribs, for medium heat remove half, and for a spicy salsa leave them in place. Arrange the pepper halves cut-side-down on the sheet with the other vegetables, then place in the oven under the broiler. Cook with the oven door ajar until the vegetables are softened and charred in spots, 6 to 12 minutes, watching carefully. Transfer the cooked vegetables to a blender, then add the garlic, cilantro, lime juice, salt, and pepper. Blend until smooth, stopping to scrape down the sides as needed. Transfer to a sealed container in the fridge for up to 2 days.

TO MAKE THE TORTILLA CHIPS
Preheat oven to 350°F/177°C, and arrange the rack in the center of the oven. Place a corn tortilla on a cutting board, and brush the top lightly with vegetable oil. Place another tortilla directly on top of the first, and brush the top with oil. Repeat the

process, making an even stack of tortillas brushed with oil. Use a large sharp knife to cut the stack of tortillas into 8 wedges. Spread the wedges on a clean baking sheet and bake until crispy, 25 to 30 minutes, tossing occasionally. While still hot, sprinkle generously with salt to taste. Serve immediately while still warm, accompanied with roasted tomatillo salsa. Enjoy!

Everything Pretzels

Makes 8 large soft pretzels • Vegan

If you love soft, giant pretzels and are a fan of everything bagels, you are in for a surprise. This is what happens when you get intense cravings for both but can't decide which to make—you combine them into one glorious treat. Introducing the everything pretzel! Topped with a savory blend of sesame and poppy seeds, minced garlic, and onion, these exceptionally soft and chewy, warm homemade twists are truly . . . everything.

FOR THE PRETZELS
1 cup (237 ml) warm water (see note)
1 teaspoon granulated sugar
2¼ teaspoons active dry yeast
2½ cups (300 g) all-purpose flour
1 teaspoon salt
vegetable oil, for greasing the bowl

FOR THE EVERYTHING TOPPING BLEND
2 teaspoons sesame seeds
2 teaspoons poppy seeds
2 teaspoons coarse kosher salt
2 teaspoons minced onion flakes
2 teaspoons minced garlic flakes

FOR THE WATER BATH
5 cups (1.2 L) water
⅓ cup (80 g) baking soda

In a glass measuring cup, combine the warm water and sugar, stirring to dissolve. Add the yeast and stir to combine. Let sit until the top is foamy, about 10 minutes. Pour into a mixing bowl, then add the flour and salt. Stir until the dough comes together, then transfer to a floured work surface and knead until smooth and elastic, 5 to 10 minutes, adding more flour as needed if the dough is sticky. Lightly brush the inside of the bowl with vegetable oil, then gather the dough into a smooth ball and place it in the oiled bowl.

Preheat the oven to 400°F/204°C for one minute, then turn it off. Place the oiled bowl in the warm oven, cover with a kitchen towel, and close the door. Let rise until the dough has doubled in size, 45 to 60 minutes.

While the dough is rising, in a small bowl, combine all the ingredients for the everything topping, and set aside. Line a baking sheet with parchment or a silicone mat. In a medium saucepan, make a water bath by combining the water and baking soda, and bring to a boil.

Once the dough has doubled in size, remove the bowl from the oven, and preheat the oven to 450°F/232°C. Transfer the dough to a floured work surface, and divide into 8 equal pieces. Roll one piece into a rope about ½-inch wide and 12 to 16 inches long. Form the rope into a circle, twisting the ends together, then fold the ends over the bottom of the circle, and press down to create a pretzel shape. Repeat with the remaining ropes of dough.

Carefully pick up one of the pretzels and place it facedown in the boiling water. Cook for 30 seconds, then lift out of the water using a spider strainer and lay it faceup on the prepared baking sheet. Repeat with the remaining pretzels. Once all the pretzels are on the baking sheet, sprinkle them with the everything topping, using all of it to cover the pretzels evenly and generously.

Bake until golden brown, 8 to 12 minutes. Serve warm or at room temperature, and enjoy!

Notes

- To make 1 cup of warm water for yeast, combine ¾ cup of cold water with ¼ cup of boiling water, and voilà: the perfect temperature for proofing.

Hummus Four Ways

Gluten-Free, Vegan

Special Tools: Food Processor

Hummus is the ultimate party food, and since it happens to be gluten-free and vegan, everyone can join in. Rich in protein and high in fiber, this smooth Mediterranean dip is healthy and nutritious—perfectly balancing out the eight-layer Schokoladen Cake (page 181) you plan on seducing your friends with at dessert time. Whip up all four hummus varieties and excite your lucky guests with an epic *mezze* spread—roasted beet, smoky eggplant, roasted garlic, and jalapeño lime. Chop up some veggies, pick out a few fancy cocktails for the evening, and we'll see you tonight at eight o'clock!

Roasted Beet Hummus

1 medium beet (about 125 g)
1 15-ounce (425 g) can chickpeas, rinsed
   and drained
3 tablespoons tahini
2 large garlic cloves (10 g), minced or pressed
3 tablespoons freshly squeezed lemon juice
1 teaspoon salt

½ teaspoon freshly ground black pepper
⅛ teaspoon ground cumin
1 to 2 tablespoons extra-virgin olive oil,
   plus more for roasting the beet
lemon zest, for garnish

Smoky Eggplant Hummus

1 japanese eggplant (about 160 g)
1 15-ounce (425 g) can chickpeas, rinsed
   and drained
3 tablespoons tahini
1 large garlic clove (5 g), minced or pressed
3 tablespoons freshly squeezed lemon juice

1 tablespoon minced parsley, plus more
   for garnish
1½ teaspoons salt
⅛ teaspoon ground cumin
3 tablespoons extra-virgin olive oil

Roasted Jalapeño-Lime Hummus

1 green jalapeño pepper, plus another
   for garnish
1 lime
1 15-ounce (425 g) can chickpeas, rinsed
   and drained
3 tablespoons tahini

1 teaspoon freshly squeezed lime juice
1 teaspoon salt
1 teaspoon chopped mint leaves, plus more
   for garnish
4 tablespoons extra-virgin olive oil, plus more
   for roasting the lime

Roasted Garlic Hummus

1 head garlic
1 15-ounce (425 g) can chickpeas, rinsed
   and drained
3 tablespoons tahini
1 tablespoon freshly squeezed lemon juice
1 small garlic clove (3 g), minced or pressed

1 teaspoon salt
½ teaspoon freshly ground black pepper
3 tablespoons extra-virgin olive oil, plus more
   for roasting the garlic
smoked paprika, for garnish

FOR THE ROASTED BEET HUMMUS

Preheat oven to 400°F/204°C. Wash the beet thoroughly (no need to peel), and trim off the stem and long root. Place on an 8-inch square of foil, brush lightly with olive oil, and wrap tightly to create a sealed packet. Place directly on the oven rack and roast until easily pierced with a knife, about 1 hour. Unwrap carefully and let cool to lukewarm. Transfer to a food processor, and add the chickpeas, tahini, garlic, lemon juice, salt, pepper, and cumin. Blend until smooth, stopping to scrape down the sides as needed, then with the motor running, add the olive oil in a slow stream. Once smooth, transfer to a bowl and garnish with lemon zest.

FOR THE SMOKY EGGPLANT HUMMUS

Preheat oven to 400°F/204°C, and line a baking sheet with parchment paper or a silicone baking mat. If you have a gas stove, lay the whole eggplant directly on top of a burner. Set heat to medium-high, and cook for about 2 minutes, until blackened on the bottom. Turn the eggplant with tongs and cook the second side for another 2 minutes. Continue until all sides of the eggplant are blackened. Transfer to a cutting board, and cut the eggplant in half

lengthwise. Lay the two halves cut-side-down on the prepared baking sheet, and roast in the oven until quite soft and tender, 12 to 15 minutes. (Alternatively, if you do not have a gas stove, you can blacken the eggplant under the broiler instead. Cut the raw eggplant in half lengthwise and place the halves cut side down on a baking sheet. Set under a broiler until the skin blackens, 3 to 4 minutes, then roast as directed for 12 to 15 minutes.) Transfer the roasted eggplant to a cutting board, let cool enough to handle comfortably, then peel off and discard the skins.

Transfer the peeled eggplant to a food processor, and add the chickpeas, tahini, garlic, lemon juice, parsley, salt, and cumin. Blend until smooth, stopping to scrape down the sides as needed, then with the motor running, add the olive oil in a slow stream. Once smooth, transfer to a bowl and garnish with minced parsley.

FOR THE ROASTED JALAPEÑO-LIME HUMMUS

Preheat oven to 400°F/204°C, and line a baking sheet with parchment or a silicone baking mat. Cut the jalapeño pepper in half lengthwise, and remove the seeds and white ribs to adjust the heat level (remove them all for a mild hummus, remove half for medium heat, and leave them intact for a spicy version). Lay the pepper halves cut-side-down on the prepared baking sheet. Cut the lime into thin slices, and arrange them on the same baking sheet in a single layer without overlapping. Drizzle the lime slices with olive oil—about ½ teaspoon per slice— and roast in the oven for 20 to 25 minutes, flipping the lime slices halfway through. Let cool on the sheet for 5 minutes.

Transfer the cooled pepper and lime slices (including the skins) to a food processor, and add the chickpeas, tahini, lemon juice, salt, and mint leaves. Blend until smooth, stopping to scrape down the sides as needed, then with the motor running, add the olive oil in a slow stream. Once smooth, transfer to a bowl and garnish with jalapeño slices and mint leaves.

FOR THE ROASTED GARLIC HUMMUS

Preheat oven to 400°F/204°C. Leave the head of garlic intact, and use a sharp knife to cut off the top ½ inch from the head, exposing the tops of the cloves. Place the head cut-side-up on an 8-inch square of foil, drizzle with a teaspoon of olive oil, then wrap tightly to create a sealed packet. Place directly on the oven rack and roast for 45 minutes. Unwrap carefully, let cool for 5 to 10 minutes, then gently squeeze the cloves out, discarding the papery skins.

Transfer the soft garlic cloves to a food processor, and add the chickpeas, tahini, lemon juice, raw garlic clove, salt, and pepper. Blend until smooth, stopping to scrape down the sides as needed, then with the motor running, add the olive oil in a slow stream. Once smooth, transfer to a bowl and garnish with a few pinches of paprika.

Ratafruitie

Serves 8 to 10

Though ratatouille is typically made by simmering vegetables in a rich garlic-infused tomato sauce, leave it to the Husbands to turn this savory dish into a luscious sweet treat—say bonjour to Ratafruitie! Similar to a dessert tart, thin slices of fresh fruit are layered in a visually stunning spiral pattern and rest on a cloud of smooth vanilla custard with a crunchy graham cracker crust. Throughout the year, Ratafruitie will change with the seasons—have some homegrown summer peaches? Throw them in! Don't like melon? Leave it out! No matter what you decide, this showstopper will turn out beautifully every time.

FOR THE VANILLA CUSTARD CREAM
2 cups (473 ml) half-and-half
8 tablespoons (99 g) granulated sugar, divided
⅛ teaspoon salt
5 large egg yolks
3 tablespoons cornstarch
4 tablespoons (57 g) unsalted butter, cubed
1½ teaspoons vanilla extract

FOR THE CRUST
1¼ cups (142 g) graham cracker crumbs (from about 9 whole crackers, or one sleeve)
¼ cup (50 g) granulated sugar
5 tablespoons (71 g) unsalted butter, melted

FRUIT IDEAS (PICK AT LEAST 5 TO 6)

Year-Round Fruits
½ cantaloupe
1 to 2 mangoes
2 to 3 kiwis

Spring/Summer Fruits
1 to 2 nectarines or peaches
½ pint of strawberries
2 to 3 plums or apricots

Fall/Winter Fruits
2 to 3 apples of different colors
2 to 3 persimmons
2 to 3 pears of different colors
a few tablespoons of lemon juice, to prevent browning

FOR GARNISH
1 fruit of choice, cut into a rose shape (see note)
1 to 2 tablespoons jelly of your choice (see note)
mint leaves

MAKE THE CUSTARD CREAM
In a small saucepan, stir together the half-and-half, 6 tablespoons of sugar, and salt over medium-high heat until simmering.

Meanwhile, in a medium bowl, whisk together the egg yolks and 2 tablespoons of sugar. Add the cornstarch and whisk until completely smooth.

Once the half-and-half mixture is simmering, take a ladleful of the hot liquid and slowly drizzle it into the bowl with the egg yolks as you whisk vigorously. Repeat with another ladleful. Then pour the contents of the bowl back into the simmering saucepan, and stir to combine. Bring to a simmer and stir for another 30 seconds until thickened and bubbly, then remove from heat and quickly add the cubed butter and vanilla extract. Stir until smooth and evenly blended. Let cool slightly, then transfer the custard cream to a heatproof bowl. Cover with plastic wrap, pressing the wrap directly on the surface of the cream to prevent a skin from forming. Refrigerate until completely chilled, at least 3 hours, or overnight.

MAKE THE CRUST

Preheat oven to 350°F/177°C. In a medium bowl, combine the graham cracker crumbs, sugar, and melted butter, and stir until evenly combined. Transfer to a 10-inch oven-safe skillet or round baking dish, and press the crumbs firmly into the bottom and about ½-inch up the sides, creating a crust. Bake for 5 to 7 minutes, then cool completely.

ASSEMBLE THE DISH

Select 5 to 6 different fruits of different colors, depending on what is available and in season. Peel them if needed—like kiwis, mangoes, or cantaloupe—and remove any seeds or pits. Cut the fruits in half, then slice them into ⅛-inch-thin half-moon slices. For fruit that turns brown quickly—such as apples and pears—dip the slices in lemon juice to retain their color.

Spread the custard cream evenly over the cooled graham cracker crust. Decide on which order you want to layer your fruit, then begin placing the fruit slices in a repeating pattern around the edge of the skillet, packing them in snugly. Once the outer circle is complete, start a second row closer to the center of the pan without overlapping. Once that row is complete, there will still be some space in the middle. You can fill it with another small row of fruit slices, or you can make a fruit rose (see note).

Place a few tablespoons of jelly in a heatproof bowl, then microwave it in short 10-second bursts until the jelly is liquified (alternatively, you can do this on the stove in a small pan). Brush the surface of the fruit slices lightly with the glaze until shiny. Garnish with mint leaves, if desired. Serve immediately or refrigerate for up to a day, and enjoy!

Notes

- Brushing the fruit with melted jelly gives it a glossy shine. Pick any flavor you like, but be sure to buy jelly (which is clear and made from fruit juice) and not jam (which has bits of fruit in it).

- To make a fruit rose, first select a soft fruit that will bend well when thinly sliced, such as a nectarine, mango, or kiwi. Cut the fruit in half and remove the seed as needed. Place one half flat-side-down on a large cutting board. Using a very sharp knife, slice it into thin ¹⁄₁₆-inch slices, keeping the slices together as you cut. Slowly slide the slices across each other, fanning them out until they make a long line of overlapping slices. Starting at one end, gently roll the slices up until they form a spiral rose shape.

Curry Deviled Eggs

Makes 12   •   Gluten-Free

Despite their name, deviled eggs are oh so heavenly. Both our grandmothers prepared them for us when we were growing up, we have continued to make them for each other throughout our relationship, and they are just so darn cute. This Indian-inspired version—mixed with garlic, curry, turmeric, cumin, and a pinch of cayenne—is intensely flavorful with a hint of devilish heat. Garnished with fresh cilantro and a sprinkle of golden curry powder, this light hors d'oeuvre is perfect before a heavy meal, and an angelic low-calorie snack the next time you get a case of the munchies.

6 large eggs
3 tablespoons mayonnaise
1 tablespoon dijon mustard
1 teaspoon white wine vinegar
2 teaspoons curry powder, plus more for
  garnish, if desired
½ teaspoon salt
¼ teaspoon ground turmeric
⅛ teaspoon ground cumin
pinch of garlic powder
pinch of ground cayenne pepper
chopped cilantro, for garnish

Place the eggs in a medium saucepan, and add enough cold water to cover by at least 1 inch. Bring to a boil over medium-high heat, then immediately turn off the stove and let the pan rest for 12 minutes. Remove the eggs from the pan, place in a strainer, and rinse with cold water to stop the cooking process. Peel and discard the shells, then cut the eggs in half lengthwise.

Scoop the egg yolks into a medium bowl, leaving the whites intact. To the yolks add the mayonnaise, mustard, vinegar, curry powder, salt, turmeric, cumin, garlic powder, and cayenne pepper, stirring until smooth and blended. Divide the filling mixture among the 12 egg halves, using a pastry bag and piping tip, a ziplock plastic bag with the corner cut off, or by simply spooning it in by hand. Garnish with chopped cilantro and a few pinches of curry powder, if desired. Serve at room temperature or chilled, and enjoy!

Notes

- The finished eggs will stay fresh covered in the fridge for up to 2 days.

Spring Tarts with Asparagus, Sun-Dried Tomatoes, and Goat Cheese

Makes 10 to 12 4-inch tarts

Set your clocks one hour ahead, and spring forward with these zesty tarts. The sun is shining and love is in the air, so open the windows, dust off those cobwebs, and throw an equinox extravaganza with sparkling cocktails and seasonal hors d'oeuvres. In this spring celebration, tender asparagus spears are lightly sautéed with garlic and sun-dried tomatoes and rest on a bed of creamy goat cheese. Sprinkled with lemon zest and red pepper flakes and nestled in a flaky, buttery crust made with fresh thyme, these irresistible mini tarts are a ray of springtime sunshine.

FOR THE CRUST

1¼ cups plus 2 tablespoons (165 g) all-purpose flour

½ teaspoon salt

1 tablespoon fresh thyme leaves, minced

½ cup (113 g) unsalted butter, cubed and chilled

¼ cup (58 g) greek yogurt or sour cream

2 teaspoons freshly squeezed lemon juice

¼ cup (59 ml) ice water

FOR THE SAUTÉED VEGETABLES

2 tablespoons extra-virgin olive oil

1½ cups (150 g) asparagus cut into 1-inch lengths

2 large garlic cloves (10 g), minced

¾ cup (100 g) thinly sliced sun-dried tomatoes

½ teaspoon salt

½ teaspoon freshly ground black pepper

FOR ASSEMBLY AND GARNISH

8 ounces (227 g) goat cheese, warmed slightly in the microwave to a spreadable texture, about 10 to 12 seconds

a few pinches of flaky sea salt

a few grinds of black pepper

a few pinches of red pepper flakes

lemon zest, for garnish

TO MAKE THE CRUST

In a large mixing bowl, combine the flour, salt, and thyme leaves. Add the cold butter cubes, and use a pastry cutter to blend in the butter until the largest pieces are the size of peas. In a measuring cup, stir together the yogurt, lemon juice, and ice water, then pour over the flour mixture. Stir until the dough comes together, using your hands to gather any loose scraps into one ball of dough. Form into a rough disc shape, wrap tightly in plastic, and refrigerate for at least 1 hour or up to 2 days.

Preheat oven to 400°F/204°C. Roll out the dough on a floured work surface until it is about ⅛-inch thick. Place a mini tart pan facedown on the dough, and cut a circle of dough about ¼-inch around the pan. Repeat and make additional circles of dough until it is all used up, gathering the scraps and rerolling as needed. Press the circles of dough into the bottom and sides of the mini tart pans, trimming off any excess. Fill as many tart pans as you have available; they can be reused after baking to make additional rounds of crusts as needed.

Arrange the tarts on a baking sheet, place a small square of foil over each one, and fill each tart with pie weights, dried beans, dry rice, or metal coins to keep the crusts from puffing up. Bake until golden and crisp, 14 to 16 minutes. Remove the weights and the foil, and let the tarts cool on a wire rack. Remove the crusts from the tart pans and repeat the process with any remaining unbaked dough.

TO MAKE THE SAUTÉED VEGETABLES

Set a large skillet over medium heat, and when hot, add the oil. Sauté the asparagus until crisp-tender, 5 to 6 minutes. Add the garlic, sun-dried tomatoes, salt, and pepper, and cook for 60 seconds, then remove from heat.

TO ASSEMBLE THE TARTS

Spread a generous layer of goat cheese in each crust, then top with spoonfuls of sautéed vegetables to fill the tart (a 4-inch tart will use about 2 to 3 tablespoons). Garnish with pinches of flaky sea salt, black pepper, red pepper flakes, and lemon zest. Serve warm, and enjoy!

Potstickers with Spicy Dipping Sauce

Makes about 40 • Vegan

Making homemade potstickers is easier than you think. There are no special tools needed, and folding them up is as simple as sealing a ziplock bag. You can make one large batch, store them in the freezer, and enjoy handmade potstickers for months—anytime the craving strikes. Also known as *jiaozi* in China or *gyoza* in Japan, these tender dumplings are filled with sautéed carrots, crisp daikon, bok choy, ginger, garlic, and scallions, then pan-fried until golden and crispy and served with a spicy dipping sauce. You will be a potsticker pro in no time!

4 tablespoons vegetable oil, divided
2 cups (200 g) finely chopped onion (about 1 medium onion)
3 cups (185 g) sliced bok choy cabbage (about 2 small cabbages)
2 cups (155 g) grated carrots (about 2 medium carrots)
1 cup (120 g) grated daikon radish (about one 6-inch piece)
⅔ cup (40 g) sliced scallions (about 3 scallions)
4 teaspoons tamari or soy sauce
2 tablespoons (24 g) minced ginger
3 large garlic cloves (15 g), minced
40 *gyoza* wrappers (see note)
Gyoza Dipping Sauce, for serving (page 279)

Place a large, deep skillet over medium heat, and add 2 tablespoons of vegetable oil. When hot, add the onion and cook until softened, about 5 minutes. Add the bok choy, carrots, daikon, and scallions, and cook for 4 minutes until softened, stirring occasionally. Add the tamari, ginger, and garlic, and cook for 1 to 2 minutes more. Remove from heat and transfer the vegetable mixture to a bowl or plate to cool enough to handle comfortably. Use the filling immediately, or transfer to a sealed container in the fridge for up to 3 days.

To make the potstickers, first prepare a work station with the *gyoza* wrappers, the bowl of filling, a small bowl filled with water to wet your fingers, and a tray lined with parchment for the finished dumplings.

Hold one *gyoza* wrapper flat in the palm of your hand. Scoop about 2 heaping teaspoons of filling into the center of the wrapper. Using your other hand, dip a finger in the bowl of water, then lightly moisten the edges of the wrapper. Fold the wrapper over, pinching and pleating the edges to seal them tightly. Place on the prepared tray, and repeat with the remaining wrappers until all the filling is used up, arranging the finished potstickers so they are not touching. They can be cooked immediately, or frozen for future use (freeze them directly on the tray, then transfer to a sealed container in the freezer for up to 2 months).

Place a large, deep skillet over medium heat, and add the remaining 2 tablespoons of vegetable oil. When hot, place the potstickers flat-side-down in the skillet in a single layer, as many as will fit comfortably without touching. Cook without stirring until deeply browned on the bottom, 2 to 4 minutes (add 1 to 2 minutes of cooking time if frozen). Without stirring, add ¼ cup of water and immediately cover the pan, as it will spatter aggressively. Cook for 2 to 3 minutes, then remove the lid and continue to cook until all the water evaporates. Serve immediately with dipping sauce and enjoy!

Notes

- *Gyoza* or potsticker wrappers are available in many grocery stores; look for them in the refrigerated section. They are circular and slightly thicker than wonton wrappers, but wonton wrappers will work if *gyoza* wrappers are unavailable.

Cheddar-Beer Fondue

Serves 4 to 6

Many tears were shed when our local fondue restaurant closed. We used to visit on birthdays and anniversaries, because what better way to celebrate than with a bubbly pot of melted cheese? The closure has been a blessing in disguise, since it compelled us to experiment in the kitchen and create our own recipe. In this Swiss appetizer, sautéed garlic and shallots are simmered with sharp cheddar cheese, creamy gruyère, and lager-style beer until smooth and melty. Warmed over a candle flame, and served with an assortment of fun dunking options, get out your fondue forks and let the dipping commence!

9½ ounces (269 g) sharp cheddar cheese, grated (about 2½ cups)
6½ ounces (184 g) gruyère cheese, grated (about 1½ cups)
1 tablespoon all-purpose flour
1½ teaspoons mustard powder
⅛ teaspoon ground cayenne pepper
2 tablespoons extra-virgin olive oil
1 small shallot (40 g) minced
2 large garlic cloves (10 g), minced
1 cup (237 ml) lager-style beer (see note)
¼ teaspoon worcestershire sauce (see note)

DIPPING SUGGESTIONS
bread cubes
apple slices
cauliflower florets
broccoli florets
cherry tomatoes
carrot sticks
celery sticks

Preheat the oven to 200°F/93°C, and place an empty fondue pot or other serving vessel inside to warm up while you prepare the fondue.

In a medium bowl, combine the grated cheddar and gruyère, then add the flour, mustard powder, and cayenne pepper. Toss to combine, and set aside.

Place a medium saucepan over medium heat and add the olive oil. When hot, add the minced shallot and simmer until soft, about 2 to 3 minutes, stirring often. Add the garlic and sauté for 30 seconds. Add the beer and bring to a simmer, then add the cheese mixture a small handful at a time, whisking with a fork between additions until smooth and creamy. Add the worcestershire sauce and stir to blend. Carefully pour the hot fondue into the warmed pot, and serve immediately with a variety of dipping options. If desired, set the pot over a heat source to keep the fondue warm. Enjoy!

Notes

- Pre-shredded bagged cheese is coated with cellulose and other additives that affect the texture of the fondue, so buying blocks of cheese and grating them yourself is recommended.

- For the beer, a light lager is preferable. IPAs and other bitter beers can overwhelm the flavor.

- Worcestershire sauce typically contains fish, but there are vegetarian varieties available at natural food stores.

Heirloom Tomato and Wild Mushroom Bruschetta

Serves 6 to 8 • Gluten-Free Option, Vegan

Special Tools: Food Processor

Bruschetta is the perfect way to begin a meal. Fresh summer flavors of tomatoes, basil, and garlic served on a crusty baguette make an appetizing appetizer that won't fill your appetite. In this easy recipe, we use garden-ripe heirloom tomatoes for extra sunshiny flavor, then sprinkle them over a garlicky wild mushroom and olive tapenade blended with lemon zest and fresh parsley. Drizzled with balsamic vinegar and topped with pinches of flaky sea salt, black pepper, and red chili flakes, your favorite Italian starter now has a tasty tapenade twist.

FOR THE SAUTÉED MUSHROOMS
2 tablespoons extra-virgin olive oil
16 ounces (454 g) mushroom variety of your
   choice, sliced
3 large garlic cloves (15 g), minced
1¼ teaspoons salt
½ teaspoon freshly ground black pepper
¼ cup (12 g) finely chopped parsley
⅛ teaspoon red pepper flakes
zest from 1 lemon
1 tablespoon coarsely chopped marinated olives
   (such as kalamata or niçoise)
1 large garlic clove (5 g), pressed

FOR ASSEMBLY
1 large baguette, gluten-free if desired
a few teaspoons of balsamic vinegar, divided
2 to 3 large heirloom tomatoes of different
   colors, coarsely chopped
8 to 10 basil leaves, thinly sliced
a few pinches of flaky sea salt
freshly ground black pepper
red pepper flakes

TO MAKE THE SAUTÉED MUSHROOMS
Place a large, deep skillet over medium heat and add the olive oil. When hot, add the mushrooms and cook until softened, 8 to 10 minutes, stirring occasionally. Add the garlic, salt, black pepper, and parsley, and cook for another 30 to 45 seconds.

Remove from heat and let cool briefly. Transfer to a food processor, add the red pepper flakes, lemon zest, olives, and raw garlic, and pulse just until finely chopped but still chunky—not a smooth paste. The mushrooms can be used immediately, or kept in a sealed container in the fridge for up to 4 days. If refrigerating, warm the mushroom mixture in the microwave or on the stove before assembling the bruschetta.

TO ASSEMBLE
Slice the baguette thinly, cutting diagonally rather than straight across to create larger slices. If desired, toast the baguette slices until crispy—in a skillet on the stove, under a broiler for 1 to 2 minutes, or in a 375°F/191°C oven for about 10 minutes.

Drizzle a tiny amount (about ¼ teaspoon) of balsamic vinegar over a slice of baguette. Scoop a generous spoonful of the mushroom mixture over the slice in an even layer. Top with a layer of chopped tomatoes and a pinch of shredded basil. Place on a serving tray and repeat with the remaining baguette slices. Sprinkle the slices with a few pinches of flaky sea salt, grinds of black pepper, and red pepper flakes. Serve warm, and enjoy!

Condiments

Dressings, syrups, and dips, oh my! Your taste buds will be over the rainbow when they sample the colorful flavors throughout the next few pages. With eight simple syrups to enhance your home bar, six salad dressings to stock your fridge, scrumptious sauces, tangy aiolis, and everything for your dipping essentials, turn the page and follow the yellow brick road to the Wonderful Chapter of Condiments.

Husbands' Aioli

Makes about ½ cup • Gluten-Free, Vegan Option

This simple aioli belongs in every grocery store in America. Whenever we steam artichokes, this is our go-to dip, and for years, I have been telling Ryan we need to bottle this million-dollar sauce so the world can know about it. Maybe one day, Husbands' Aioli will appear on every shelf across the country, but until then, the secret recipe is revealed here for the first time. This tangy dip comes together in seconds, making a delicious drizzle for steamed vegetables and a smooth spread for sandwiches. Make a batch now—before it becomes a household name!

—*Adam*

½ cup (113 g) mayonnaise or vegan mayo
1 tablespoon white wine vinegar
¼ teaspoon garlic powder
¼ teaspoon smoked paprika
¼ teaspoon dried dill
¼ teaspoon salt
¼ teaspoon freshly ground black pepper

In a small bowl, combine all the ingredients and stir to blend. Use immediately or transfer to a sealed container in the fridge for up to a week.

Notes

- To make this Vegan: use vegan mayonnaise.

Gyoza Dipping Sauce

Makes about ½ cup • Gluten-Free Option, Vegan

If dumplings could talk, they would ask where this spicy sauce has been all their lives. A match made in heaven, this bright Japanese condiment gives potstickers (page 272) some zing and makes spring rolls sing! Try it as a zesty marinade for tofu, or a simple sauce for your next stir-fry—just have your cameras ready, because there is nothing more entertaining than a singing spring roll.

¼ cup (60 ml) rice vinegar
¼ cup (60 ml) tamari or soy sauce
½ teaspoon sesame oil
¼ teaspoon red pepper flakes
⅛ teaspoon garlic powder
⅛ teaspoon ginger powder

Notes

- To make this Gluten-Free: use tamari instead of soy sauce.

In a small bowl or measuring cup, stir together all the ingredients. Let sit for 15 minutes before serving to allow the flavors to blend. Use immediately or keep in a sealed container in the fridge for up to a week.

Eight Simple Syrups

Gluten-Free, Vegan

With these eight simple syrups to choose from, you will never have to go out for drinks again. Combined with your favorite spirits to make festive cocktails, these assorted tonics will quench everyone's thirst and turn happy hour into the happiest of hours. With cool Cucumber Mint to help rejuvenate on a hot day, and Spicy Jalapeño that will surely heat things up, pick out some stylish cocktail garnishes, set out a tip jar, and watch how quickly your friends fill it up.

CLASSIC
1½ cups (355 ml) water
1½ cups (297 g) granulated sugar

VANILLA LAVENDER
1½ cups (355 ml) water
1½ cups (297 g) granulated sugar
½ of 1 vanilla bean, split in half, seeds scraped
    into the pan
1 tablespoon dried lavender

CUCUMBER MINT
1½ cups (355 ml) water
1½ cups (297 g) granulated sugar
½ large cucumber (130 g), thinly sliced
15 to 20 mint leaves

LEMONGRASS THYME
1½ cups (355 ml) water
1½ cups (297 g) granulated sugar
2 stalks of lemongrass, coarsely chopped
2 to 3 thyme sprigs

BROWN SUGAR CINNAMON
1½ cups (355 ml) water
1½ cups (315 g) brown sugar
2 cinnamon sticks, crushed

SPICY JALAPEÑO
1½ cups (355 ml) water
1½ cups (297 g) granulated sugar
1 medium-size jalapeño pepper, sliced

ROSEMARY
1½ cups (355 ml) water
1½ cups (297 g) granulated sugar
4 to 6 rosemary sprigs

STRAWBERRY GINGER
1½ cups (355 ml) water
1½ cups (297 g) granulated sugar
1 pound (454 g) strawberries, sliced
2 ounces (57 g) sliced ginger (about a 4-inch
    piece)

TO MAKE CLASSIC SIMPLE SYRUP
In a small saucepan, combine the water and sugar. Bring to a simmer over medium heat, stirring to dissolve the sugar. Once all the sugar is dissolved and the mixture is clear, turn off the heat. Let cool briefly, then transfer to a sealed container in the fridge to chill. The syrup will stay fresh for up to 2 weeks.

TO MAKE FLAVORED SIMPLE SYRUP
In a small saucepan, combine the water, sugar, and desired ingredients. Bring to a simmer over medium heat, stirring to dissolve the sugar. Once simmering, cover the pan, turn the heat as low as possible, and simmer gently for 10 minutes. Turn off the heat and let the mixture steep, covered, for 15 to 20 minutes. Pour through a fine-mesh strainer to remove any solids, then transfer to a sealed container in the fridge to chill. The syrup will stay fresh for up to 2 weeks.

Notes

- Need some classic simple syrup in a hurry? You can combine equal parts water and sugar in a glass and stir until the sugar dissolves—no stove necessary. It takes several minutes of stirring, but it works!

Six Salad Dressings

Making salad dressing is as easy as pouring a bowl of cereal. With these six elegant options, you can breathe new life into those packed work lunches, save a few extra calories by enjoying a bowl of tossed greens for dinner, or treat yourself to a colorful garden salad for a light afternoon snack. From the tangy Vegan Lemon Ranch Dressing to the Classic Italian Vinaigrette, make all six dressings, stock your fridge, and create the salad bar of your dreams.

Vegan Lemon Ranch Dressing • Gluten-Free, Vegan

1 cup (225 g) vegan mayonnaise
¼ cup (59 ml) milk of your choice
1 teaspoon lemon zest
1 to 2 tablespoons freshly squeezed lemon juice
1 tablespoon minced parsley
½ teaspoon salt
¼ teaspoon freshly ground black pepper
½ teaspoon garlic powder
¼ teaspoon onion powder
⅛ teaspoon smoked paprika

In a small bowl, whisk together all the ingredients until smooth. Taste for salt and lemon, and adjust as needed. Transfer to a sealed container in the fridge for up to a week.

Vegan Sriracha Ranch Dressing • Gluten-Free, Vegan

1 cup (225 g) vegan mayonnaise
¼ cup (59 ml) milk of your choice
3 tablespoons plus 1 teaspoon (50 ml) sriracha
   hot sauce
1 tablespoon minced parsley
½ teaspoon salt
¼ teaspoon freshly ground black pepper
½ teaspoon garlic powder
¼ teaspoon onion powder
⅛ teaspoon smoked paprika

In a small bowl, whisk together all the ingredients until smooth. Transfer to a sealed container in the fridge for up to a week.

Mandarin-Lime Vinaigrette • Gluten-Free, Vegan

½ cup plus 1 tablespoon (133 ml) freshly
  squeezed mandarin orange juice
3 tablespoons freshly squeezed lime juice
6 large garlic cloves (30 g), minced or pressed
1½ teaspoons salt
1½ teaspoons freshly ground black pepper
¾ cup (177 ml) extra-virgin olive oil

In a small bowl, combine the orange juice, lime juice, garlic, salt, and pepper. While whisking, slowly add the oil and whisk to blend. Transfer to a sealed container in the fridge for up to a week.

Classic Italian Vinaigrette • Gluten-Free

¼ cup (59 ml) white wine vinegar
1 large garlic clove (5 g), minced or pressed
1 teaspoon salt
1 teaspoon freshly ground black pepper
¼ teaspoon granulated sugar
2 tablespoons (15 g) finely grated pecorino
  romano cheese
¾ cup (177 ml) extra-virgin olive oil

In a small bowl, combine the vinegar, garlic, salt, pepper, sugar, and pecorino romano cheese. While whisking, slowly add the oil and whisk to blend. Transfer to a sealed container in the fridge for up to a week.

Creamy Avocado-Cilantro Dressing • Gluten-Free, Vegan Option

Special Tools: Food Processor

1 medium avocado (160 g), peeled and pit
  removed
½ cup (125 g) greek yogurt
1 large garlic clove (5 g), minced or pressed
1 cup (48 g) coarsely chopped cilantro
3 tablespoons lime juice
1 teaspoon salt
½ teaspoon freshly ground black pepper
2 tablespoons extra-virgin olive oil
¾ to 1 cup (177 to 237 ml) water, to thin

In a food processor or blender, combine the avocado, yogurt, garlic, cilantro, lime juice, salt, pepper, and olive oil. Pulse until blended, stopping to scrape down the sides of the bowl as needed, then with the motor running, add the water until the desired consistency is reached. Transfer to a sealed container in the fridge for up to a week.

Notes

- To make this Vegan: use vegan mayo or sour cream instead of greek yogurt.

Zesty Sesame-Ginger Dressing • Gluten-Free Option, Vegan Option

¼ cup (59 ml) rice vinegar
1½ tablespoons tamari or soy sauce
1 large garlic clove (5 g), minced or pressed
½ tablespoon honey
1 tablespoon (16 g) grated fresh ginger
¼ teaspoon freshly ground black pepper
1 teaspoon sesame seeds
½ cup (118 ml) extra-virgin olive oil
¼ cup (59 ml) sesame oil

In a small bowl, combine the vinegar, tamari, garlic, honey, grated ginger, pepper, and sesame seeds. While whisking, slowly add the olive oil and sesame oil and whisk to blend. Transfer to a sealed container in the fridge for up to a week.

Notes

- To make this Gluten-Free: use tamari instead of soy sauce.

- To make this Vegan: use maple or agave syrup instead of honey.

Smoky Tamarind Barbecue Sauce

Gluten-Free Option, Vegan

Special Tools: Immersion Blender or Standard Blender

For years, we have been on a quest to find the best barbecue sauce. We have climbed the highest mountains and scoured the seven seas searching for the perfect match, but most store-bought brands aren't quite right—they are too sweet, too acidic, or filled with enough preservatives to stock a chemistry set. Thankfully, we realized that making our own could not be easier, and now we're bottling it by the gallon. This bold sauce is perfectly balanced—tart from tamarind paste, subtly sweet, and smoky with a hint of peppery heat. It is the star of our Meatless Western Bacon Cheeseburgers (page 106), the secret ingredient in our Barbecue Baked Beans (page 151), and a divine dip for Garlic Mashed Potato Tots (page 251). Our condiment quest is complete, and this ruby-red treasure made it all worth it.

1 tablespoon extra-virgin olive oil
1 medium onion (320 g), chopped
2 large garlic cloves (10 g), minced
1 cup (285 g) tomato paste
1 tablespoon tamarind paste (see note)
¼ cup (59 ml) apple cider vinegar
2 tablespoons molasses
6 tablespoons (80 g) brown sugar
2 tablespoons yellow mustard
¼ cup (59 ml) tamari or soy sauce
1½ tablespoons liquid smoke
1 tablespoon chili powder
pinch of ground cayenne pepper

Pour the oil into a medium saucepan, and place over medium heat. When hot, add the onions and sauté until softened, 7 to 9 minutes. Add the garlic and cook 1 minute. Add all the remaining ingredients and stir until blended. Cover, bring to a simmer, and cook for 10 to 15 minutes, stirring occasionally. Purée the sauce—either using an immersion blender or a standard blender—then let cool and keep refrigerated in a sealed container for up to 3 weeks.

Notes

- Tamarind paste or pulp—also used in our Avocado Egg Rolls with Tangy Tamarind Dipping Sauce (page 254)—is sold in jars in some Asian grocery stores, or you can easily make it yourself. Peel a few tamarind pods, breaking up the fruit with your hands. Place the fruit in a small bowl, pour boiling water over the top to cover, and let sit for 30 minutes. Drain the fruit, remove the seeds, and press the pulp through a fine-mesh strainer to remove the fibers. You will be left with a smooth, tangy paste that is ready to use, and any leftovers can be refrigerated for up to 2 weeks.

- To make this Gluten-Free: use tamari instead of soy sauce.

Acknowledgments

To our family and friends, for supporting us during the making of this book and for understanding each time we had to cancel plans and spend our evenings and weekends working.

To Leigh Eisenman, for finding us and bringing this cookbook to life and for being the best literary agent two husbands could ever have.

To Laura Apperson, for making this entire process a pleasure from start to finish and for encouraging us with creative ideas and helpful edits.

To Elizabeth Lacks, for believing in our cookbook from the first day and for bringing us into St. Martin's Press.

To Rachel Saltzman, our close friend and fearless manager, who handles any situation with style and has been with us from the beginning.

To Emma K. Morris (@emmakmorris), for all your great ideas and the fun photoshoots that never felt like work.

To Chris and Sara, our diligent copy editors who made the editing process fun and easy.

To Ginny and Doug Erickson at Erickson Surfaces (@ericksonsurfaces), for all your beautiful handmade photography backgrounds that appear throughout this book.

To Meg Van Der Kruik (@thismessisours), for opening your home that day and letting us take photos in your gorgeous kitchen.

To Jonah and Jamie Malarsky (@firechiefcharlie), for taste-testing, giving us your valuable opinions, and enthusiastically taking dozens of desserts off our hands.

To Christine Carlson (@c.r.a.v.i.n.g.s) and Rebecca Firth (@displacedhousewife), for your friendship, for all your great advice, and for making us laugh all the time.

To Julie and Dan Resnick, Kevin Masse, and the Feedfeed (@thefeedfeed), for leading a thriving community of foodies filled with cooking creativity and endless inspiration.

To Sarah Phillips (@food), for your friendship, support, and encouragement.

To Alexandra Stafford (@alexandracooks), for sharing your life-changing bread recipe with us.

To Deb Perelman (@smittenkitchen), who was the first cooking blogger we ever followed and the person who inspired us to launch our website.

To everyone who has supported us on our blog and on social media and has made our recipes at home.

Corrections Page: We thought it would be helpful to add a page on our website that will list any corrections or mistakes that may appear in this book. As meticulous and organized as we are, we are not perfect, so in case there are any errors, you will find a list of corrections at www.husbandsthatcook.com/oops. There is a place to comment, so please let us know if you find any mistakes in these pages.

Website: Visit us at www.husbandsthatcook.com and sign up for our email list to stay up to date with more Husbands' recipes and all the latest news. Come say hello, and let us know if you have any questions or comments—we would love to hear from you! Also, we can't wait to see what you make from the book, so use the hashtag #husbandsthatcookbook on social media so we can see your creations!

Index

Page numbers in *italics* refer to recipe photographs.